DATE DUE

DISCARD

Phenomenology
and existentialism

Also by Reinhardt Grossmann
Meinong

Phenomenology and existentialism

An introduction

Reinhardt Grossmann
Professor of Philosophy, University of Indiana

ROUTLEDGE & KEGAN PAUL
London, Boston, Melbourne & Henley

First published in 1984
by Routledge & Kegan Paul plc

14 Leicester Square, London WC2H 7PH, England

9 Park Street, Boston, Mass. 02108, USA

464 St Kilda Road, Melbourne,
Victoria 3004, Australia and

Broadway House, Newtown Road,
Henley-on-Thames, Oxon RG9 1EN, England

Set in Palatino, 10 on 12pt,
by Hope Services, Abingdon, Oxon
and printed in Great Britain
by T. J. Press (Padstow) Ltd
Padstow, Cornwall

Library of Congress Cataloging in Publication Data

Grossmann, Reinhardt, 1931–

Phenomenology and existentialism.
Includes index.
1. Phenomenology—History—Addresses, essays, lectures.
2. Existentialism—History—Addresses, essays, lectures.
3. Philosophy, Modern—Addresses, essays, lectures.
I. Title.
B829.5.G7   1984   142'.7   84-4783

British Library CIP data also available

ISBN 0-7102-0270-9(c)
ISBN 0-7102-0291-1(p)

Contents

Contents

Contents

Contents

Preface

This book is based on lectures which I have given for the last ten years or so. This explains its style. Some other features, I think, require a little more explanation.

Different philosophers have quite different conceptions of what philosophy is all about. I am no exception, and my particular conception of philosophy has shaped my treatment of Husserl, Heidegger, and Sartre. In brief, I believe that all important philosophers–whether they know it or not and whether they admit it or not–deal with certain traditional problems. There is a, sometimes hidden, continuity to philosophy. No matter how revolutionary a philosophical movement may at first appear to be, and Phenomenology and Existentialism certainly claimed to be revolutionary, a closer look reveals that the same old problems are merely discussed in a new way. I selected three such problems–the problem of knowledge, the problem of existence, and the problem of freedom–in order to provide some focus to the discussion, and because I believe that they were of major concern to Husserl, Heidegger, and Sartre, respectively.

But philosophical books are written, not only with a definite conception of philosophy in mind, but also from a particular point of philosophical view. My philosophical view is not easily described in contemporary terms. Although I was schooled in what is now called the 'analytic' tradition, I was also taught to appreciate Plato and Aristotle, Aquinas and Scotus, Descartes and Berkeley. I hope to show with this book that one so schooled can appreciate Heidegger and Sartre as well. It is surely silly to assume that only an Existentialist, say, can understand another Existentialist; as silly, I might add, as to believe that all Existentialists talk nonsense.

Finally, there is the fact that I argue, rather vehemently at times, for my own philosophical views. This will undoubtedly offend those who believe that an introductory text should present an unbiased picture. In defense of my polemical style, I can only plead that I find it very difficult to develop the dialectic of a particular problem—the arguments and counter-arguments, the choices and limits—without taking a definite stand myself. I assure the reader that I sound much more dogmatic than I am. And I invite him to develop the arguments further than I have done, refuting my contentions in the process. This is the very stuff of which philosophy is made.

It goes without saying that Husserl, Heidegger, and Sartre have thought and written about things other than knowledge, existence and freedom. Just as it is obvious that there are other Phenomenologists and Existentialists. After all, this is merely an introduction to, not a survey of, Phenomenology and Existentialism. My main criticism of most of the introductions and anthologies in this field is that they contain bits and pieces from numerous sources from Dostojewski to Marcel, without ever following up on any one topic, with the result that the student cannot possibly appreciate the complexity of the issues, or be impressed by the manner in which philosophical problems grow out of each other.

While writing this book, I consulted many times with my colleague Paul Spade, who taught a similar course in the department. I would like to thank him for sharing with me his knowledge of and enthusiasm for some of the more notorious philosophers of our time.

R. Grossmann

Bloomington, Indiana

Part I

The background

1. Descartes: a new conception of the mind

(1) *The traditional distinction between substance, essence and accident*

In order to understand the fundamental ideas of phenomenologists and existentialists, we must consider their origins. René Descartes' (1596–1650) philosophy is the source of many of the problems which led to the development of various philosophical movements during the last three hundred years. Phenomenology and Existentialism are no exceptions. Descartes was a modern philosopher. He proposed views contrary to those of the tradition; views which still influence the thought of contemporary philosophers. But he was also steeped in the very tradition which he opposed. He had, as it were, one foot in the tradition and one foot in a new era of philosophy. We consider him to be the father of modern philosophy.

The tradition I am speaking of consisted of the Scholastic philosophy of Descartes' time. It consisted of a most complicated, most elaborate, most comprehensive system of ideas going back to St Thomas Aquinas (1224/5–1274) and, ultimately, to Aristotle (384/3–322 B.C.). You may compare it to a most complex Rube Goldberg-type contraption fashioned from Tinker Toys. Descartes, to stay with this picture, thought that this towering edifice needed a slight adjustment. He removed one of the parts and replaced it by another. As it turned out, the replaced part was crucial to the structure. Without it, the whole structure collapsed. The history of philosophy since Descartes can be viewed as consisting of various attempts to erect a new comprehensive system which incorporates some of Descartes' views.

According to the tradition, everything there is can be divided into two basic categories of things, called 'substances' and 'accidents', respectively. These are the traditional terms, but I shall sometimes adopt a more modern terminology and speak of *individual things* and their *accidental properties*. Everything there is, then, is either an individual thing or else an accidental property of an individual thing. Examples of individual things are: a hair on Napoleon's head, the sun, the Tower of London, Socrates, and the typewriter I am using. Examples of accidental properties are: the color of Napoleon's hair, the mass of the sun, the height of the Tower of London, Socrates' sense of humor, and the shape of my typewriter. Substances are distinguished from accidents, according to the tradition, by the fact that they are *independent existents*. They are not dependent for their existence on accidents, while accidents can only exist as accidents of substances.

A material substance is conceived of by the tradition as a composite of *matter* and *essence*. The matter of a material thing is some sort of formless stuff. This undifferentiated stuff receives its structure from the essence. The essence is the feature, characteristic, or property which is responsible for the fact that some matter is Napoleon's hair, while other matter is the sun. In a way, the essence of a material substance is a property of that substance, and I shall often speak of essential, as opposed to accidental, properties. But we must keep in mind that this property is much more intimately connected with the substance than its accidental properties are. It is, in a sense, a *part* of the substance and not merely added on to it from the outside like an accident is. From this point of view, one may say that a substance has two kinds of property, essential and accidental properties. The essential property is part and parcel of the substance itself; it determines the inner structure of the substance. The accidental properties, on the other hand, are added on to the whole, compromised of matter and essence, in such a way that the substance would still be what it is, this particular kind of thing rather than that one, without the

4

accidental properties. I realize that I am not too precise, and I apologize. But the view I am trying to describe is simply not very clear. In particular, it has difficulties in making a sharp distinction between the essential and the accidental properties of substances, and it is rather vague both on the nature of the relationship between substance and essence, and on the quite different relationship between substance and accident. Or perhaps I should say that within the tradition, there are several versions of how these things are to be understood.

In terms of these traditional distinctions, we can now describe the small piece in the monumental Tinker Toy structure which Descartes replaced. A human being, according to the tradition, consists of a body and a soul. And now comes the crucial point: *The soul is conceived of as the essence of the body.* The relationship between a human being and his soul (mind, spirit) is the relationship between a substance and its essence. (This essence, it was stressed, can exist separated from the body.) According to Descartes, on the contrary, the mind is conceived of, not as the essence of the body, but as a substance in its own right. A human being, according to Descartes, is thus a combination of two individual things, namely, of a body and a mind. The relationship between body and mind is, not the relationship between substance and its essence, but a relationship between two substances. Each one of these two substances, consequently, must have its own essence, the mind just as much as the human body. Descartes' innovation consists in his claim that minds are individual things (substances) and not essences of individual things.

(2) *Descartes' distinction between bodies and minds*

According to Descartes' new philosophy, there are three kinds of individual thing: one kind uncreated, and two kinds created. The uncreated individual is God. The two created kinds are bodies and minds. Every individual (other than God) is either a body or a mind. Of course, there are many bodies which are not combined with minds. My typewriter is one of them. Curiously, Descartes held the rather absurd view that animals are mere bodies, comparable, say, to complicated pinball machines,

5

rather than combinations of bodies with (rudimentary) minds. There are also, presumably, minds which are not combined with bodies. Angels are of this sort.

Descartes did more than just claim that minds are substances, he also told us how they differ from bodies. Bodies have an essential property that distinguishes them from minds. This property is *extension*. Minds, on the other hand, share an essential property which all bodies lack. This property is *thought*. Bodies and only bodies are extended. This means that they and only they have a shape, that they and only they are located in space. Minds have no shapes. Nor do they exist somewhere in space. My typewriter, for example, has a certain shape, a shape hard to describe other than by saying it is the shape of an old typewriter. It is also located on my desk, and the desk is in my office, and my office is in a certain building, and the building is in Bloomington, and Bloomington is so many miles south of Indianapolis. Minds, as I said, are different in this respect from bodies. They are, quite literally, nowhere. My mind is not square; nor does it have any other shape. And it is not located so many inches above my shoulder, in this room, in Bloomington, south of Indianapolis.

But is this really true? Is my mind not located in my head rather than in one of my big toes? Descartes would answer, I think, that we are tempted to locate our minds where our brains rather than our toes are because we have learned from experience that changes in our brains rather than in our toes cause changes in our minds. If the amputation of a big toe would inevitably cause a cessation of all mental processes, we would be inclined to locate the mind in the toe rather than in the head. We do not observe minds in space. Our inclination to think of them as being located in heads is due to two facts. Firstly, brains are literally located in heads. Secondly, changes in the brain (in the nervous system) cause changes in the mental processes. It remains, therefore, true that minds, in contrast to brains, are not literally located anywhere.

Bodies are spatial. Minds think. What does Descartes mean, precisely, by defining minds as thinking substances? Here is one of his explanations: 'What is a thinking being? It is a being which doubts, which understands, which conceives, which affirms, which denies, which wills, which rejects, which imagines also, and which perceives.' (*Meditations on First Philosophy*, Second Meditation). Thinking, it is clear, is for Descartes a very general mental activity. It encompasses such quite different mental phenomena as conceiving, willing, imagining, and perceiving. I shall anticipate our later terminological needs and introduce another technical term. I shall speak of *mental acts* of conceiving, of mental acts of willing, mental acts of imagining, etc. Thought, then, consists of various mental acts. Descartes lists only a very select group of mental acts, a fact which will occupy us later. But we should notice that he leaves out emotions, and he omits remembering, desiring, questioning, and many other kinds of mental act. If we add these kinds to our inventory of mental acts, we can say that a mind is an individual which has mental acts like desiring, perceiving, hating, fearing, affirming, remembering, imagining, etc.

Bodies have shapes and are at places, but they do not perceive, desire, etc. Minds do all of these things, but they are not spatial. Descartes does not mention it, but there is also a 'glue' that binds these two realms together. This glue is *time*. Bodies as well as minds are temporal things. Both kinds of individual are in time. Bodies and minds have durations, and they are also temporally located, that is, they stand in temporal relations to each other. Caesar's body existed *before* Napoleon's. But Caesar's thoughts also occurred *before* Napoleon's. And Caesar made certain plans *while* (at the time when) he (his body) crossed the Rubicon. Bodily and mental processes are both in time. One may occur earlier than the other, or later, or simultaneous with the other. To repeat, time is the glue of the universe .

Descartes' new conception of minds as totally different individual things from bodies has profound consequences for the rest of the Scholastic system. It does not jibe with other parts of the system or, at least, it brings into sharp focus longstanding shortcomings of the traditional view. This is the reason why the whole edifice comes tumbling down. In particular, it poses two important philosophical problems: the problem of the causal interaction between mind and body and the problem of representation by ideas. We shall briefly explain these problems in the next two sections.

(3) *The problem of causal interaction*

According to Descartes, bodies and minds are essentially different. They do not exist together in the same space as two billiard balls do. Yet Descartes also insists that body and mind interact with each other. For example, our ideas of external bodies are caused by these bodies. But how can a body, either the external body of the perceived object or the brain itself, act upon something which is not even in space? How can a change in the properties of a brain cause a change in the essentially different properties of the mind? To Cartesians, the interaction was a fact, but a fact that posed a mystery.

Two views clash at this point. There is, on the one hand, the new Cartesian conception of the mind as a thinking, non-spatial, substance. There is, on the other, an old notion of causality at work. According to this notion, the paradigm of a causal interaction is the bumping between two billiard balls or the pulling of an object by a string. I shall call this the 'push-pull model of causality'. It is clear that this model cannot be applied to body and mind. A body can neither push a mind nor pull it. It cannot touch it, bump into it, or hit it. Hence, on this model, a body cannot causally interact with a mind. But such causal interaction is a fact. Something, obviously, has to give. It is fair to say that most Cartesians simply knew no way out of this dilemma. Some boldly declared that causal interaction between body and mind is a matter which cannot be explained by reason, but only by faith. Others felt forced to deny that interaction ever takes place. Our ideas are not in our minds, caused by external objects, they held, but are in God.

Eventually, the issue was resolved–as resolved as any issue ever can be in philosophy–by David Hume's (1711–76) introduction of a new conception of causality (See David Hume, *A Treatise of Human Nature*, Oxford University Press, 1967.) The old push-pull model was abandoned in favor of a notion of causality as a constant conjunction of events. Speaking most generally, the notion of cause is supplanted in modern science by the notion of *lawfulness*. This is not a topic which we can take up in this context, but I shall hint at what is at stake for future reference.

It is clear that changes in the nervous system of a person, in his brain, cause changes in his mental life. A prefrontal lobotomy, for example, will make a person docile, unemotional, and slow down his mental processes. These facts are investigated by a great number of physiologists, chemists, and psychiatrists. But these scientists do not search for direct action by a brain on a mind in analogy to two billiard balls hitting each other. Rather, they look for laws which will connect changes in the brain with changes in the mind. Such a law may be of the following kind: *whenever* you stimulate a certain region of the brain with electrical impulses, then the subject of the experiment will see a red flash before his eyes. Or it may be of this sort: *whenever* a person dreams, *then* his eyes will make certain rapid movements. A law of this sort is of the form: whenever such-and-such changes take place in the nervous system of a person, then (simultaneously or some time later) such-and-such changes will take place in his mental processes. As you can see, all that is asserted is a certain regular connection between bodily processes and mental processes. No pushing or shoving is envisaged. As you can also see, the Cartesian mind-body dualism is perfectly compatible with this modern conception of causality as lawfulness.

(4) *The problem of representation by ideas*

The second main problem of the Cartesian philosophy arises because Descartes' insistence that body and mind are essentially different clashes with the Scholastic conception of knowledge in general and of perception in particular. According to this conception, as we have seen, a material substance is composed of an essence and of matter. The essence determines what kind of material thing it is. It is thought of as a principle of organization. In addition to its essence, an individual also has numerous accidental properties. Now comes the important point. When a human being knows, that is, perceives a material object, the essence of the object is supposed to exist in his mind. The perceiver and the perceived object share a common property, namely, the essential property of the perceived object. One and the same thing, the essence of the object, exists in the material world, as the essence which informs this piece of matter, and also in the mind of the perceiver, as a concept of this object.

How does the essence get into the mind? The process is supposedly very complicated. The material object, through a medium, somehow causes a material impression on the sense organ. This impression causes a material image. Then the active part of the mind goes to work on this image and extracts from it the essence of the perceived object. Fortunately, we need not bother trying to understand this process in detail. What matters for our purpose is, firstly, that in perception the essence of the perceived object is quite literally in the mind of the perceiver; and, secondly, that therefore the mind and the object share a common property.

Recall now Descartes' insistence that body and mind are essentially different. It is clear that Descartes' view does not agree with the Scholastic account which we have just outlined. Since body and mind are radically different, they could not possibly share a common property, as required by the Scholastic account of perception. Body and mind have absolutely nothing in common and, hence, could not possibly share the essence of the perceived object. Let us agree to call the essence *as it exists in the mind of the perceiver* a 'notion' of the perceived object. In this terminology, Descartes's philosophy has no room for notions. Knowledge of the perceptual object cannot be by means of *notion*. It must be by way of *idea*. When you perceive an elephant, then there exists in your mind, according to the Cartesian, the idea of this elephant. How this idea arises in your mind is again a complicated process. The physical part of this process, the stimulation of the sense organ and the transmission of this stimulation to the brain, is viewed in mechanical terms. How the mechanical changes in the brain give rise to the idea is, as we noted in the last section, a serious problem for Descartes. But no matter how the idea may be caused, this idea is not the essence of the perceived elephant. This idea, according to Descartes, is not even *like* the elephant. How, then, can it possibly *represent* an elephant?

Let us approach this problem from another angle. The Scholastic and the Cartesian agree that the perceived object is somehow 'in' the perceiving mind. Both hold that something in the mind corresponds to the perceived object. According to the

Scholastic, this something is a notion; according to Descartes, it is an idea. How is this mental entity related to the elephant? The Scholastic has an answer at hand, unsatisfactory as it may turn out to be in the long run. The notion of the elephant is the essence of this elephant, as it exists in the mind. The Cartesian, on the other hand, has no ready answer. The idea of the elephant is not the same as its essence. The idea is a property of a thinking substance, while the essence is a property of an extended substance. The idea cannot even be *alike* or *similar* to the essence of the elephant. Since body and mind have nothing in common, how could they be alike or similar?

The problem of how ideas represent, just like the problem of how body and mind interact, was never solved by the Cartesians. But it had to wait even longer for a solution than the problem of causal interaction. It was not until the second half of the nineteenth century that Franz Brentano (1838–1917) and his students seriously took up the question once again of how ideas represent their objects. One of Brentano's students was Edmund Husserl (1859–1938), the founder of phenomenology.

(5) *The distinction between ideas and sensations*

In addition to ideas, minds have other modifications called 'sensations'. But these modifications, according to the Cartesian, do not represent anything. They are not, like ideas, *of* anything. They, unlike ideas, have no objects. They are caused in the mind, it is true, but they do not convey knowledge of the external world. Examples of sensations are colors, odors, tastes, sounds, tactual feelings, heat, cold, etc. Examples of sensations are, as you may notice with some surprise, all sensory properties of objects, all the properties of the objects around us which we can perceive by means of our eyes, ears, noses, mouths, and hands. I shall call these properties from now on 'perceptual properties'. In the Cartesian tradition, these properties are sometimes called 'secondary qualities' (of perceptual objects). But this terminology is misleading. According to the Cartesian, these so-called secondary qualities are not qualities of perceptual objects at all: they are mere sensations in the mind.

Secondary qualities are contrasted with primary qualities.

Examples of primary qualities mentioned by Descartes are: size, shape, number, and motion and rest. Material substances have these and only these properties. What is 'out there' in the way of material substance has a certain size, a shape, and it is in motion or at rest. But it is not red or green, it has no taste, it is neither hot nor cold, etc. It is the primary qualities which are supposed to be known by way of ideas. Ideas are said to represent these qualities. According to this distinction between primary and secondary qualities, we have ideas of shapes, but we do not have ideas of colors. Shapes are properties of material objects; colors are only sensations in a mind.

You can hardly fail to see how doubtful this distinction between shape and color really is. Not only is it doubtful, but it leads almost immediately to the rather absurd view that there are no material objects at all. George Berkeley (1685–1753), not too long after Descartes, came to precisely this conclusion. He pounced on Descartes' admission that colors are only sensations in minds and argued that whatever speaks for this admission also shows that shape (as well as size, number, and motion and rest) is only a sensation in the mind. Thus all qualities, primary as well as secondary qualities, are only sensations in the mind. But if all of the alleged properties of material objects are not properties of such objects at all, what sense can it make to speak of the things which have these properties, that is, of the material objects themselves? All there are, according to Berkeley, are these sensations in minds, and what we ordinarily think of as perceptual objects–an apple, for example–are nothing but bundles of such sensations. In this perfectly straightforward and lucid fashion, Berkeley comes to the surprising conclusion that houses, mountains, rivers and all other perceptual objects have an existence only in the mind.

But, of course, houses, mountains, rivers, and trees do not exist in our minds. And if Descartes' distinction between primary and secondary qualities, between ideas and sensations, leads to Berkeley's conclusion, then we must take a critical look at the reasons for the distinction. I think that there are three main reasons which explain why Descartes as well as many later philosophers and scientists have clung to the view that colors 'are only in the mind', while certain other properties 'are truly out there'.

The first reason consists in what I shall call–tongue in cheek, to be sure–'the scientist's fallacy'. This logical howler is committed by some scientists when they do not carefully watch what they are saying and by many philosophers when they deliberately obfuscate the issues. The general line of reasoning is as follows. One asserts that, say, objective colors are nothing but reflected light waves (of a certain length). 'Out there', then, are only light waves. Where does that leave the colors as we literally see them with our eyes? Well, if they are not 'out there', then they must be in the mind. Colors, *as we see them* literally with our eyes, are mere sensations in our minds. Now, the particular fallacy I have in mind occurs at the beginning of this line of thought, when one asserts that colors are nothing but reflected light waves. What the scientist really discovers is a most surprising law: differently colored surfaces reflect light waves of different lengths in such a fashion that to different colors there correspond different wave lengths. It is this law from which one then concludes, fallaciously, that colors are nothing but light waves. Consider another example. We have also discovered that the hotter a fluid or gas is, the faster its molecules move. From this perfectly astounding law, one concludes, again fallaciously, that heat is nothing but molecular motion. And here is still another example: from the fact that whenever there is lightning, then there is an electrical discharge, one concludes that lightning is nothing but an electrical discharge.

There is a pattern to this logical mistake. In each case, the scientist discovers a law of the form: whenever something has a certain property, P, then it has the property Q, and conversely. For example, whenever a surface is olive green, then it reflects light of a certain wave length, and conversely; or whenever a gas has a certain temperature, then its molecules move with a certain velocity, and conversely. And from this law, one concludes without further ado that the property P *is nothing but* the property Q. For example, one concludes that olive green is nothing but a certain wave length; that a certain temperature is nothing but molecular motion of a certain sort. But it is obvious that one cannot conclude from the fact that two properties go hand in hand, so to speak, that therefore the one property is really the other. Perhaps the extent of this logical mistake can be

13

illustrated by the following hypothetical case. Assume that everything olive green in the universe is square, and conversely. Assume, in other words, that olive green and square go hand in hand, as I just put it. Does it follow that there is no such color as olive green, but only the property of being square? Obviously not. This example shows that the illogical scientist has a curious prejudice. I could have asked, rhetorically, does it follow that there is no property of being square, but only the color olive green? One may just as well mistakenly conclude that light waves are nothing but colors as that colors are nothing but light waves, or that molecular motion is nothing but heat as that heat is nothing but molecular motion.

The second reason for holding that colors as perceived are only sensations in the mind also derives from modern science. It rests on the twin discoveries that material objects consist of elementary particles and that such particles are not colored. Descartes knew nothing of positrons, of course, but he, too, thought of material objects as consisting of smaller and smaller bodies. And he, too, believed that these smaller bodies had no colors. But let us stick to the more modern version of physics for our example. Elementary particles, we are told, have a number of properties—for example, they have mass, electrical charge, and a number of very esoteric properties like spin—but they are not colored. Furthermore, ordinary perceptual objects like apples consist of elemetary particles. From these two facts, one concludes that apples cannot be colored. Colors, therefore, are only in minds.

In this case, the crucial argument is of the following form: (1) An apple consists of elementary particles; it is a complicated structure of such particles; (2) elementary particles have no colors. Therefore, an apple has no color. It is not hard to see that the conclusion does not follow from the two facts (1) and (2). One needs another premise, another assumption. Let us insert the following principle: (3) a structure (a whole) can only have those properties which its constituents (its parts) have. Now, from (1), (2), and (3) it follows indeed that apples cannot be colored. The logic of our argument is sound. But assumption (3) is quite obviously false. Take the most simple counterexample. Imagine a square with the two diagonal lines drawn. This square consists of four triangles, but it has the shape square. It has a shape, in other words, which none of its spatial parts has. Or consider the apple of our example. An apple is not an elementary particle. Rather, it is a complicated structure of such particles. Why, then, should it not have properties which elementary particles do not have? Surely, I can take a healthy bite out of the apple, but I cannot take a healthy bite out of an elementary particle! Just the opposite of principle (3) is true: a structure has many properties which its parts do not have. This disposes of the second reason for believing that colors are only in minds.

The third reason is rather complicated and of a more philosophical nature. Assume that you look at the rectangular top of a desk from different angles. What you see from these different angles, according to the argument, are different shapes of the top. For example, from several feet away and at an angle from six feet down, you will see a trapezoidal shaped desk top. From directly above, suspended from the ceiling, on the other hand, you will see a rectangular top. And so on. Now, every one of these perspectives is equally 'correct', equally 'normal', equally 'standard'. But if this is so then what is the true shape of the desk top? Is it the trapezoidal shape, or the rectangular shape, or some other shape? One concludes that we have no reason to ascribe one of these shapes rather than any other to the desk top. And from this result, one concludes further that the desk top has no shape at all, that shape is not one of its properties. Of course, the same line of reasoning is supposed to apply to color and to other perceptual properties of the desk top. Given the lighting conditions of the room, for example, it may be that the top looks brown from one angle, grey from another, and black from a third. I used the example of shape rather than color in order to make clear how Berkeley could have used this argument against the Cartesian assertion that shape, in distinction to color, is a primary quality.

Let us assume that the argument is sound as far as the conclusion is concerned that we cannot know the true shape of the desk top. How does it then follow that the top has no shape at all? Obviously it does not. And hence it does not follow that shape must be a sensation in the mind. Nor are there any plausible assumptions which we may add in order to get from our inability to know the shape of the top to the conclusion that it has no shape. At best, therefore, this argument shows that we cannot know the perceptual properties of perceptual objects, but not that they do not have such properties or that such properties exist in minds.

But does it really show that much? I do not think so. I believe that we know the properties of perceptual objects–within the margin of perceptual error, of course–that we know their colors and their shapes. The desk top is rectangular; it is not trapezoidal. And it is, say, brown; it is neither grey nor black. Something must be wrong with the argument. We shall see later on precisely what has gone wrong when we discuss Husserl's theory of aspects. I am afraid that you shall have to wait until then.

(6) *The attack on substance: Berkeley*

With Descartes, modern philosophy begins. Yet Descartes philosophizes exclusively within the framework of the substance, essence, accident distinction. Shortly after Descartes, an attack on this distinction is launched. I want to impress on you how important this attack is. Descartes, we saw, has one foot in the tradition: he never questions the substance, essence, accident distinction. But he also has one foot in the future: he thinks that minds are independent substances. That there are material substances, and that they have essences and accidental modifications, was an accepted view. But now a fundamental break with this tradition takes place. In the wake of Descartes' philosophy, the very notion of material substance is attacked from two sides. On the one side are the so-called 'British Empiricists' who maintain that substances cannot be known. On the other side are so-called 'Rationalists' who despair of making philosophic sense of the notion of a substance. Both sides propose to supplant the category of substance by that of a bundle of properties. Before we look at this two-pronged criticism, let me try to explain as clearly as possible how the opposing views differ.

According to the traditional view, a view to which Descartes still subscribes, an apple is a material substance which *consists* (in part) of an essence and which *has* certain accidental properties. Among these accidental properties are its color, its taste, its consistency, its smell, etc. We can therefore distinguish between the apple, on the one hand, and its accidental properties, on the other. These two kinds of thing are somehow related to each other. This relation is expressed by the copula 'is' or some form of it. What the relation is, is never adequately explained by the tradition. Nor is this surprising. Relations in general received scant attention. But even though the precise nature of the relation between substance and accident was never fully articulated, it is clear that it is not a whole-part relation, like the relation between substance and essence. A substance in some sense has its accidents, but it does not consist of them. A substance is not a whole which has accidents in its parts. Let me impress on you this dogma by repeating: a substance *has* accidents, but does not *consist* of them.

The bundle view, by contrast, holds that an individual thing, the apple of our example, is a bundle of properties, including its accidental properties. The apple is conceived of as a whole of some sort, a whole which consists of all the properties which we ascribe to it. The most fundamental difference between the substance and the bundle view concerns, therefore, the nature of the predication relation. The bundle view conceives of this relation as a whole-part relation, the substance view does not. I think you can see how the bundle view inevitably destroys the distinction between essence and accident. If accidents are just as much part of the individual as its essence is, then they are just as essential to its inner structure as the essence! What we get, therefore, is a view which conceives of an individual thing as a bundle of properties all of which are equally important to the individual. Now, I happen to agree with the bundle view that the distinction between essential and accidental properties cannot be defended. But I also believe, with the substance view, that the relation between an individual and its so-called accidental properties is not a whole-part relation. My view is that none of the properties of an individual, so-called essential or accidental, is a part of the individual. But this is not the place to argue for my position. We shall return to it later in connection with the Platonic distinction between particulars and universals. What we are interested in is the nature of the criticism which the Empiricists heaped upon the substance view.

Descartes invites their criticism by making a very important albeit mistaken claim for material substances. Material substances, he maintains, can be recognized as the same independently of all of their perceptual properties. This is the point of his famous wax example in the Second Meditation. We are invited to consider a fresh piece of wax which has just been taken from a hive. It smells of honey, it is white, has a certain shape and consistency, etc. Now, this piece of wax is held close to a fire: the taste of honey evaporates, the odor vanishes, its color changes from white to black, it changes shape and consistency. We shall assume that all of its original perceptual properties have changed. Do we have the *same* piece of wax after all of these changes have taken place? Descartes says: 'no one denies it, no one judges otherwise.' And then he asks: 'What is it then in this bit of wax that we recognize with so much distinctness? Certainly, it cannot be anything that I observed by means of the senses, since everything in the field of taste, smell, sight, touch, and hearing is changed, and since the same wax nevertheless remains.' He concludes that the piece of wax 'was neither that sweetness of honey, nor that odor of flowers, nor that whiteness, nor that shape, nor that sound, but only a body which a little while ago appeared to my senses under these forms and which now makes itself felt under others.' And he concludes further that this body is not known by the senses, but by a different faculty of the mind which he calls 'understanding'.

It is certainly true that the piece of wax is not identical with *any one* of its properties. It is not the same as this sweetness of honey or as that odor of flowers. It is also true that the piece of wax is not identical with *either one* of the two bundles of properties, the bundle at the hive and the bundle after it has been held to the fire. For, if it were identical with one of them, it would have to be identical with the other, since we are assuming that it is the same piece of wax. Descartes is right in both regards. But he is wrong when he goes on to conclude that the piece of wax, the substance, is not known by the senses, but by the understanding. He is mistaken when he concludes that there is a special faculty of the mind, different from perception, by means of which we can recognize the same piece of wax directly, independently of all of its properties. We can easily prove that Descartes is mistaken. If there were such a faculty, then we should be able to tell whether or not a piece of wax which is now shown to us is the same as a piece of wax which was shown to us earlier, *even if we have not observed it continuously*. But we are obviously not able to do this. Consider a simpler case. Assume that I show you a white billiard ball and then, a little while later, a white billiard ball again. You will not be able to tell whether the latter is the same as the one which I first showed you. And this proves conclusively that you cannot recognize an individual thing as the same directly and by means of a special mental faculty. Of course, if you can watch the billiard ball which was first shown uninterruptedly until I show you a ball for a second time, then you know whether or not it is the same. What you have observed, by means of the senses, is the spatio-temporal position of the ball.

We conclude from our thought experiment that there is no such faculty as the understanding which allows us to re-identify individual things directly. We can only recognize an individual thing as the same on the basis of its properties, including its spatio-temporal properties. And we know about these properties through perception. An opponent of Cartesian material substances, however, may argue as follows. According to Descartes, a material substance is something which can be recognized directly, independently of all perceptual properties. But we have just seen that individual things cannot be so recognized. It follows, therefore, that individual things cannot be material substances. There simply are no such entities as material substances in the Cartesian sense of the term. Here, then, you have one of the three main arguments against material substances put forth by the Empiricists. It is an argument which Descartes himself invites by his exaggerated claim in behalf of a faculty of understanding.

Another argument is invited by the description which John Locke (1632–1704), one of the British Empiricists who still believes in material substances, gives of such substances. He says:

> The idea then we have, to which we give the *general* name substance, being nothing but the supposed, but unknown, support of those qualities we find existing, which we imagine cannot subsist, *sine re substante*, without something to support

them, we call that support *substantia*; which, according to the import of the word is, in plain English, standing under or upholding. (*An Essay Concerning Human Understanding*, Book II, xxiii, sec. 2)

Locke here declares that substances are unknowable. Well, if they are unknowable, then we don't know that they exist. And if we do not know that they exist, then we cannot assert that individual things are substances. Why does Locke believe that material substances are unknowable? He does not state his reasons. But we may speculate that he may have had the following argument in mind. A substance, apart and distinguished from all of its properties, cannot be known. It cannot be known, because one can know a thing only through its properties. Put differently, in order to know a substance, one must know what properties it has. But the substance, considered by itself, has no properties. Hence, one cannot know it. This argument is obviously unsound. If it were sound, then it would follow that one cannot know anything whatsoever, substances or anything else. For, consider any entity E, and distinguish between E, on the one hand, and its properties on the other. Now it is impossible to describe *what E is* without mentioning some property or another and, hence, it is impossible to know what E is divorced from all of its properties. According to the argument, for example, we could not know elephants because we cannot know what they are; and we cannot know what they are because we do not know what properties they have when considered divorced from all of their properties. But, of course, we know what elephants are because we know (some of) their properties. And in the same sense we know what material substances are because we know (some of) their categorial properties. According to Descartes, for example, they are characterized by having extension. Thus while we admit that material substances cannot be known in the sense of known to be the same directly without recourse to their properties, we do not admit that they cannot be known in the sense of known to have such-and-such properties.

There is still another, a third, important sense of knowable which plays a role in the Empiricist's attack on material substances. Berkeley claims that material substances are unknowable in that we are never *acquainted* with them. (Note that some languages have different words for knowledge in the sense of knowing something about and knowledge in the sense of acquaintance. In German, one distinguishes between 'wissen' and 'kennen'.) According to Berkeley, we are acquainted with the sensible properties of perceptual objects, but not with their alleged material substances. Witness the following dialogue:

Phil. This point then is agreed between us–that *sensible things are those only which are immediately perceived by sense.* You will further inform me whether we immediately perceive by sight anything besides light and colors and figures; or by hearing, anything but sounds, by the palate, anything besides tastes; by the smell, anything besides odors; or by touch, more than tangible qualities.

Hyl. We do not.

Phil. It seems, therefore, that if you take away all sensible qualities, there remains nothing sensible?

Hyl. I grant it.

Phil. Sensible things therefore are nothing else but so many sensible qualities or combinations of qualities.

Hyl. Nothing else. (*Three Dialogues Between Hylas and Philonous,* Indianapolis, Bobbs-Merrill, 1965; beginning of the First Dialogue)

Hylas conceded too much when he immediately agrees that we perceive nothing but sensible qualities. This is simply not true. We see, not only colors, shapes, and sizes, but we also see apples, mountains, rainbows, and billiard balls. None of these things is a sensible property. What we perceive are individual things and their properties. It looks as if Berkeley means to deny one of the most obvious truisms, namely, that we perceive such individual things as apples.

But note that Philonous claims that sensible things are nothing but combinations (bundles) of qualities. Granted that an apple is not a sensible property–not even a complex property, for what would it be a property of?–could it not be a bundle of such properties? This particular apple, which I shall whimsically call 'Oscar', is indeed conceived of by Berkeley as a bundle of sensible qualities: it consists, he maintains, of a certain color, a certain smell, a certain taste, etc. Another apple consists of slightly different sensible properties. For example, its taste may be the same as Oscar's, but it has a different shape; or its shape may be the same as Oscar's, but it has a different color and taste; and so on. Thus Berkeley, it may be said, clearly distinguishes between sensory properties, on the one hand, and bundles of such properties, on the other. Oscar, he would admit is not a sensory property, but is a bundle of such properties.

We grant Berkeley his distinction but point out that he has to face the following dilemma. Either Philonous really means it when he claims at the beginning of our quotation that all we can perceive are sensible properties or else he does not. If he does not mean it, if we can perceive things other than sensible qualities, then we shall insist, as we have before, that the things other than properties which we perceive are individual things like the apple, Oscar. Berkeley, in other words, has done nothing to convince us that we cannot be acquainted with material substances. As regards the other horn of the dilemma, if Philonous does mean to say that we cannot perceive anything but sensory properties, then it follows, upon his own view, that we cannot perceive apples, for an apple is not a sensible quality, but rather a bundle of such qualities. In this case, it follows not only that we cannot see apples conceived of as material substances, but that we cannot see them even if we conceive of them, like Berkeley, as bundles of properties.

Let me summarize. I distinguished between three different senses in which an individual thing may be said to be known. Contrary to Descartes' claim, an individual cannot be directly recognized. But we do not have to maintain that it can be so recognized in order to defend the notion of a material substance. It suffices if we hold that such a substance can be known in two ways. It can be known in that we can know things about it; we can know its properties. We can know that a particular body is an elephant; and we can know that all and only bodies are extended. Furthermore, we are also acquainted with material substances in perception. It is simply not true that we can only perceive perceptual properties. We also perceive the things which have these properties. When we see an apple, we perceive *something* which has a certain color, a certain taste, a certain shape, etc.

I think, therefore, that the Empiricist's challenge of the substance philosophy can be met. Nevertheless, the bundle view became more and more popular. There were other reasons for this popularity as well. For one, the great philosopher Leibniz built his philosophical system around it. Let us take a look at his reason for rejecting the substance view.

(7) *The attack on substance: Leibniz*

The substance view, I pointed out a moment ago, does not explain what relationship there is between a substance and its accidents. It is only clear on this point: the relationship is not a whole-part relation like the relation between substance and essence. It is much less 'intimate' than a whole-part relation; it is 'external' rather than 'internal'. Now, just as Berkeley emphasized long-standing doubts about the *knowability* of material substances, so Gottfried Wilhelm Leibniz (1646–1716) stressed long-standing doubts about the *intelligibility* of the relation between substance and accident. And he claimed that this relationship must be understood, in opposition to the tradition, as a whole-part relation:

> We must consider, then, what it means to be truly attributed to a certain subject. Now it is certain that every true predication has some basis in the nature of things, and when a proposition is not an identity, that is to say, when the predicate is not expressly contained in the subject, it must be included in it virtually. This is what the philosophers call *in-esse*, when they say that the predicate is in the subject so the subject term must always include the predicate term in such a way that anyone who understands perfectly the concept of subject will also know that the predicate pertains to it.
> (*Discourse on Metaphysics*, in *Philosophical Papers and Letters*, trans. L. E. Loemker, University of Chicago Press, 1956, vol. 1, pp. 471–2)

Leibniz speaks here of subjects and subject terms, of predicates and predicate terms, but what he says can easily be translated into our terminology. The properties of an individual, he claims, are *included* in the individual; they are parts of it. Thus the relationship between a property and the individual which has the property is a *part-whole* relation. Somewhere else, Leibniz says that he is able to understand what truth is only if he conceives of the predication relation as an inclusion relation, so that the predicate is included in the subject. The mystery of predication disppears if we conceive of predication as a part-whole relation. What could be more intelligible than the relationship between a whole and one of its parts.?

This conception of predication implies the bundle view and, hence, a rejection of the substance view. Leibniz thus joins hands with Berkeley, although you can hardly find two more different philosophers or philosophies. Both philosophies signal the end of the reign of substance philosophy. A revolution takes place in metaphysics, and the end of this revolution is not yet in sight.

Let us look at some of the fruits of this revolution for later reference. Here is an apple lying in front of me on my desk. I shall continue to call it 'Oscar'. According to Berkeley, it consists of a certain color, a certain taste, a certain consistency, etc. Oscar, in other words, is a complex entity which consists of a great number of properties. If we indicate a complex entity consisting of properties by writing down corners like this '⟨'and this '⟩', we can try to represent Oscar in the following way:

$$Oscar = \langle F, G, H, ... \rangle,$$

where F, G, H, etc. are the properties which Oscar has. F, for example, is the particular taste which Oscar has. (In order to keep things simple, we assume that Oscar tastes the same throughout his body; similarly for color and for other properties.) To say that Oscar has this taste is to say that F is a part of $\langle F, G, H, ... \rangle$. But now we must note an important complication. Oscar did not always have this taste. When he was still ripening on the tree, he was very sour. It is only *at this particular time* that he has the property F. At an earlier time, Oscar did not have the property (the taste) F, but had some other property instead. Oscar does not just have the properties which he has at this moment, when he is before me on my desk, but has all the properties he ever had and ever will have. I think that you can see that Oscar must consist of a *temporal succession of bundles of properties*. He is a *temporal* whole consisting of bundles. Let us

24

refer to a temporal whole by writing down brackets like this '[' and this ']' and let us indicate the temporal succession by subscripts. Then we get the following formula for Oscar:

Oscar = $[\langle F_1, G_1, H_1, ... \rangle, \quad \langle F_2, G_2, H_2, ... \rangle, \quad \langle F_3, ... \rangle, \quad \langle ... \rangle]$.

Recall Descartes' piece of wax. We saw earlier that it cannot be identical with either the bundle of those properties which it has when taken from the hive or with the bundle of properties which it has after it has been close to the fire. We now realize that, according to the bundle view, it is identical with a temporal whole consisting of numerous bundles, including the two just mentioned.

The list of properties which make up Oscar is very large. It includes all of the properties which he has had, which he has, and which he will have. And it contains, not only Oscar's colors at various times, but the most insignificant properties of his as well. For example, it includes the property that he was picked (at a certain time) by a boy named 'Martin'. It must contain this property; for it is true that Oscar was picked by Martin. The list must contain everything that is true of Oscar. This is one of the consequences of the bundle view.

Another is, as I have already mentioned briefly, that the distinction between essential and accidental properties disappears. Among the properties which constitute Oscar, there will be the essential property of being an apple. But there will also be the accidental property of having been picked by Martin. Now, if Oscar had not contained the property of being an apple, he would not have been Oscar, this apple. This follows from the principle that temporal wholes of bundles are identical only if the properties of the one whole are precisely the same as the properties of the other (and the temporal succession is the same). But from this principle it follows also that if Oscar had not been picked by Martin, he would not have been Oscar. A whole which does not include the property of being picked by Martin is not the same whole as Oscar. The bundle view abolishes the distinction between essential and accidental properties by making all properties, even the accidental ones, essential to an individual's being what it is. Let us from now on call the sum total of all of Oscar's properties his 'nature'. Every property, even the most insignificant one, enters into Oscar's nature.

Turn now from Oscar, the apple, to Adam, the first man. How does the bundle view agree with the Christian account of Adam's creation? Leibniz gave a lot of thought to this question and came up with the following explanation. According to the Christian theology, God did not create *a man*, but created a specific man, namely, Adam. God could have created some other possible person, but this person would have been a specific person, too. If God had created just *a* man without creating a specific man, then He would not have known whom specifically, He had created. And this is absurd. In short, God had a specific man, Adam, in mind when He created him. Put differently, God had a specific *concept* of whom He wanted to create. This concept, in order to be the concept of Adam, must have included every last property of Adam, including the number of hairs on his chest. It must have been a concept of Adam's *nature*. As a matter of fact, as Leibniz and other philosophers think of it, this concept *is* Adam's nature. When God created Adam, He freely chose to endow the concept of Adam with existence. Adam was created when God added existence to the concept. Thus we must once more revise our formula for an individual thing; we must add existence to the nature:

$$Adam = ([\langle \quad \rangle, \langle \quad \rangle, \ldots]; existence).$$

The parentheses indicate that we are dealing with a '*combination*' of a nature with existence. An individual is thus a *combination* of existence with a *temporal whole* which consists of *bundles of properties*.

I said a moment ago that the concept *is* the nature of Adam. The idea behind this identification is that as long as Adam's properties only exist in God's mind, they form a concept of Adam. When He adds existence to these properties, they become the nature of Adam. One and the same thing, in the traditional way, is supposed to exist both in a mind as a concept and in the world as a nature.

What has happened to Berkeley's simple substitution of bundles of properties for material substances? It may have looked as if he merely supplanted one category by another. But we realize now that things are much more complicated than they seemed to be. Adam, first of all, belongs to the category of *combination*: he is a combination of a temporal whole with existence. Secondly, this combination involves a *temporal whole* and a very peculiar entity, namely, *existence*. Existence, as you can see, is not treated like a property among properties. It does not belong to Adam's nature. But if it is not a property, what is it? To what category does it belong? These are questions that must eventually be answered. Martin Heidegger (1889–1976), as we shall see, makes them the centerpiece of his philosophy. Thirdly, the temporal whole consists of *bundles* of properties. This assay of individuals, therefore, involves three kinds of structure (whole) in addition to existence: bundles, temporal wholes, and combinations. And this raises the questions of what kind of an entity a structure is in general and how these three kinds of structure differ in particular. I consider it to be one of the most amazing features of the history of modern philosophy that these two questions never came up until recently, that is, until the end of the nineteenth century. Edmund Husserl (1859–1938), as we shall also see later, tries to answer them.

Back to Adam and Leibniz's story of his creation. Leibniz's story has at least two very unpleasant consequences. It is part of Adam's nature that he eats from the apple. Any nature, otherwise like Adam's but without the property of eating from the apple which Eve provides, is simply not Adam's nature. And if God had created a person without this property, He would have created a person other than Adam. But if Adam's nature includes eating from the apple, then God created a person who will eat from the apple. God, of course, knows what belongs to the nature of His prospective creation. God thus knew that Adam would eat from the apple. But if God knew this, how could He possibly be indignant when it happened? Why would he warn Adam not to eat from the apple? Why would he cast him from Paradise? Why, indeed, would he create Adam in the first place, rather than a person whose nature does not include sinning? God, it is true, does not *decide* that Adam should sin. But he does pick out for creation a nature which includes sinning. Leibniz has a problem. He must give some explanation of why God chose Adam's nature over other possible, less sinful, natures for creation. In more general terms, he must try to explain why God created this world rather than some other possible world, a possible world without cancer, without floods, and without concentration camps. Leibniz admits that this world is not perfect, but he claims that it is, nevertheless, *the best of all possible worlds* which God could have created. I recommend that you read Leibniz's defense of his rather hopeless case (*Theodicy*, trans. E. M. Huggard, London, Routledge & Kegan Paul, 1952).

The other unpalatable consequence of Leibniz's story of the creation of Adam is that Adam *has no choice but to sin*. Adam is not *free* not to eat from the apple. In order to distinguish this kind of freedom from other kinds, I shall speak of 'metaphysical freedom'. Every action of Adam's down to the most insignificant scratching of his head, is determined at the moment of Adam's creation by his nature. *As surely as Adam is Adam*, he will eat from the apple and he will scratch his head. Could Adam possibly not have eaten from the apple? No! Anyone who does not eat from the apple is not Adam. And what holds for Adam, holds presumably for all of us. Everyone of us is a combination of a nature with existence. And each nature contains every single one of our properties. *Thus man is not free*. All of our actions are determined. As we shall see, Leibniz's view is anathema to existentialists like Jean-Paul Sartre (1905–1980).

2. Brentano: the thesis of intentionality

(1) *Brentano's distinction between mental and physical phenomena*

Franz Brentano is one of the most remarkable figures in the history of philosophy. He was a brilliant philosopher. He was also, together with Wilhelm Wundt (1832–1920), a founder of the science of psychology. Most importantly, he had a host of distinguished students. Through these students, he became the grandfather of Husserl's phenomenology, of Meinong's theory of objects, and of Kotarbinski's reism, to mention just a few influential movements.

The most famous of Brentano's doctrines is the thesis that all and only mental phenomena are *intentional*. In order to understand this thesis, let us return for a moment to Descartes' characterization of a mental substance as a thinking being. We saw that by a thinking being Descartes means a being which performs a number of mental acts: it is a being which doubts, which affirms, which perceives, etc. Within the framework of Descartes' ontology, this means that the mental substance has a number of modifications. Mental acts are conceived of as properties of minds. Now the first thing we must note is that Brentano's students reject the substance view and embrace the bundle view. A mind is conceived of, not as a substance, but as a bundle of properties. But these properties, secondly, are really thought of as individual things. A particular mental act of affirmation, for example is conceived of, not as a property of a certain mental substance, but as an individual thing, which is part of a complicated whole, composed of many such individual things, that is, mental acts. Properly speaking, Brentano and his students do not think of a mind as a bundle of properties, in the sense of 'bundle' which we have so far used, but think of it as a whole, as a structure of a different sort, namely, as a whole consisting of individual things. Let me hasten to add that they were not at first as clear about the nature of this kind of whole as they should have been.

According to Descartes, minds have the essential characteristic that they think. Translated into Brentano's philosophy, this amounts to saying that minds consist in essence of individual mental acts. But this raises a new question: how are these mental individual things, these mental acts, distinguished from material individuals? Brentano continues Descartes' inquiry into the nature of the mind by trying to answer this further question. Minds, we know from Descartes, are different from bodies by having mental acts. But what distinguishes mental acts from bodies? Brentano puts the question this way: what distinguishes between mental and physical phenomena?

He starts out by giving examples of mental things:

> Every idea or presentation which we acquire either through sense perception or imagination is an example of a mental phenomenon. By presentation I do not mean that which is presented, but rather the act of presentation, thus hearing a sound, seeing a colored object, feeling warmth or cold, as well as similar states of imagination are examples of what I mean by this term. I also mean by it the thinking of a general concept, provided such a thing actually does occur. Furthermore, every judgment, every recollection, every expectation, every inference, every conviction or opinion, every doubt, is a mental phenomenon. Also to be included under this term is every emotion: joy, sorrow, fear, hope, courage, despair, anger, love, hate, desire, act of will, intention, astonishment, admiration, contempt, etc. (*Psychology from an Empirical Standpoint*, trans. Antos C. Rancuredo, D. B. Terrell and

Linda L. McAlister, New York, Humanities Press, 1973, pp. 78-9)

What a change from the few mental acts mentioned by Descartes! And notice all of the emotions which are mentioned. But there is also something strange about this list which I wish to point out to you. Brentano speaks of hearing, seeing, feeling, etc. What he seems to be referring to are mental acts of *perception*. But he calls these acts 'acts of presentation'. What are the objects of these presentations? Well, what are the objects of perception? What do we see, what do we hear, etc.? We see trees, and mountains, and clouds, and other perceptual objects; and we hear cars, trains, melodies, etc. Brentano says that seeing a colored *object* is an act of presentation, but he also says that hearing a *sound*, not a perceptual object, is an act of presentation. Here we have two kinds of object: we may be said to see trees and hear cars, but we may also be said to see colors and to hear sounds. As I shall continue to use the term 'perceive', we perceive trees and their colors and shapes, and we perceive cars and the noises they make. But Brentano, as it turns out, thinks of the objects of presentations only as sensory properties. What we are presented with in perception are colors and shapes, not colored objects and shaped objects. Furthermore, these sensory properties are identified with sensations in the mind. Brentano is under the spell of the argument from science according to which colors are, at best, sensations in minds, but not objective properties of independent bodies.

Let us look at Brentano's examples of physical phenomena: 'Examples of physical phenomena, on the other hand, are a color, a figure, a landscape which I see, a chord which I hear, warmth, cold, odor which I sense; as well as similar images which appear in the imagination' (*ibid.*, pp. 79-80). This assortment is even stranger than the previous one. The only example which seems to fit is the landscape. But this is exactly not the kind of example which Brentano wants. Rather, what he has in mind as examples of physical phenomena are the sensory properties we just mentioned. But if these sensory properties are conceived of as sensations in minds, then how could Brentano possibly think of them as physical phenomena? I shall solve this puzzle in a moment. If you are inclined to think that I must be wrong, that Brentano could not possibly have thought of sensations as physical, remind yourself that he also mentions images as examples of physical phenomena.

Having given examples of what he means by mental and physical phenomena, Brentano next tries to find defining characteristics of these two groups of things. And the first distinguishing characteristic he mentions is this: every mental phenomenon, as distinguished from all physical phenomena, either is an act of presentation or else is built upon one. This criterion reveals one of Brentano's fundamental convictions. Brentano believes that every mental act other than a presentation, presupposes such a presentation. Before such an act can occur, an act of presentation must precede it. He says: 'This act of presentation forms the foundation not merely of the act of judging, but also of desiring and of every other mental act. Nothing can be judged, desired, hoped or feared, unless one has a presentation of that thing' (*ibid.*, p. 80). Brentano's view, in short, is this. In order to judge something or other, this something or other must first appear before the mind; similarly, in order to fear something, one must have an idea of what it is that one fears, that is, the object must be before the mind; in order to desire something, to give one more example, a desired object must first be brought before the mind by an act of presentation. It is the function of acts of presentation to supply the mind with objects. Other acts then fasten upon these objects: they are judged, feared, desired, etc. I do not think that Brentano's view is correct, and we shall return to it eventually when we discuss Husserl's theory of eidetic intuition.

Next, Brentano briefly alludes to the Cartesian characterization of bodies as being extended, that is, as being spatial. He does not argue that this feature fails to distinguish between bodies and minds, but merely remarks that the distinction is not universally accepted. And then he goes on to give what we now consider to be the fundamental thesis of the intentionality of mental acts:

> Every mental phenomenon is characterized by what the Scholastics of the Middle Ages called the intentional (or mental) inexistence of an object, and what we might call, though not wholly unambiguously, reference to a content,

direction toward an object (which is not to be understood here to be a thing), or immanent objectivity. Every mental phenomenon includes something as object within itself, although they do not all do so in the same way. In presentation, something is presented, in judgment something is affirmed or denied, in love loved, in hate hated, in desire desired, and so on. (*Ibid.*, p. 88)

Every mental phenomenon is directed toward an object. This thesis sums up such undeniable facts as that there is no idea which is not an idea of something or other, that there is no desire which is not the desire for something or other, that there is no belief which is not the belief in something or other, that there is no seeing which is not the seeing of something or other, and so on. Once pointed out, the thesis of intentionality is a truism. But its philosophical ramifications, as we shall see, are monumental.

As it stands, however, the thesis is flawed in two respects. Firstly, and most importantly, it is merely true for mental acts, not for mental entities in general, as Brentano claims. There are mental phenomena which are not intentional, which do not have an object. Thus mental phenomena divide into two groups, those that are intentional and those that are not. The former are what we have always called 'mental acts'. Among the latter are such mental things as sensations, feeling, and images. Secondly, the thesis remains incomplete as long as no account of the special directedness of all mental phenomena is provided.

All mental acts, we agree with Brentano, are intentional. This distinguishes between mental acts, on the one hand, and all other things, on the other. In particular, it distinguishes between mental acts and material bodies. An apple, for example, has no object as a desire has; it is not directed toward anything else. But intentionality, we object to Brentano, is not the defining characteristic of the mental in general. There are mental things which are not mental acts, which are not intentional. Recall Brentano's strange classification of images as physical. We can now understand it. An image, say a visual image of your father's face, is not intentional as a mental act of imagining is. It is merely a picture which becomes a picture *of* something–and hence truly a picture–through an intentional act of imagining. When we clearly distinguish between the visual phenomenon which we call 'an image' and the mental act of imagining something or other by means of this image, then we see that while the act is intentional, the image itself is not. The latter gets its direction only through the former. But if an image is not intentional, and if all mental phenomena are intentional, then it follows that images cannot be mental. And since they must be either mental or physical, it follows, as Brentano claims, that they are physical. We know, of course, what is wrong with this argument: it is not true, as Brentano believes, that *all* mental phenomena are intentional. Perhaps another example will better convince you of this. Consider a pain, a toothache, and distinguish between the pain and your feeling it. The act of feeling a pain, of experiencing a pain, is clearly intentional; it is directed toward an object, namely, the pain. But the pain itself is not intentional; it has no object. If Brentano were correct in his general thesis, then we would have to classify pains as physical phenomena; and this would surely be incorrect.

Images and pains, I have so far argued, are mental without being intentional. Let me now add sensations (sense-impressions) to this list. The colored sensation which you experience when you look at an apple is clearly a mental phenomenon, but it is not intentional. Again, the act of experiencing this visual sensation is, of course, intentional; it has an object, namely, the sensation. But the sensation itself is not. At this point of our exposition, extreme carefulness and precision is in order. Most philosophers, traditional as well as modern, do not sufficiently distinguish between the following kinds of thing, and Brentano is no exception. There are, firstly, *perceptual objects* like our paradigm apple. These are the kinds of thing which we can perceive. There are, secondly, *physical objects* of which the perceptual objects, according to the latest theory of physics, consist. These physical objects are elementary particles, or psi-functions, or what have you. We cannot perceive these physical objects, but we can perceive their effects, for example, on photographic plates. Thirdly, there are *sensations* which we experience (not perceive) when we perceive perceptual objects. When we see an apple, for example, we experience a certain visual sensation which has size, color, and shape. This visual sensation changes its size with the distance from the apple, it changes its shape with the perspective on the apple, and it changes its color with the lighting conditions. Of course, the apple does not change its size, nor its shape, nor its color, when we walk around it and look at it from different angles. The visual sensation which we experience when we look at an apple is a function, not only of the apple before us, but also of the conditions of our perception, including the condition of our eyes and of our nervous system. Perhaps the best example of the independent variability of sensation and perceived object is afforded by perspective. If you learn to draw in perspective, what you learn is to draw, not the shape of the perceived object, but the shape of the visual sense impression which is caused in you by the perceived object when you stand at a certain distance from it and view it from a certain angle. For example, if you look at a rectangular desk top from a few feet away, you will experience a trapezoidal sensation. You can easily check on the shape which a smaller or taller person experiences by putting yourself at his eye level.

Color, contrary to the Cartesian school of thought, is an objective property of perceptual objects. But it is also a property of visual sensations. Both non-mental and mental things can be colored: an apple is red, and so may be the visual sensation which I experience when I look at it. And you can easily see that your visual sensation may change color without the apple's changing color by putting on dark blue glasses: the apple will still be red, but your sense-impression will now have a different color. To hold that color is merely a sensation in the mind is, from our point of view, doubly mistaken. It is mistaken, firstly, because color is a property of *material things* (perceptual objects like apples). And it is mistaken, secondly, because color is a *property* of sensations (and perceptual objects), not a sensation itself.

Let us return to Brentano. Recall his examples of physical phenomena: he mentions a color, a figure (shape), a landscape (this is the strange one), a chord, warmth, cold, and odor. I think that what he had in mind are perceptual properties and that the landscape slipped in by mistake. A particular color, at any rate, is said to be an example of a physical phenomenon. From our point of view, this is again doubly mistaken. It is mistaken, firstly, because colors are, not only properties of material objects (perceptual objects), but of *sensations* as well.

And it is mistaken, secondly, because colors are *properties* of perceptual objects and sensations, and are not themselves individual things.

Brentano holds that all mental phenomena are intentional. I have argued that there are at least three kinds of thing which are mental without being intentional, namely, feelings, images, and sensations. But I also agreed with Brentano that mental acts, this most important kind of mental phenomenon, are intentional. This is what distinguishes mental acts from all other individual things: they have objects. By 'the thesis of intentionality' I shall from now on understand the narrower claim. It is a claim which all Phenomenologists and Existentialists embrace.

(2) *Kinds, contents, and objects of mental acts*

Mental acts have objects. But what, precisely, does this having of an object consist in? Compare the two sentences:

(1) Martin believes that the earth is round,

and (2) Marcy sees that her cake is ready

with the following two sentences:

(3) Martin is the brother of Marcy.

(4) Marcy is taller than Martin.

In (3) and (4), we assert that certain *relations* hold between Martin and Marcy, namely the relation of being a brother of in (3) and the relation of being taller than in (4). A comparison between these two sentences and (1) and (2) suggests that the latter, too, mention relations, namely, the relation of believing and the relation of seeing, respectively. (1) asserts that a relation of believing holds between Martin, on the one hand, and the state of affairs that the earth is round, on the other. (2) asserts that a relation of seeing holds between Marcy, on the one hand, and the circumstance that the cake is ready, on the other. And this suggests further that the intentionality of mental acts consists in that they are relations. To say that every mental act has an object, one may think, is to say that every mental act, since it is a relation, has a second term. Its first term is, of course, the person or, more accurately, the mind which experiences the mental act. A (two-term) relation always holds between two things. Martin cannot just be a brother without being a brother of someone; Marcy cannot just be taller, she must be taller than someone else; and Luckys cannot just taste better, they must taste better than something else. Strictly analogously, Martin cannot merely believe, but must believe something; Marcy cannot just see, but she must see something; and Romeo cannot just love, but must love someone.

I think that this insight into the nature of intentionality is essentially correct, but it needs a few refinements. Firstly, a particular mental act cannot really *be* a relation, since it is an individual thing which occurs at a certain moment in time. Rather, it must *involve* a relation to an object. Consider Martin's belief that the earth is round. At a certain moment in time, there occurs in Martin's mind an act of believing. This, as I said, is an individual thing. Now, this mental act is an act of believing that the earth is round rather than, say, that it is flat or that two plus two equal four. This means that this particular mental act is *related* to the state of affairs that the earth is round rather than, say, to the state of affairs that it is flat or to the state of affairs that two plus two equal four. There is thus a unique and most important relation, which I shall call 'the intentional nexus', between individual mental acts, on the one hand, and their objects, on the other. In our second example, this very same relation obtains between one of Marcy's mental acts of seeing and the state of affairs that her cake is ready. We can now give a revised formulation of the thesis of intentionality: mental acts and only mental acts stand in a unique relation, the intentional nexus, to something else. A mind is intentional in so far as it harbors mental acts which are intentional.

We must, secondly, refine our first rough sketch by noting that the objects of mental acts, as we ordinarily talk, are not necessarily states of affairs or circumstances. We assert that we saw *an elephant*, that we remember *Paris*, or that we desire *Hedy Lamar*. We clearly imply that the objects of these acts are individual things: an elephant, a city, and an attractive woman. But it may be said that the three assertions are really incomplete; they don't tell the whole story. What we really saw was some such circumstance as that an elephant stood on his two hind legs, and what we really remember is some such state of affairs as that we walked the streets of Paris, and what we really desire is some such circumstance as that Hedy Lamar dances a tango with us. I think that it is indeed true that most of our important mental acts, for example, all of our perceptions, intend states of affairs rather than individual things, properties, and the like. But I shall not argue for this contention now. It is not all that important for our present inquiry, but will become crucial when we discuss Husserl's notion of eidetic intuition.

Thirdly, we must still further refine our first refinement of the nature of intentionality. The intentional nexus does not really hold between a mental act and its object, but holds between a property of the mental act and its object. Let me explain. Martin believes that the earth is round. Assume that Eric shares this belief; he, too, believes at a certain moment that the earth is round. There occur therefore two different acts of believing, one in Martin's mind and one in Eric's mind. Yet, these beliefs have something in common; they share a common property, just as two white billiard balls share a color. This property characterizes them as mental acts with the *same* object. The Brentano school of philosophers calls this property 'the content of the mental act'. Just as all white billiard balls in the world at this moment share a color, so all acts of believing that the earth is round share a common content. And it is really the content of a mental act which gives it the direction toward a particular object. The intentional nexus, according to this view, holds between the content of a mental act and a certain object. A mental act has the particular object which it has because it has the particular content which it has. For example, Martin's belief is a belief that the earth is round rather than a belief that the earth is flat because it has a certain property rather than another; it has a certain content rather than another. The content of a mental act thus determines completely what object the act has.

Fourthly and lastly, individual mental acts form kinds. Martin's and Eric's acts of believing do not only share a common content, but they are also of the same kind: they are both acts of believing. Someone else, Paul, may doubt that the earth is round. In this case, his mental act of doubting has the same content as Martin's and Eric's acts of believing and, hence, the same object, namely, the circumstance that the earth is round. But his act is of a different kind. It is not, as Martin's and Eric's acts are, an act of believing, but is an act of doubting. This means that while Martin's and Eric's acts share the property of being believings, Paul's act has the property of being an act of doubting. It shares this property with all other individual acts which are acts of doubting. Every mental act has thus two important properties. It has a property which determines what particular object the act has. I called this property 'the content' of the act. And it has a property which determines what particular kind of act it is, whether it is a believing, or a doubting, or a desiring, or a remembering, or a seeing, etc. I shall call this property, for obvious reasons 'the kind' to which an act belongs.

Summing up our four refinements, we must distinguish between:

(a) an individual mental act, say A_1;
(b) the particular content, C_1, which this act has;
(c) the specific kind, K_1, to which it belongs;
(d) the unique object which the act has, O_1;
and (e) the intentional nexus, I, which obtains between C_1 and O_1.

I shall use Figure 2.1 to represent that an act A_1 intends an object O_1.

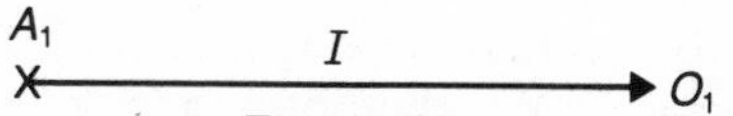

Figure 2.1

The cross at the left represents the particular act A_1; the arrow represents the intentional nexus; it points at the object O_1. The content of the act is not depicted in order to keep the diagram as simple as possible; the kind will be indicated, if it is important, by just writing down 'seeing', or 'believing', etc.

Here, then, is our last and final formulation of the thesis of intentionality: only mental acts have those peculiar properties which we called 'contents', and only contents stand in that most unique relation, the intentional nexus, to other things. In this, therefore, consists the radical uniqueness of the mind: it alone among all of the furniture of the world *has before it* a world; a world to be explored, to be feared, a world to care about.

(3) *The nature of the intentional nexus*

I said earlier that one of the main problems of the Cartesian philosophy is to explain how ideas can represent their objects without resembling them. Brentano and his students finally found a solution: an idea represents its object by intending it. Put differently, the relation between an idea and its object is, not a relation of identity or resemblance, but rather the intentional nexus. Applied to ideas, the distinctions of the last section come to this: there is an act of having an idea; an act of presentation (as Brentano would say); this act has a certain content which is the idea proper; this content (the idea proper) stands in the intentional nexus to an object; and there is, finally, this object.

A solution of Descartes' problem had to wait for several hundred years, I think, because of two circumstances. Firstly, there is the fact that relations, in the sense described above, have only been accepted very recently as forming a basic category of their own. Even philosophers like Berkeley and Leibniz, who supplanted substances by bundles of properties, were suspicious of relations and tried to eliminate them. But an explanation of the intentionality of mental acts is impossible without recognition of relations. Secondly there is the fact that a relational account of the intentionality of acts runs into a profound difficulty, namely, into what I shall call 'the problem of nonexistent objects'. We shall have a look at this problem in the next section, but let me hint at what is at stake. Consider the idea of a golden mountain. This idea, like all ideas, has an object, namely, a golden mountain. According to the relational account of intentionality, this means that this idea is the content of various individual mental acts of having this idea, and that this content stands in the relation *I* to a golden mountain. But how can this idea stand in a relation to a golden mountain when there is no golden mountain? How can the relation *I* obtain between an idea, on the one hand, and something that does not exist at all, on the other? How can there ever be a relation between something that exists and something that does not exist? Does a relation not require that the things between which it holds exist? We seem to be faced with the following dilemma. We must either insist that a relation can connect with something that is not there at all, or else we must give up the relational account of intentionality.

Relations, I said, were neglected by the Aristotelian tradition of which Descartes is a member. But they were also shunned by the new bundle-philosophers. There are many reasons for this disregard. Let me mention two; one for the tradition, one for the moderns.

Plato was the teacher of Aristotle; he was the older of these two. Let us therefore assume that at one time he was taller than Aristotle, but that Aristotle eventually grew to be taller than Plato. At t_1, then, Plato is taller than Aristotle, while at t_2, Aristotle is taller than Plato. Now, assume further that you can conceive of change (in a substance) only in terms of a thing's changing its properties. How can you possibly explain that Plato was at one time taller than Aristotle, and now is no longer taller than Aristotle? Plato, it is clear, has not changed at all; he has not changed his height. Yet, what was true of him at one time, is no longer true of him. If there were relations, then we would have to say that Plato has changed. But, quite obviously, he has not changed. Hence there cannot be any relations. The way out of this difficulty is quite clear to us modern philosophers. We must distinguish between two kinds of change, change in property and change in relation. While it is true that Plato has not changed in one sense, it is also true that he has changed in another. Plato has not changed his height, but he has changed in relation to Aristotle. Things, in short, can change in different ways. But to see this clearly, one has to acknowledge the ontological uniqueness and independence of relations.

There is no room for relations in the bundle view of individual things. An apple is conceived of as consisting of a number of properties; these properties are 'in' the apple; they are parts of it. Now suppose one apple, A, is to the left of another apple, B. A certain shade of red, the color of A, is a part of the bundle which is A; a certain shade of green, the color of B, is a part of the bundle which is B. But of what is the relation of being to the left of a part? This relation *holds* or *obtains between* A and B and, hence, is quite obviously neither a part of A, nor a part of B, nor a part of both A and B. According to the bundle view, there is simply no place for it to be. Thus the bundle view must either try to make room for it somewhere, or else must deny that there are relations. Usually, it does the latter.

Those who denied the existence of relations had to explain the structure of relational facts. It is a fact, as far as our examples go, that Plato is (at one time) taller than Aristotle; and it is a fact that

A is to the left of *B*. If there are only individual things and their properties, then these two facts must somehow consist of facts which involve only these two categories. A standard view has it that relations are the creation of mental acts of comparison. Take our example of Plato and Aristotle. According to this view, at some time, Plato has a certain height and Aristotle has a certain height. The height of Plato is, of course, conceived of as a property of his; and so is Aristotle's. Now if someone compares the height of Plato with the height of Aristotle, his mind somehow creates the relation of being taller than between them and arrives at the judgment that Plato is taller than Aristotle. Similarly, *A* is said to be located at a certain place, while *B* is at another place. These places may be conceived of as properties of *A* and *B* or as individuals. In either case, the judgment that *A* is to the left of *B* is allegedly arrived at by a mind's comparing the places of *A* and *B* with each other.

This attempt to reduce relations to properties and mental acts of comparison is not very promising. What, precisely, is this presumed property of height which Plato has? Is it the property of being, say, six feet tall? If so, then we deal no longer with a property, but rather with a relation, namely, with the relation of *being as tall as* a measuring device of six feet in length. To attribute to Plato this height is to attribute a certain relation to him and something else. The alleged property of height turns out to be a disguised relation. Almost all of the properties which qualify as material for acts of comparison turn out to be disguised relations. In our second example, there is a different difficulty. There is simply nothing in or about the place of *A*, conceived of either as a property of *A* or as an individual point in space, which would afford the slightest clue as to where it is relative to the place of *B*. Why, then, does a mind not arrive at the judgment that *A* is to the right of *B*?

Like everything in metaphysics, the issue of whether or not relations break up into properties is profound and complicated. I do not think that they do. And I shall adopt without further ado the view that relations form a third fundamental category, in addition to individuals and their properties. How do relations differ from other things? What are their essential characteristics? Well, the most obvious feature is that they obtain between two or more things, while properties are predicated of one thing. So far, we have only considered two-term relations, but there are also relations with more than two terms. For example, the *between* relation is a three-term relation: A is between B and C.

Perhaps the most astounding feature of relations is the fact that they bring order into the world. If there were no relations, there could be no measurement and, hence, no science. To get a glimpse of this compare the two sentences:

(1) Plato is taller than Aristotle,

and (2) Aristotle is taller than Plato.

It is clear that if (1) is true, (2) must be false, and conversely. Thus it makes a big difference whether Plato occurs as the first term of the relation or Aristotle is its first term. We cannot just turn the names around and get the same fact. This feature is often described by saying that relations (among all of the things there are) have a *direction*. Every (two-term) relation comes, so to speak, with two different hooks, so that it makes a difference which one of two things is hooked onto the relation by which one of the two hooks. Another way of putting the same thing is to say that every (two-term) relation comes with two distinct places. If we depict these places by a circle and a square, respectively, we can depict the relation in this way:

$$\bigcirc^R \square$$

Now, to say that the relation has a direction is to say that the fact:

$$\text{Ⓐ}^R \boxed{B}$$

is never identical with the fact:

$$\text{Ⓑ}^R \boxed{A}$$

no matter what R is, or what A and B are.

To see what all of this has to do with order, we must introduce one more distinction. Relations can be divided into symmetric and non-symmetric ones. A relation is symmetric if and only if it holds between B and A, in that order, as long as it holds between A and B, in that order. An example of a symmetric relation is the relation of parallelism between lines. If line A is parallel to line B, then it is obviously also the case that line B is parallel to line A. Another example is the relation of being a spouse. If Tom is the spouse of Jane, then Jane is the spouse of

Tom. Notice that the relation of being a husband is not symmetric: if Tom is the husband of Jane, Jane is not the husband of Tom. A non-symmetric relation is simply a relation for which the condition just stated does not hold: from the fact that the relation holds between A and B, in that order, it does not follow that it also holds between B and A, in that order. Among the non-symmetric relations, the really interesting ones are the so-called 'asymmetric' relations. A relation is asymmetric if and only if the following is always the case: if the relation holds between A and B, in that order, then *it does not hold* between B and A, in that order. I called asymmetric relations interesting because it is this kind of relation which is responsible for the order in the world. As you can easily see, the relation of being taller than is asymmetric, and so is the relation of being to the left of. The intentional nexus is asymmetric: if I holds between a content C_1 and an object O_1, then it does not hold between O_1 and C_1. An example of a non-symmetric relation which is not asymmetric is the relation of being a brother of. If A is the brother of B, then B may not be the brother of A, but the sister of A. Hence the relation is not symmetric. But it is also not asymmetric, for B may be the brother of A. One more example, coupled with a lament. The relation of being in love with is not symmetric, but imagine the amount of misery and despair that would have been prevented in the history of the world if it were symmetric!

Not every asymmetric relation gives you an interesting ordering. The relation must fulfill other conditions as well. Just compare the taller than relation in this respect with the intentional nexus. The former allows you to arrange all people, for example, in a certain order from the smallest to the tallest. The latter does not yield a similar series. But if we assume that contents themselves are objects of other contents, then we can order a series of mental acts according to their relative position in the series. A certain act, A_1, with content C_1, intends another act, A_2, with content C_2, which intends a third act, A_3, with C_3, and so on.

After this excursion into the ontology of relations, let us return to our main concern, the intentional nexus. We have seen how unique relations are. Without them, there is no direction and without direction, there is no order. And without order, as we shall later see, there is no structure. We can therefore hardly overestimate the ontological importance of relations. If we cheerfully and with open arms, so to speak, welcome relations to our inventory of the categories, then nothing stands in our way of conceiving of the intentionality of mental acts in terms of the intentional nexus. The intentional relation I is a two-term, asymmetric relation which conjoins a mind and a world. It is the bridge which spans the abyss between the inner life of your mind and the independent world around you.

(4) The problem of nonexistent objects

A relational account of the intentionality of mental acts, however, runs immediately into the formidable problem of nonexistent objects. This problem arises because the nature of relations clashes with the nature of intentionality. Relations seem to require existing terms, while mental acts can intend nonexistent objects and circumstances. Can these two features be reconciled? I do not think so.

Brentano's response to the problem is rather complicated and ingenious, but in the end comes down to abandoning a relational account of intentionality. In the typical Aristotelian vein, he proposes to treat all relations as a special kind of property. According to Brentano, when John thinks of Paris, then there occurs a certain act of thinking in his mind, and this act has a certain property, namely, the property of being-a-thinking-of-Paris. This property, he also holds, does not concern or involve Paris. To think of Paris, is to think *in a certain way*, not to think *of a certain object*. Thinking of Paris is like feeling tired, in that feeling tired is a way of feeling rather than a feeling of something. When John on another occasion thinks of the golden mountain, he thinks in a certain way rather than of a certain object. His thinking has then the property of being-a-thinking-of-a-golden-mountain. Of course, this property is different from the property of being-a-thinking-of-Paris, and the two acts of thinking are distinguished by means of this difference. Just as the latter property does not involve Paris, so the former does not concern the golden mountain. The problem of nonexistent objects is 'solved' by denying that John stands in some kind of relation, the intentional nexus, to the golden mountain when he thinks of the golden mountain. He does not even stand in some kind of relation to Paris, when he thinks of Paris. This is a most radical solution to the problem, for it amounts to the view that the mind does not really relate to anything, that there is no world *for* a mind. Ultimately, it must lead to the conclusion that there is not even a world, but merely a self-contained mind, observing its ever-changing properties.

Actually, Brentano's strange act-properties cannot even be genuine properties of minds. The reason is that Brentano thinks of change, in the Aristotelian fashion, as accidental change in a substance. Recall our assumption that at one time Plato was taller than Aristotle and that, at another time, he was shorter than Aristotle. According to Brentano's view, this is to say that Plato first had the property of being-taller-than-Aristotle and later lost this property. Yet, as Brentano sees it, Plato has not really changed at all. He concludes, therefore, that a property like being-taller-than-Aristotle cannot be a genuine property. If it were a genuine property, then Plato would have changed as soon as he loses it. What holds for this property, holds for all those strange act-properties like thinking-of-Paris: none of them can be a genuine property. What a quandary! In order to escape from the problem of nonexistent objects, Brentano replaced relations by properties. But now it turns out that these alleged properties, since they invite relational change, cannot really be properties.

You may think that the problem is solved if we hold that the intentional nexus holds when the object exists and does not hold when it does not. Thus when John thinks of Paris, the content of his act of thinking is related to Paris, since Paris exists. But when he thinks of the golden mountain, then the content of his thought is not related to the golden mountain, since there is no such thing. But this will not do. The intentionality of mental acts is a phenomenon that holds with equal force for acts with nonexistent objects and acts with existent objects. A thought of the golden mountain is a thought *of* the golden mountain and not, say, a thought *of* Pegasus (the winged horse that sprang from Medusa at her death). The object of the one thought is different from the object of the second. The intentionality of mental acts, their *having* objects, has absolutely nothing to do with the *existence* of their objects. If you deny that John is in some fashion or another related to the golden mountain when he thinks of it, then you must explain in some other way why his thought is a thought *of* the golden mountain rather than *of* the winged horse that sprang from Medusa at her death.

A solution to the problem of nonexistent objects quite different from Brentano's was proposed by the famous British philosopher Bertrand Russell (1872-1970). He agrees with us that intentionality must be grounded in the intentional nexus. Since he also believes that all of the terms of a relation must exist, he boldly concludes that every object of every mental act must have some sort of being. He distinguishes, therefore, between two forms (kinds, stages, modes) of being. There is, firstly, the genuine article, namely *existence*. Paris has this kind of being, but the golden mountain does not. And then there is, secondly, a general kind of being, just called 'being', which even the golden mountain and Pegasus have. Here is how Russell describes his distinction:

> *Being* is that which belongs to every conceivable term, to every possible object of thought–in short to everything that can possibly occur in any proposition, true or false, and to all such propositions themselves. ... The homeric gods, relations, chimeras, and four dimensional spaces all have being, for if they were not entities of a kind, we could make no propositions about them. Thus being is a general attribute of everything, and to mention anything is to show that it is. Existence, on the contrary, is the prerogative of some only among beings. (B. Russell, *The Principles of Mathematics*, New York, Norton & Co., 1964, p. 449)

According to Russell, the golden mountain has being–there is a golden mountain–but it does not exist. Mount Everest, on the contrary, has, not only being, but also existence. The problem of nonexistent objects is solved in the following way. The intentional nexus has always two terms; both of its terms have, at least, being. Its first term, the content, has also existence. Its second term, the object, sometimes has existence and sometimes does

The background

not. But even if the object does not exist, it has at least being. Thus we do not have a relation which connects the content with nothing.

I do not think that this solution is correct. It seems to me to be no less a blow to common sense to have to acknowledge the existence of a relation which can hold between a content and something that has mere being than to have to admit that the intentional nexus holds between a content and something that has no being at all. The problem of nonexistent objects arises because we believe ordinarily that a relation must hold between *existents*. Russell's solution clashes with this belief. But it tries to smooth over this clash, it tries to hide it, by introducing the notion of being. But we are just as baffled by the claim that the intentional nexus can hold between a content and the golden mountain when the latter is said to have being as when it is said not to exist. We must not be fooled by the word 'being', as it occurs in this context. The golden mountain, Russell agrees, does not exist. There really is no such thing at all. You will search for it in vain the world over. What, then, could it possibly mean to say that it nevertheless has being? I suspect that this means nothing more than that one can nevertheless think of it, wish for it, discuss its existential status, etc. If so, then Russell's solution amounts to nothing more than the disguised admission that the intentional nexus can connect minds with what is not there, what does not exist, what really has no being.

This brings us to a third attempt to solve the problem. This way out was proposed by one of Brentano's students, the Polish philosopher Kasimir Twardowski (1866–1938). Like Brentano himself, Twardowski denies one of the two propositions which together create the problem. Brentano, as we have seen, denies that intentionality is a matter of relations. Twardowski denies that relations must have existing terms. Our ordinary intuition, nourished by examples of spatial, temporal, and family relations, is simply mistaken. While it is true that these paradigms of relations require existing terms, not all relations are of this sort. In particular, the intentional nexus is an exception. It is not true, as other philosophers have contended, that there are objectless ideas. It is not true, for example that the idea of the golden mountain has no object. The belief that it does not have an object is created because of a confusion:

48

The confusion of the proponents of objectless ideas consists in that they mistook the nonexistence of an object for its not being presented. But every idea presents an object whether it exists or not, just as every name designates an object, regardless of whether the latter exists or not. Although it is therefore correct to assert that the objects of certain ideas do not exist, one says too much if one also asserts that no objects fall under these ideas, that these ideas have no objects, that they are objectless. (K. Twardowski, *On the Content and Object of Presentations*, trans. R. Grossmann, The Hague, Martinus Nijhoff, 1977, p. 22)

Twardowski's point is that we must sharply distinguish between two questions. There is, firstly, the question of what a given idea represents, what its object is. There is, secondly, the quite different question of whether or not this object exists. Every idea has an object or, more generally, every mental act has an object. Thus the intentional nexus always holds. But not every object exists. Thus the intentional nexus does not always connect with an existent.

In this context, Twardowski advances a most fascinating argument for a distinct but related thesis. Assume that someone denies that the golden mountain, *since it does not exist*, can ever be before a mind. What does he then believe not to exist? Surely, not the idea of the golden mountain, for this idea is neither made from gold nor a mountain, and does most certainly exist. He must therefore be denying the existence of something that is made from gold and is a mountain, and this can only be the golden mountain. But then the golden mountain must be before his mind. The argument is even more impressive when we take as our example the idea of the round square, that is, of something which combines, as one says, contradictory properties. The only thing, so Twardowski argues, of which one can deny existence when one denies the existence of the round square is the round square itself, that is, of a thing which combines the contradictory properties of being round and also square. If this is so, then the round square itself must be before the mind. I called this a fascinating argument because it implies, among other things, a very important ontological thesis, namely, the thesis that nonexistent things have properties. It implies, for example, that the golden mountain, though it does not exist, is golden and is a mountain. It even implies that the round square, though it is a contradictory thing and certainly does not exist, is nevertheless both round as well as square. And it implies that Pegasus, although there is no such thing, nevertheless has wings. I believe that this part of Twardowski's view is false. But it was accepted by many of Brentano's students and it is one of the cornerstones of Husserl's Phenomenology.

Of the three solutions of the problem of nonexistent objects, I think that Twardowski's is the correct one. We must acknowledge the existence of 'abnormal' relations, that is, of relations with nonexistent terms. As it turns out, the intentional nexus is not the only relation of this kind. Other abnormal relations hold between states of affairs. Consider the relation represented by the connective 'or' as it occurs in the sentence: 'The earth is flat *or* the earth is not flat.' This sentence represents a fact since it is true. It is also a fact that the earth is not flat. But the sentence 'The earth is flat' is not true and, hence, does not represent a fact; there is no such circumstance as that the earth is flat. But this nonexistent circumstance is nevertheless related by the connection *or* to the fact that the earth is not flat, so that it forms, together with the latter, the compound fact. In short, the nonexistent state of affairs that the earth is flat is related by *or* to the fact that the earth is not flat. Even stranger is the relation *neither-nor*. Consider the fact that the earth is neither flat nor shaped like a cube. This fact is of the form: *neither P nor Q*. Here neither *P* nor *Q* is a fact; both are nonexistent circumstances! And here is a third example of an abnormal relation: the relation which holds between the circumstance that the earth is flat and the compound fact that the earth is flat or the earth is not flat. The former, I shall say, is a *constituent* of the latter. A nonexistent state of affairs can be a constituent of a fact.

Thus as soon as we turn away from every-day relations–spatial, temporal, and family relations–we discover, not just one, but a whole nest of abnormal relations. Most of these relations do not concern the mind. And this shows that 'abnormality' is not the hallmark of the mind. The intentional nexus, it is true, exists only in a world with mental acts. But relations like *or* and *neither-nor* are part of the furniture of the non-mental world. Even if there were no minds and never had been any, it would still be a fact that the earth is flat or the earth is not flat.

(5) *The infinite regress argument against mental acts*

There is an old argument against the existence of mental acts that goes back to Greek philosophy. It tries to show that the assumption that there are mental acts leads to an infinite regress of other mental acts and must therefore be rejected. Assume that there exists one mental act, A_1, in a given mind. Now, if A_1 is part of that mind, then that mind is aware of A_1; for a mind is aware of every mental act that occurs in it. But this means that there must occur a second mental act, A_2, which is the awareness of A_1; for to be aware of something means for a mental act of awareness to occur. But since A_2 is part of that mind, it, too, is known by the mind. And this means that there must occur a third mental act, A_3, in that mind, namely, the awareness of A_2. And so on. Thus the occurrence of A_1 in a mind implies the occurrence of an infinite series of further acts in that mind. But infinitely many mental acts never occur in a given mind. Hence there can occur not even a single act. Therefore, there are no mental acts.

This argument rests on two crucial assumptions:
  (1) A mind is aware of every mental act that occurs in it. (We might say, with an allusion to Berkeley, that for mental acts, to be is to be experienced).
  (2) The awareness of a mental act always consists in another mental act.

If you accept both of these premises, you cannot escape from the regress. If we further grant, as I do, that infinitely many mental acts cannot indeed ever occur in a mind, we will be forced to deny the existence of mental acts. Thus our choice is clear: We must deny one or the other of these two premises (or, of course, both). Brentano was well aware of this objection to mental acts and chose to reject (2). I think that (1) is the culprit. Let us first look at Brentano's way out.

Brentano accepts (1). He insists that there can be no mental act of which the mind in which it occurs is not aware. But this awareness, he declares, does not consist in another mental act, contrary to (2). But how can we possibly be *aware* of an act, A_1, without an act of awareness? In what, if not a mental act, does the awareness of A_1 consist? Brentano must answer this question. And answer he does. He says that the awareness of A_1 consists in A_1 itself. Every act, according to this peculiar doctrine, is an awareness of itself. Every act, therefore, has two objects, a primary object and a secondary object. The primary object is the ordinary object of the act; the secondary object is always the act itself. Consider the act of hearing a certain tone. The primary object of this act is the tone, its secondary object is the hearing itself. Or consider the desire to fly to Rio. The primary object is that one is on a plane to Rio; the secondary object is the desire itself. Every mental act is like a snake with two heads, one of which always bites its own tail. We can depict Brentano's conception of the self-awareness of every mental act in Figure 2.2.

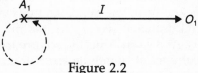

Figure 2.2

It is clear that Brentano's view avoids the infinite regress. When a certain mental act occurs, the hearing of a tone, the mind is indeed aware of this mental act. Yet this awareness does not consist in a second mental act, but consists of the act itself. Hence no second mental act need occur in the mind. There is no infinite series of further mental acts of awareness. But even though it escapes from the regress, Brentano's view seems to me to be quite obviously mistaken. Consider once again the act of hearing A_1. There is an awareness of A_1. But in what does this awareness consist? Not, we are told, in another act of awareness. No, it is A_1 which intends A_1. But this means, if I understand it at all, that there is a *hearing* of a *hearing*! It seems quite evident to me that one cannot hear one's acts of hearing. What do they sound like? What pitches do they have? But if one cannot hear one's act of hearing, then it cannot be the case that an act of hearing can be its own (secondary) object. And what holds for an act of hearing holds for all mental acts other than acts of awareness: none of these acts can be its own object.

My argument only shows that acts *other than awarenesses*

cannot be their own objects. And this suggests a revised version of Brentano's view. One could hold that every mental act is known to the mind in which it occurs by a second mental act of awareness, but that this second act is always its own awareness. For example, the act of hearing, A_1, is experienced by its mind through a second act, A_2, which is an act of awareness. But this second act has two intentional objects. Its primary object is the act A_1; its secondary object is A_2 itself. The infinite regress is avoided and yet, a mind is aware of every act that occurs in it. But I do not think that this revision is correct either. This time, however, I have no decisive objection. It just seems to me that no mental act is ever its own object, not even an act of awareness. If so, then we must search for a different response to the infinite regress argument.

The correct response, I submit, is to reject premise (1): it is not true that a mind is aware of every act which occurs in it. In particular, I think that a mind at a moment always contains precisely one act of which it is not aware. This is an act of experiencing; it belongs to that kind of indefinable mental act through which we are acquainted with the ingredients of our minds. By means of this act, one experiences whatever there is to one's mind at a given moment, but one does not experience this experience itself. I can best explain my view if I introduce a few terminological conventions.

A *mental state* (always: at a moment), I shall say, comprises all there is to a mind (at that moment). It consists of everything that makes up a given mind. A *mind*, as an entity which lasts through time, is conceived of as a succession of such mental states. Now, and this is the important part, a mental state has two main ingredients: it consists of an act of experiencing, on the one hand, and everything that is experienced by this act, on the other. It consists, to put it differently, of an act of experiencing and the object of this act. I shall call the sum total of what is experienced by that act the *'conscious state'* (at that moment). Thus a *mind* consists at a given moment of a *mental state*, and a *mental state* consists of an *act of experiencing* and what is experienced, namely, a *conscious state*. Every mental state has the diagram of Figure 2.3.

I depict the conscious state as a circle because there are many things which one experiences at a given moment, and all of

Mental state

A_1 (Experience)   Conscious state

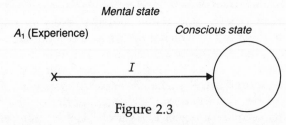

×—————————— I ——————————▸

Figure 2.3

these mental phenomena will be inside the circle. Notice that no arrow points at A_1, the act of experiencing. This means that there is no act whose object is A_1. Hence A_1 is not itself experienced: the mind is not aware of it. Therefore, there is no infinite regress.

Let us consider a concrete situation in order to fill in some details. Assume that someone sees that an elephant is crossing the street. What does his mental state look like? The basic diagram is, of course, like the one of Figure 2.3. The conscious state will in this case contain an act of seeing. The mind experiences, among other things, an act of seeing. The mind will also experience certain visual sensations caused by the elephant's presence. I shall depict all of these sensations, visual, auditory, etc., by small squares. The elephant, we may assume, trumpets with its trunk and smells rather strongly. Furthermore, the person in question also experiences a great number of kinesthetic sensations. These sensations are present most of the time and I shall not mention them again. Furthermore, there may be a toothache at the time. In this case the conscious state will also contain a feeling of pain. I shall depict feelings by small circles. To sum up, in our example, the conscious state will (at least) contain a mental act of seeing, various sensations, and some feelings. The diagram is Figure 2.4.

Mental state

A_1 (Experience)   Conscious state

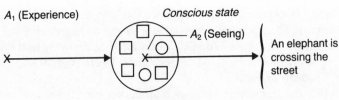

Figure 2.4

Another example. Assume that someone imagines that he is walking down the avenue called 'Ramblas' in Barcelona. In this case, his conscious state will contain a visual image of his walking down that street. I shall represent images by little triangles. And it will also contain an act of imagining, as distinct from the visual image. Thus we get a diagram like Figure 2.5:

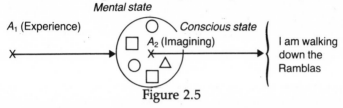

Figure 2.5

One final example. Let us assume that someone remembers a past desire of his to fly to Rio. What he experiences at the present time is, of course, an act of remembering; it is not the desire. He does not have this desire now, but merely remembers it now. Thus what is contained in the conscious state is the memory, not the desire. The desire is the object of the act of remembering and therefore occurs at the tip of the arrow which issues from the remembering. All this is diagrammed in Figure 2.6.

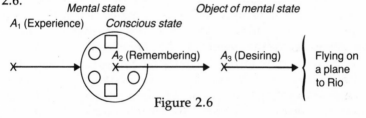

Figure 2.6

By rejecting the assumption that we are aware of every mental act which occurs in our minds, we have averted the infinite regress. But we have also gained our first understanding of the structure of the mind. A mind is a succession of mental states. A mental state consists of the experience of various mental acts, sensations, feelings, and images. In short, it consists of the experience of a conscious state. The ingredients of a conscious state are conscious or, better, we are conscious of them. But to call them 'conscious' is to say nothing more than that they are *experienced*. If it were possible, I would call the conscious state the 'experience state'. But this sounds too strange. Since I am stuck with the term 'conscious state', I must next explain how my terminology fits in with the Freudian conception of *unconscious* mental acts. This explanation will hopefully prepare us for the Existentialists' analysis of the role which anxiety plays in our mental life.

(6) *The nature of 'unconscious' mental acts*

Let me emphasize at the very beginning that a mental act which is unconscious in the Freudian sense of this word is *not* unconscious in our sense of 'unconscious'. We can easily avoid confusion by putting the matter this way: an *unconscious* act in the Freudian sense is nevertheless *experienced* (and, hence, part of the conscious state). I fervently wish Freud had never spoken of *unconscious* desires. A more misleading terminology can hardly be imagined. But it is much too late to change the jargon of psychoanalysis. What we can and must do is to get clear about what Freud meant when he so infelicitously spoke of unconscious wishes, desires, and the like.

In one sentence, an unconscious desire is a desire which a person *experiences*, but which the person does not *recognize* for what it is. A conscious desire is a desire which a person experiences and which the person knows for what it is. This is all there is to the heart of the Freudian notion of the unconscious. How many misunderstandings Freud could have avoided, had he only put the matter this way: some of our desires we recognize for what they are, we correctly identify them and their objects; others, we are mistaken about. But, as I said, it is too late now to cry over spilled milk. Let us proceed in our exposition of the Freudian view.

A young girl, whom we shall call 'Anna', enters the bedroom of her father one morning in order to ask him a question. It is summer, and her father sleeps during the summer months in the nude. As she enters the bedroom, her father is just getting out of bed. She sees him in the nude and suddenly feels a strong sexual desire for him. She realizes that she is experiencing this kind of desire for him and feels terribly ashamed and horribly guilty. She remembers that the night before, at the dinner table, the family had discussed the fact that a girl-friend of Anna's hates her father so much that she hasn't spoken a word to him in six weeks. And now the thought occurs to Anna that what she experiences may not be a sexual desire at all, but rather a hatred similar to the one which her girl-friend feels toward her own father. All of this happens in the blinking of an eye. The thought that she hates her father greatly reduces Anna's feelings of shame and guilt. And this reduction in shame and guilt is a powerful reward for thinking the thought. Since the thinking of this thought is thus greatly rewarded, Anna *learns* to think it. Whenever she feels a desire for her father on later occasions, she responds with the thought: 'I hate him so much that I get all upset.' When her mother asks her why she avoids her father, why she never wants to be alone with him anymore, why she does not hug him when he comes home, etc., she 'confesses' that she hates him.

In the Freudian terminology, Anna has *repressed* her desire for her father. It is now *unconscious*. At one point, when she first experienced it, the sexual desire was conscious. Then Anna repressed it, and now it is unconscious. As I have described the process of repression, it is a straightforward case of learning: Anna learns to misidentify her desire. The reward for this learning is a reduction in shame and guilt. As you can see, there is nothing mysterious about this Freudian notion of the unconscious and the process of repression. Anna's desire is still experienced by her, it is still a part of her conscious state, it is still there. A repressed, unconscious, desire is just as much part of a conscious state as an unrepressed, conscious one. *But Anna has learned, because it makes her feel less ashamed and less guilty, to misidentify what she experiences*: she believes that it is hatred rather than a sexual desire.

The story of Anna can later take different turns. Here is one possible course of events. Anna's father is a kind and loving parent. She has absolutely no reason to hate him. Anna realizes this and feels now guilty about hating such a wonderful father. The thought that she sexually desires her father is by far more terrifying than the belief that she hates him, but even this belief is not acceptable to her. Hence she may once again misidentify her feeling. She may convince herself that it is not really hatred she feels for her father but rather fear of him. This new misidentification is rewarded in the same manner as the first one, namely, by a reduction in guilt. She does not have to feel guilty for hating such a kind and devoted father because it is not hate after all which she feels for him. But once again, Anna has jumped from the fire into the frying pan; for now she has to explain to herself the reasons for her fear. The troubles of a neurotic person, as you can see, are never over. Perhaps she will read sinister threats into harmless remarks by her father. She may magnify small differences and frictions. She may eventually invent a complicated story about her father's persecution of her and his intention to do away with her. At this point, her behavior will have become rather bizarre and she will be forced to see a psychiatrist.

The psychiatrist is faced with the task of curing Anna's neurotic behavior. For example she never eats anything touched by her father or any of his friends. She locks her door at night; refuses to ride in a car with a male; and so on. It is easy to see how a cure would be effected: the process of repression simply has to be reversed. If Anna can learn to face up to the fact that she desires her father, she will no longer behave as if she were afraid of him or as if she hated him. In short, Anna has to learn to face the truth about herself. The truth shall make her free of neurosis.

As far as our conception of a mental state is concerned, Freud's lesson is clear: to experience a desire–to have it–is not the same as to know that you have it or what its object is. We experience many desires, fears, wishes, and the like, which we repress, that is, which we learn to misidentify to ourselves, because we feel ashamed of them. Freud's insight, once pointed out and properly explained, is but an obvious truth.

(7) *The importance of structures*

Freud, by the way, attended some of Brentano's lectures at the University of Vienna. Brentano, as I already mentioned, had many famous students. One of these was Alexius Meinong (1853–1920). Meinong taught later at the University of Graz in Austria. Meinong founded there the first psychological laboratory of Austria. One of Meinong's students was Christian von Ehrenfels (1859–1932), and it is an article by von Ehrenfels which is commonly considered to mark the beginning of *Gestalt psychology*. Brentano, you might say, was the great-grandfather of this psychological movement.

Before we turn to Ehrenfels' article, let me briefly remind you of what I said earlier about the so-called bundle view. The notion of a material substance, we saw, was supplanted by that of a bundle or collection of properties. An apple, Berkeley's famous example, is conceived of as a bundle of perceptual properties. But no one seriously discussed the question of to what category bundles belong, or the question of whether there are other kinds of whole in addition to bundles, or the question of how different wholes can be similar to each other, etc. Questions of this sort were of great concern to Brentano's students. Gestalt psychology is a product of that concern.

The concern is about the nature of wholes or, as I shall say, *structures*. The Gestalt psychologists discovered the category of structure. But this philosophical discovery was put to psychological use. In particular, it was applied to the psychology of perception. What we perceive, to put the theory in a nutshell, are not mere *sets* of perceptual stimuli, but are *structures* of stimuli. Consequently, what we experience are not mere *sets* of sensations, but *structures* consisting of sensations. This basic insight was often summed up in the slogan: a whole is more than the sum of its parts! In our terminology, it becomes the ontological law: a structure is not the same as the set of its parts. Ehrenfels calls our attention to this law:

> The proof for the existence of *Gestaltqualitaeten* (Gestalt qualities) in our sense of the term, at least in regard to visual and auditory presentations, is provided by the similarity of spatial figures and melodies with completely different tonal or spatial foundations (which is pointed out by Mach in the passage cited earlier). This fact cannot be reconciled, as we shall show now, with the conception of spatial and tonal configurations as mere sums of tonal and spatial determinations.
>
> For, it can be asserted at once that different complexes of elements, if they are nothing else but the sums of these, must be the more similar, the more similar their individual elements are to each other. However, that this condition is

not fulfilled for melody and spatial configuration can be
proven decisively by example. (Ch. von Ehrenfels, 'Über
Gestaltqualitaeten', *Vierteljahrsschrift für wissenschaftliche Philosophie*, 3 (1890), pp. 258–9)

Ehrenfels then gives an example and concludes with these
words:

> Thus there can be no doubt that the similarity of spatial and
> tonal configurations rests on something other than the
> similarity of the elements with whose collection in conscious-
> ness they appear. Those configurations must therefore be
> something other than the sums of the elements.–The strin-
> gency of this proof seems to us unavoidable. (*Ibid.*, p. 260)

His argument is that a melody, for example, cannot be a set of
tones. If it were a mere set of tones, then the similarity between
two transpositions of the same melody would have to be a
function exclusively of the similarity between the tones of the
two transpositions. But examples show that this is not the case.
Hence a melody cannot be a set of tones.

I think that Ehrenfels' argument is sound. It proves, for
example, that a spatial figure is not a set of its parts. Tones must
stand in certain *relations* to each other in order to form a given
melody; and spatial parts must be *arranged* in a certain fashion to
yield a given figure. Ehrenfels' point can be made more directly.
The same set of tones, when the tones are played in different
temporal orders, yields quite different melodies. It follows that
it cannot be identical with one of these melodies. Similarly, the
same set of four squares, when differently arranged, yields once
a rectangle, once a square. Hence it cannot be identical with one
of these two figures. This argument presupposes that a set, in
distinction to a structure, is completely determined by its
elements. A set S_1 is the same as a set S_2 if and only if the
elements of S_1 are the same as the elements of S_2. The
arrangement of the elements, to put it loosely, does not matter.
Think, for example of four squares, a, b, c, and d, once arranged
in the fashion of Figure 2.7, once in the fashion of Figure 2.8.
The squares which form Figure 2.7 are the same as the squares
which form Figure 2.8. Hence the two sets of squares are the

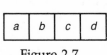

Figure 2.7   Figure 2.8

same: both sets have the elements *a*, *b*, *c*, and *d*. But a structure is different from a set. Although the structure of Figure 2.7 consists of the same squares as the structure of Figure 2.8, the two structures are not the same. The structure of Figure 2.7 is a rectangle, while the structure of Figure 2.8 is a square. A structure is not even completely determined by its non-relational parts together with its relational parts, that is, by the set of its non-relational and relational parts. To see this, you merely have to compare the structure of Figure 2.9 with that of Figure 2.10.

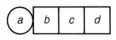

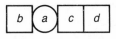

Figure 2.9   Figure 2.10

We assume that both structures consist of the same non-relational parts, namely, the circle *a* and the three squares *b*, *c*, and *d*. We assume further that both contain the same relation, namely, the relation of being to the left of. Yet it is clear that the two structures are not the same. In Figure 2.9, the circle *a* occurs to the left of square *b*, while in Figure 2.10, *b* occurs to the left of *a*.

What this last example shows is that three conditions must be fulfilled so that a structure T_1 is the same as a structure T_2:

(1) the non-relational parts of T_1 must be the same as the non-relational parts of T_2;

(2) the relations of T_1 must be the same as the relations of T_2;

and (3) the same non-relational parts must stand in the same relations to each other in T_1 and T_2.

A melody is not a set of tones, a spatial figure is not a set of spatial parts. Both are structures. As soon as one has a firm grip on the category of structure, one realizes that structures are everywhere and that every science, nay, every inquiry, is ultimately an inquiry into the structure of things. The real numbers, arranged according to size, form a structure; and so do the atoms in a molecule. Every plant is a structure; and so is every animal. The planets form a structure; and so do whole solar systems. The Congress of the United States is a structure, and so is the Communist Party of Cuba. My family is a structure; and so is the color body arranged in the three dimensions of hue, lightness, and saturation. There exists even a general theory of structures. That theory is algebra. Why, then, may you ask, did it take so long to grant philosophical respectability to structures? Well, philosophers knew, of course, that there are structures. But they did not realize that structures form an irreducible category of entity. In order fully to recognize the uniqueness of structures, one must have a firm grasp of the uniqueness of relations. And I have mentioned repeatedly that relations have only recently come into their ontological own. The discovery of the philosophical significance of relations, to no one's surprise, goes hand in hand with the discovery of the philosophical significance of structures.

Generally speaking, things are *similar* when they share a common property. Two white billiard balls are similar in color because they share the same color. They are also similar in shape because they are both round. Two structures can be similar in this way too. Two chess boards, for example, are similar in shape because they are both square. But structures, of all the things there are, can also be similar to each other in a different and fascinating way. They can be *isomorphic* to each other. It is this unique categorial feature of isomorphism which makes structures so interesting to the mathematician. Two structures, T_1 and T_2, are said to be isomorphic to each other if and only if three conditions are fulfilled:

(1) for every non-relational part of T_1 there is precisely one non-relational part of T_2, and conversely;
(2) for every relation of T_1 there is precisely one relation of T_2, and conversely;
(3) the parts of T_1 which correspond to the parts of T_2 stand in the relations of T_1 to each other which correspond to the relations of T_2, and conversely.

Let me illustrate this notion of isomorphism. Consider the two series of even and of odd positive integers arranged by size:

2   4   6   8 10 12 ...
1   3   5   7   9 11 ...

These two series are isomorphic to each other. To every even number there corresponds one odd number, and conversely. You can see this from the way the numerals have been arranged, the odd numerals underneath the even numerals. (We must not confuse, of course, the numbers with the numerals: I cannot possibly 'write down a number', but I can write down a numeral; and there is also *another* numeral for the *same* number three, namely, 'iii'.) Secondly, to the relation which orders the even numbers, namely, the relation of being the next larger even number, there corresponds the relation of being the next larger odd number. Thirdly and finally, whenever two even numbers stand in the former relation to each other, the co-ordinated odd numbers stand in the latter relation to each other, and conversely. For example, 10 is the next larger even number after 8; 10 is co-ordinated to the odd number 9, 8 to the odd number 7; and 9 is the next larger odd number after 7.

The notion of isomorphism is so fascinating because it explains how one complex thing can somehow *represent* another complex thing; for a structure may be said to *represent* another structure, if it is *isomorphic* to it. Language, for example, may be said to be (in some way) isomorphic to the world. And since it is isomorphic to the world, it can be used to speak about it. Without some kind of isomorphism between a system of signs and the structure of the world, a language would be impossible. Gestalt psychologists also thought that there may be an isomorphism between the perceptual stimuli which we perceive, on the one hand, and the brain processes during perception, on the other. But this is a story which we cannot pursue now. I merely wish to call your attention to the fact that isomorphisms have played an important role in the philosophy of language and in the psychology of perception.

(8) *Four dogmas of Gestalt psychology*

Ehrenfels and his followers were correct: a whole (Gestalt) is more than the sum of its parts! As we put it in our terminology: a structure is not the same as the set of its parts. With this dogma of Gestalt psychology we cannot but agree. But there are three additional theses on which most Gestalt psychologists insist. The first of these is the assertion that a whole (Gestalt) may have properties which none of its parts has. A whole, as one sometimes says, has *emergent* properties. I think that this dogma is true as well and, moreover, obviously so. It is obvious that the series of even positive integers has properties which none of its non-relational and relational parts has. For example, it consists of infinitely many integers; it has a beginning, but no end; etc. An ordinary structure like your car, to give an example closer to home, has many properties which none of its parts has. To begin with, you can drive it to work. And it has also a certain shape and size. Nevertheless, there have been quite a few philosophers who have fought the second dogma of Gestalt psychology tooth and nail. They challenged it with a thesis of their own, the thesis of reducibility: every alleged property of a whole is in reality a property of its parts or a relation between its parts. This version of the thesis of reducibility (as usual, there are a number of quite different formulations in circulation) amounts to the claim that wholes really have no properties. All there is to a whole, are the properties of its parts and the relations between them. If I am right with my examples, then this claim is not only false, but obviously so. Why, then, would anyone want to defend it?

In the background, there lurks a powerful motive. What these opponents of the second dogma wish to attack is the notion that there are such things as the will of the people, the ideology of the working class, and the ethos of the Nordic race. Take the so-called working class. It consists of a group of people with various kinds of social, legal, economic, etc. relations between them. It may therefore be thought of as a structure. So far, so good. But can we speak of a belief of this structure, unless we simply mean the beliefs of its members? It is quite clear to me that this group, as a group, has no beliefs, no desires, no perceptions, in short, it experiences no mental acts. Of course, the members of the groups have beliefs, desires, and perceptions; and these beliefs, desires, and perceptions may more or less agree with each other. But properly and precisely speaking, a group of people is not the kind of thing which can have a belief or a desire, only individual human beings can have beliefs and desires. The opponents of the second dogma correctly object to those much too frequent attempts to anthropomorphize such structures as the Communist Party, the French state, or the Nordic race. But they throw the baby out with the bath water when they base this objection on the thesis of reducibility. While it is true that these structures do not have the human features often attributed to them, it is also true that, in general, structures can have properties of their own, even emergent properties.

The third dogma of Gestalt psychology is that a whole (Gestalt) cannot be analyzed. This assertion, in contrast to the first two dogmas, is in my opinion mistaken. It rests on a faulty notion of analysis. Or, better, it misunderstands what analysis can and cannot achieve. Let me explain. A whole cannot (must not?) be analyzed, so the view goes, because analysis destroys its object. What you have as a result of analysis is no longer the whole with which you started, but a mere sum of its parts. Hence analysis is of no help when you want to understand a whole.

Now, it is true that the result of analysis is always a list of parts, that is, a *set* of parts. To analyze a structure means to list its non-relational and relational parts. For example, an analysis of the series of even positive integers yields a list of the numbers and the relation of being the next larger even number. An analysis of a car results in a list of all of its parts together with a list of all of the relations in which these parts stand to each other. This is the very meaning of analysis. But if the result of analysis is always a set of parts, then it is true that the result is not the same as the structure with which you started. The set consisting of even integers and the mentioned relation is not the same entity as the series of even numbers. The set consisting of all of the parts of the car and all of the relevant relations is not a car. In this sense, but only in this sense, is it true that analysis 'destroys' its object (unless, of course, its object is a set). But this does not imply that analysis is worthless, that it should not be undertaken, that it cannot be applied to structures. It is true that analysis by itself will not tell you what properties a structure has. But we are at times interested in what parts a given structure has. And analysis is the only method which will give us an answer to this particular question. If you want to know of what a structure *consists*, analysis and only analysis will be able to help you. Analyses of structures are, therefore, not only possible, but indispensable for their understanding.

Finally, there is a fourth dogma of Gestalt psychology, according to which a whole (Gestalt) is not determined by its parts, but, to the contrary, determines the nature of its parts. Like most dogmas, you can make of this one what you will. One thing is clear: It follows from the condition under which structures are the same that a structure is *completely determined* by (1) what non-relational parts it has, (2) in what relations these parts stand to each other, and (3) by what parts stand in what relations to what other parts. If the fourth dogma is meant to deny this fact, then it is surely false. But a different interpretation can be put on it in the light of the following quotation from an article by Max Wertheimer (1880–1943), one of the theorists of Gestalt psychology:

> What is given to me by the melody does not arise (through the agency of any auxiliary factor) as a *secondary* process from the sum of the pieces as such. Instead, what takes place in each single part already depends upon what the whole is. The flesh and blood of a tone depends from the start upon its role in the melody: a *b* as leading tone to *c* is something radically different from the *b* as tonic. It belongs to the flesh and blood of the things given in experience, how, in what role, in what function they are in the whole. (Max Wertheimer, 'Gestalt Theory', in *A Source Book of Gestalt Psychology*, Willis D. Ellis (ed.), New York, Humanities Press, 1967, p. 5)

A *b* as leading tone to *c*, Wertheimer asserts, is something radically different from the *b* as tonic. Thus the whole, the melody, determines what the *b* is rather than the other way around. There is some truth to this. The *b* which leads to *c* is different from the *b* as tonic by virtue of the fact that it is *related* in a certain way to the *c*, while the tonic *b* is not so related to *c*. Similarly, a woman who is a mother is quite a different person from a woman who is not. The former is related to a child; the latter is not. What a thing is, we can generalize, depends, not only on the properties which it has, but also on the relations in which it stands to other things. (Remember what we learned earlier about two kinds of change!) Parts of structure, *as parts of structures*, stand in important relations to each other. They are therefore in one sense different from what they would be without their structures. A part of a structure is characterized, not only by the properties which it has, but also by the relations in which it stands by virtue of the fact that it is part of a structure.

Gestalt psychologists have sometimes gone even farther and asserted that a part of a structure owes, not only its relations, but also its properties to the structure. For example, it has been held that the color of an area changes with the color of the background in which it is embedded. But this is surely false. That it is false follows straightforwardly from the condition for identity of structures. And we can convince ourselves directly that it is mistaken by measuring the length of the waves reflected by the area when it is embedded into differently colored backgrounds. What may be the case, and what may have misled some Gestalt psychologists, is that the area *looks different* when seen against differently colored backgrounds. Thus it may be true that a circle which is green (and which remains green, no matter what colored background we choose for it!) may *look* grey against one background and green against another. But this does not prove, of course, that the color property of the circle changes with the whole in which it appears. It only proves that how we perceive a part of a whole depends on the whole in which it occurs. Optical illusions are a case in point.

I have distinguished between four important theses of Gestalt psychology, the four cornerstones, if you wish, of this important theory. We have seen that they allow for different interpretations. I have tried to show in what sense each thesis is true and in what sense it is false. We had to go rather deeply into this topic because many Existentialists appeal to the tenets of Gestalt psychology in order to bolster their own views. We shall see how Sartre falls back on the dogma that the whole determines its parts in order to defend human freedom.

3. Kierkegaard: a different conception of man

(1) *Man as the rational animal*

Traditional wisdom has it that man's essential characteristic is the ability to think. Man belongs, to use the classic terminology, to the *genus* animal. What differentiates him from all other animals is his rationality. Hence the definition of man as rational animal. There can be no quarrel with this general conception. Man and man alone has the ability to *mean* something and to *understand* something by a noise or a mark. Man and man alone, therefore, has a language. Man and man alone asks questions about the world around him and the mind within him. And man and man alone tries to answer these questions by observation and reason.

But these truths must not obscure the fact that there is more to a human mind than the so-called intellectual faculties. Recall how Descartes describes a mental substance: 'A *thinking* being. But what is a thinking being? It is a being which *doubts*, which *understands*, which *conceives*, which *affirms*, which *denies*, which *wills*, which *rejects*, which imagines also, and which *perceives*.' I have italicized some words in order to stress that Descartes clearly conceives of the mind in this context as a rational instrument. There is not an emotion among the items of his list. Compare Descartes' examples in this regard with Brentano's: 'Also to be included under this term [mental phenomenon] is every emotion: joy, sorrow, fear, hope, courage, despair, anger, love, hate, desire, act of will, astonishment, admiration, contempt, etc.' What a variety of mental acts! As surely as man has the capacity to think, as surely does he have the ability to love and hate, to rejoice and to despair, to hope and to fear.

This rough and ready distinction between reason and emotion gives us an equally rough and ready way of distinguishing between Phenomenology, on the one hand, and Existentialism, on the other. Both of these philosophical movements owe much to Brentano's philosophy of mind. The thesis of intentionality is a cornerstone for both. But Phenomenology tends to stress the cognitive while Existentialism emphasizes the emotional side of the mind. Phenomenologists are mainly interested in how we acquire knowledge; Existentialists are mainly interested in how we respond emotionally. While Husserl gives us a theory of knowledge, Sartre describes the emotions. Needless to say this distinction must be taken with a grain of salt. There are other differences between Phenomenology and Existentialism. And it is not true, for example, that Phenomenologists show no interest in emotions. But it does help, I think, to view both movements as having a common background in Brentano's view of mental acts, but divergent interest in the two sides of the human mind, reason and emotion.

The classic conception of man as the rational animal found its cultural expression in the so-called Age of Enlightenment. Influenced by a rapid progress in science, especially in Newtonian physics, the thinkers of the Enlightenment had a boundless faith in the power of reason. Reason was not only to be the key for the solution of scientific problems, but for the solution of all human problems as well. The method of science, according to these sages, was to be applied, not only to physics, chemistry, and medicine, but also to history, religion, and morality. Reason, in the form of the scientific method, was viewed as the magic wand by means of which ignorance, injustice, prejudice, and superstition were to be eliminated. We cannot but marvel at the confidence with which these thinkers set out to change the hearts and minds of people by scientific means. The history of the last two hundred years has clearly shown that scientific progress is not paralleled by moral improvement. However, we must equally beware of the disdain for science and technology which is sometimes a reaction to the boundless naiveté about the origins of evil shown by the proponents of the Enlightenment. It is, of course, true that the affairs of man are not as simple as the motions of the planets, and that they may not lend themselves to a merely 'mechanical' explanation. But it is equally true that they cannot be understood or changed by other than rational means. The thinkers of the Enlightenment may have underestimated the task of constructing a science of man and his society. They may have been too optimistic in believing that the laws of human conduct can be as easily discovered as the laws of physics. But they were right, nevertheless, in their conviction that only by rational means can we understand and change man's behaviour.

The naive view of the power of science met with some derision even at the height of its time. One of the most passionate and famous critics of the belief in the powers of reason was the Danish philosopher Søren Kierkegaard (1813–55). Truth, he asserted, has no natural affinity to reason. Truth and reason do not fit together like hand in glove. Rather, truth is alien to reason. It must be brought to reason from the outside. This is why a teacher in the human form of Christ is necessary to *reveal* the truth to us. In this fashion, Kierkegaard confronts the Greek philosophy of knowledge with the Christian doctrine of revelation. Now, if truth is alien to reason, so another strand of Kierkegaard's thought runs, then we can only acquire it by *deciding* to accept it. Truth becomes a matter of choice rather than of reason. And since it is a matter of choice, it becomes subjective; for choice, of course, is subjective choice, the agonizing choice of the individual. I think that you can see from this sketchy description how some of the main themes of Existentialism emerge from Kierkegaard's philosophy. There is the stress on the individual and contempt for the group. There is the emphasis on choice and, hence, on freedom. And there is the theme that man is what he chooses to be, just as his truth is what he chooses it to be.

Kierkegaard: a different conception of man

(2) *The importance of being anxious*

I shall not pursue these ideas of Kierkegaard's any further. I want to concentrate on just one point, namely, on his insistence that anxiety (dread) is of the essence of the human condition.

To the heart of the matter. I submit that Kierkegaard holds (at least) four important theses about the nature of anxiety. I shall list them and quote for each one of them a few lines from Kierkegaard.

(1) *Anxiety is a defining characteristic of human beings.* Human beings, and only human beings, can experience anxiety. Animals can be afraid, but they cannot be anxious. Kierkegaard claims: 'One does not therefore find dread in the beast, precisely for the reason that by nature the beast is not qualified by spirit.' (*The Concept of Dread*, trans. Walter Lowrie, Princeton University Press, 1973, p. 38). A little later, he remarks: 'That there are people who do not notice any dread must be understood in the sense that Adam would have sensed none if he had been merely an animal' (*ibid.*, p. 47). And then there is this startling claim: 'If a man were a beast or an angel, he would not be able to be in dread. Since his is a synthesis he can be in dread and the greater the dread, the greater the man' (*ibid.*, p. 139).

(2) *Anxiety is not the same as fear.* (You have noticed that I use 'anxiety' where the translator of Kierkegaard uses 'dread'. Just treat these two words in this context as synonymous.) Anxiety must be sharply distinguished from fear: 'One almost never sees the concept dread dealt with in psychology, and I must therefore call attention to the fact that it is different from fear and similar concepts which refer to something definite, whereas dread is freedom's reality as possibility for possibility' (*ibid.*, p. 38).

(3) *The object of anxiety is nothingness.* This nothingness is sometimes said to be fate and sometimes said to be guilt. Here are some representative quotations. 'If then we ask further what is the object of dread, the answer as usual must be that it is nothing' (*ibid.*, p. 86; compare also p. 55 and p. 69). 'Dread and nothing regularly correspond to one another. So soon as the actuality of freedom and of the

spirit is posited, dread is annulled. But what then is
signified more particularly by the nothing of dread? It is
fate' (*ibid*.). Later on, Kierkegaard connects nothingness
with guilt: 'But here the nothing of dread denotes
something else than fate. It is in this sphere that the
formula "dread-nothing" appears most paradoxical, for
after all guilt is something. It is correct, nevertheless, and
so long as guilt is the object of dread it is nothing' (*ibid*., p.
92).

(4) *Anxiety reveals the possibility of freedom*. Kierkegaard
distinguishes between objective and subjective anxiety.
Objective anxiety is the anxiety felt by innocence; it is the
anxiety which reveals the possibility of freedom. Subjective
anxiety, on the other hand, is a consequence of sin. He
says: 'Thus dread is the dizziness of freedom which occurs
when the spirit would posit the synthesis, and freedom
then gazes down into its own possibility, grasping at
finiteness to sustain itself' (*ibid*., p. 55). And somewhere
else he says: ' . . . dread having been defined as freedom's
appearance before itself in possibility' (*ibid*., p. 99).

So much for the four theses which I attribute to Kierkegaard.
Now, in the formulation of thesis (3), I was not quite faithful to
Kierkegaard's words. He does not use the term 'nothing*ness*',
but merely speaks of 'nothing'. I formulated (3) with an eye on
the later Existentialists who unabashedly contrast nothingness
with being. And I did it with an eye on the following thought.
According to Brentano's thesis of intentionality, every mental
phenomenon has an object. Anxiety is undoubtedly a mental
phenomenon. But it does not seem to have an object. When one
is anxious, one is nervous, excited, restless, and so on, but one
is not directed toward a specific object as one is, for example, if
one is afraid of spiders. Anxiety thus seems to be an exception to
Brentano's rule. We have therefore the following option: we
either admit that Brentano's thesis is false (in its full generality),
or else we continue to search for an object of anxiety. If one
takes the latter route, one may reason as follows: anxiety has no
object (it seems). Hence, nothing is the object of anxiety.
Therefore, the object of anxiety is nothing. Thus anxiety has an
object after all, namely, nothing. And to bring out that this is an
object, we shall speak of nothing*ness* instead: the object of

anxiety is nothingness. Brentano's thesis is saved and Kierke-gaard's thesis (3) is vindicated. Two birds with one stone!

We shall have to discuss the Existentialist's notion of nothingness at great length later on. For the moment, let us resist the urge to make nothing into something, namely, into the object of anxiety. Is there any other way to save Brentano's thesis? It is a rather startling fact that there is indeed a rival to the Existentialist's rescue attempt. This account comes from an entirely different direction, namely, from psychoanalysis. I shall call it a 'Freudian view of anxiety'.

(3) *A Freudian interpretation of Kierkegaard's theses*

Anxiety, according to this view, does indeed have an object. Brentano is correct. But its object has been *repressed*, so that it is not known to the anxious person. We may put it bluntly: anxiety is nothing but fear whose object has been repressed! In reality, there are not two mental phenomena, fear and anxiety, but only one, namely, fear. Anxiety and fear do not constitute two kinds of mental act. But a person may either know what he is afraid of or he may not, because he has repressed the object of his fear. If he has repressed it, then it seems to him that he has a fear with no object. He is afraid without knowing what he is afraid of. He lives in fear, but does not fear anything in particular. If you have ever been really afraid, you know what a horrible feeling it is. Now try to imagine what it must be like to be afraid all or most of the time without knowing what you are afraid of. If you succeed, you will have a notion of the misery which a neurotic person experiences.

Anxiety is fear whose object has been repressed. From Anna's case in the last chapter, we learned how repression works. We saw how a desire becomes unconscious by being repressed. The same mechanism works in the case of an object of fear. When Anna realizes that she has a sexual desire for her father, she becomes horribly afraid that she may act upon her desires, that she may do something to fulfill her desire. She becomes terrified by the thought that she may act in a certain way. When she asks herself 'What am I so horribly afraid of?', however, she cannot admit to herself that it is the possibility of her behaving in a certain fashion. To admit that she may act in accordance with her desire is too shameful for her. She therefore learns, being rewarded by a reduction in shame and guilt, not to recognize the object of her fear. She is afraid that she may act out her desires, but she does not recognize that this is what she is afraid of. The object of her fear has been repressed.

In our example, we must clearly distinguish between the act of desire, on the one hand, and the fear, on the other. These two acts have quite different objects. The desire is for a sexual intimacy with the father; the fear is of a certain promiscuous kind of action on Anna's part. We have assumed, for the sake of illustration, that the *act of desire was repressed, while the object* of the fear was repressed. It is clear that there exist three possibilities for repression of a mental act: (1) the act may be repressed, (2) the object of the act may be repressed, and (3) both act and object are repressed. For example, a person may realize that she is peculiarly affected by a certain person or situation, but may not realize what it is that she feels about this person or situation. Or else a person may realize that she has a desire, but may not recognize the object of the desire. Or, finally, she may correctly identify neither the mental act nor its object.

From a Freudian point of view, then, there is some truth to Kierkegaard's thesis (3). In a sense, anxiety, in distinction to fear, has no object. It has not object, as far as the person is concerned who is anxious, because this person has repressed the object of his fear. But we can go on and also give a Freudian interpretation of the rest of Kierkegaard's theses. It is clear that anxiety must be distinguished from fear just as thesis (2) states. To be afraid is not the same thing as to be anxious. Anxiety is not a separate mental act, different from fear, it is true, but there is a difference between knowing what you are afraid of and not knowing what you are afraid of.

Even thesis (1), according to which anxiety is exclusively a human phenomenon, makes sense from the Freudian point of view. A dog, for example, may be said to be afraid of cars, but it cannot be anxious. It cannot be anxious, because it cannot repress the object of fear. And it cannot repress the object of fear, because it cannot feel ashamed and guilty about what it wishes to do. In order for Anna to repress the object of her fear, she must be able to feel that it would be wrong, shameful, disgraceful, nasty, etc., to act in a certain fashion. She must have a *moral sense*. If we can agree that animals do not have a moral sense, that they do not and cannot distinguish between right and wrong, then we can also agree that they cannot repress anything and, hence, that they cannot feel anxious. That anxiety is characteristic of the human condition, and only of the human condition, is ultimately due to the fact that human beings and only human beings can distinguish between right and wrong.

To say that anxiety is characteristic of the human condition is to say, not that every human being must experience it or must experience it all of the time, but rather that some human beings *can* feel it. It is not essential to being a human being that you experience anxiety or that you are neurotic, contrary to what Kierkegaard seems to think. There are quite a few human beings, it seems, who are reasonably happy, not tormented by repressed desires, and not tortured by unbearable guilt. Some of us are afraid of quite a number of things, but not in dread. To think of anxiety as the *typical* human feeling is as wrong as to think of jealousy in this manner. It is true that a great number of people, at one time or another, are in the grip of this emotion. But it is also clear that many people are never jealous or are only rarely jealous. A human mind, we should insist, is a complicated thing, capable of many different emotions, feelings, fears, moods, etc. Whether a given person experiences more sorrow than happiness, more anxiety than contentment, depends on many factors. It would be a mistake to generalize from one's own experience to all others. Kierkegaard, it has often been surmised, had more than an average share of anxiety. He was therefore haunted by this phenomenon. And he could therefore give a better description of it than anyone else. But he was mistaken if he thought that anxiety is *the* essential feature of the human mind.

Last but not least, there is Kierkegaard's claim that anxiety is the possibility of freedom. Perhaps better expressed, through anxiety, we become aware of our freedom. Our possibilities are revealed to us. Anxiety, to put it the way Existentialists do, confronts us with our freedom and makes us dizzy at the prospect of our posssibilities. The anxious person, as Sartre says, has 'a vertigo of possibility'. (*The Transcendence of the Ego*, trans. Forrest Williams and Robert Kirkpatrick, New York, Farrar, Straus and Giroux, no date, p. 100.) Let me put this idea my way. If a person feels anxiety, he is forced to recognize his freedom. The anxious person has been confronted with the fact that he is capable of doing things which he never thought possible. For example, Anna, in repressing both her desire and the object of her fear, has to face what she is capable of doing, namely, make sexual advances toward her father. She considers this action to be a genuine possibility; otherwise, she would not have to repress the object of her fear. A person who is convinced that he cannot possibly engage in a certain action is not afraid that he may perform it. But this realization, the realization that she could act in such a horrible way, reveals to Anna how distant the horizon of her possibilities is. It is as if she says to herself: 'My God, if I could do a thing like that, then I am capable of doing anything.' Anna has a vertigo of possibility!

To sum up. If an action is considered to be so horrible, so despicable, so shameful that it has to be repressed, then it reminds us of what we are capable of doing. And this reminder reveals to us the extent of our freedom.

Kierkegaard's characterization of anxiety, as we have seen, fits in very nicely with a Freudian conception of it. But there is one huge difference between the two. From a Freudian point of view, anxiety is a sign of neurosis. It indicates that the person in question is not quite honest with himself or herself. It shows that he hides something from himself. And the person, most likely, will also lie to himself about a number of other things; for example, about certain desires or aversions. In short, anxiety is proof that reality has been denied. There is therefore no reason for being proud of being anxious; no reason to brag about one's neurosis. To lie to oneself is just as immoral as it is to lie to others. Kierkegaard, by contrast, thinks of anxiety as essential to being a human being. For him, it is not a symptom that something has gone wrong. (But subjective anxiety, we must remember, is according to him a consequence of sin!) In general, Existentialists tend to view anxiety in positive terms. They think of it mainly as the gateway to freedom.

Part II

Edmund Husserl: the problem of knowledge

4. The distinction between particulars and universals

(1) *The world of being and the world of becoming*

We began Part I, as you may remember, with the fundamental distinction between substance, essence, and accident; a distinction which goes back to Aristotle. This time, we shall begin with an equally important distinction, a distinction that goes back even farther to Aristotle's teacher Plato (about 427–347 B.C.). According to the Platonic tradition, everything there is, is either a *particular* or a *universal*. (These are not Plato's terms, but they fit better into our discusssion.) Plato maintained that there are two realms, the realm of becoming and the realm of being. The realm of becoming comprises *changing* things, things which 'become' smaller or larger, hotter or colder, more colorful or less colorful. These are the things which are 'in space and time'. Obviously, in order to change, a thing must have a duration; it must be temporal. The world of becoming, I shall say, is populated with particulars. In the world of being, on the other hand, dwell what Plato calls 'forms', and what I shall call universals. Forms are not in space and time. They are unchanging. They *are*, but they do not *become*. Since they are not in time, they are eternal. To the world of being belong such properties as smallness and largeness, hotness and coldness, colors and shapes, but also such lofty properties as justice, honesty, beauty, and truth.

Plato's distinction overlaps in certain ways with Aristotle's. An individual thing, the apple Oscar, is a particular, according to Plato, and a material substance, according to Aristotle. In general, individual things are conceived of in the Platonic tradition as particulars, and in the Aristotelian tradition as substances. What is the difference? Well, conceived of as a substance, the apple is a combination of matter and essence. Its essence is said to be a part of the apple, giving it a certain internal structure. Conceived of as a particular, on the other hand, Oscar has no internal structure; it is not a complex thing, consisting of matter and essence. Its essence, the property of being an apple, is a universal (form) in the world of being, divorced from Oscar, dwelling in a different realm. And so are its other properties, its color, taste, etc. Both, the essential property as well as the accidental ones, are conceived of as universals. Thus there is no distinction between essence and accident in the Platonic tradition. Properties are conceived of as universals, that is, as eternal and unchanging. What about the essences and accidents of the Aristotelian tradition, are they universals in the same sense? This is perhaps the most important question for the Aristotelian tradition.

Consider the property of being round. We shall assume that there are two white billiard balls, called 'Max' and 'Moritz', which are both round. Max and Moritz are individual things. According to the Aristotelian tradition, they are substances; according to the Platonic tradition, they are particulars. According to both traditions, they are in space and time. In Plato's terminology, they belong to the world of becoming. But what about the property roundness, does it belong to an entirely different realm of being? Is it a universal? Of course, we know that it is conceived of as an accident rather than an essence. This means that it is not part of the billiard balls; it belongs to them 'externally' only. But whatever its relationship to the billiard balls may be, there is the additional question of whether roundness belongs, together with Max and Moritz, to the spatio-temporal world or to a separate world of eternal entities. If Plato is correct, then roundness is not located anywhere in space or time. You cannot find it east of Chicago; you may search for it the world over, but you will never find it at a certain place. Nor can you assign to it a place in the history of the universe. It did not come into existence at any particular time, nor will it perish eventually.

Since the time of Plato, there have been philosophers who have denied that there is a world of being. They have held that what there is, all of it, belongs to the world of becoming. What there is, is in space and/or time. (I must say 'and/or' because mental acts, for example, are thought of as being temporal but not spatial; they belong to the world of becoming without being in space.) These philosophers are called '*nominalists*'. Those that follow in Plato's footsteps and believe that there are universals are called '*realists*'. Most philosophers in the Aristotelian tradition inclined towards Nominalism. Accidents and essences, they held, are just as particular as the substances to which they belong. There were exceptions; there always are. But on the whole, Nominalism has been more popular than Realism among Aristotelians.

Before we take a second look at the issue between Nominalists and Realists, let us take care of two peripheral points. As I have formulated the issue, it concerns the question of whether or not the property roundness, for example, is in space and time. What is not at stake is whether or not this property exists. But there have been philosophers who, in order to deny that roundness is a universal, have simply denied that there is such a property to begin with. This may sound incredible to you, but I can assure you that at this very moment, some professors of philosophy profess to believe that while there is such a word as 'round', there exists no corresponding property. I think that this belief is not only false, but absurd. The second point is this. Turn your attention to the property of being a mermaid. Assuming that there never have been any mermaids and that there never will be any, is there nevertheless such a universal as the property mermaid? Does there exist, in the realm of being, side by side with the property of being an elephant, the property of being a mermaid? Or do only those properties exist which are exemplified (at some time) by some individual? (The property of being a dinosaur, please notice, is different from the property of being a mermaid, for there were dinosaurs in the past.) Plato seems to have held that even unexemplified properties, like the property of being a mermaid, belong to the realm of being. But I think that this is mistaken. I shall take for granted from now on that every universal is (at some time) exemplified, and that every particular exemplifies a universal.

Can the property of being round be located somewhere? Surely, you may say, roundness is right over there where Max and Moritz are. And it is, generally, wherever round things are. And it does not exist over here where the rectangular book is. Hence, you conclude, roundness is not a universal. Plato is wrong. Roundness must be a particular. But if you are clever enough to think of this argument, you are probably also astute enough to be able to guess what Plato's answer would be. Since I am a Realist, I would reply to you—since I do not want to presume to speak for Plato on a matter of such importance—that what you can hold in your hand and what is quite literally and without equivocation located in space is, not the property roundness, but a round object. Max and Moritz, it is true, are over there; you can point at them. But roundness is not over there, and you cannot point at it. Try it! And then ask yourself: am I not pointing, really, at the round object? Is this not what my attempt at pointing at roundness comes down to? I think that it does. Max, this particular individual thing, *is* round; he *has* the property in question. The book before me on my desk does not. Thus *there exists at a certain place*, at a certain time, a certain individual thing, namely, Max; and Max *has* the property roundness. Since Max *has* this property, one may mistakenly think that the property 'is where Max is'. Hence one may mistakenly think that it is in space just as Max is. So, if I am correct, to say that the property roundness is over there is a philosophically misleading way of saying that *something* is over there which is round. And to say that you can point at a property with your finger is a misleading way of saying that you can point at *something* with your finger which has this property. (Recall a similar situation when we talked earlier about the spatial location of a mind 'where the brain is'.)

My defense of Plato's realism rests on the assumption that particulars, like Max, are connected with their properties, like roundness, in a unique and intimate fashion. Because Max *has* this property, pointing at Max may be mistaken for pointing at roundness. I shall call this relationship between an individual thing and one of its properties 'exemplification'. Max *exemplifies* roundness; and so does Moritz. The book before me does not exemplify roundness; rather, it exemplifies the property of being rectangular. This is cumbersome and inelegant, I know, but it will allow us to put certain questions and problems more precisely. The first and foremost of these is: what is the nature of exemplification? What kind of relation is it?

(2) *The riddle of the nature of exemplification*

In order to see how important this question is for a realist, you merely have to reflect that exemplification is the only bond between the world of being and the world of becoming. Without this bond, the world would fall apart into two unconnected realms. it would not even make sense to speak of *a* world anymore. There would be *two* worlds, totally isolated from each other, and totally alone. It behooves a realist, therefore, to have a clear conception of exemplification. Plato, I believe, never did have one. Nor did any other realist until recently. As a consequence, one of the most effective arguments of the nominalists against realism has always centered around the nature of exemplification. The view that there are universals must be abandoned, one usually claims, because no sense can be made of the relationship between particulars and universals. Plato himself was fully aware of this kind of criticism. (Compare, for example, *Philebus*, 15 B.C.; and *Parmenides*, 131 A.D.) I shall introduce you to it in the words of a famous Roman philosopher, Boethius (480–524):

> But if any genus is one in number, it cannot possibly be
> common to many. For a single thing, if it is common, is
> common by parts, and then it is not common as a whole, but
> the parts of it are proper to individual things, or else it passes
> at different times into the use of those having it, so that it is
> common as a servant or horse is; or else it is made common to
> all at one time, not however that it constitutes the substance
> of those to which it is common, but like some theatre or
> spectacle, which is common to all who look on. But genus can
> be common to species according to none of these modes; for it

must be common in such a fashion that it is in the individual wholly and at one time, and that it is able to constitute and form the substance of those things to which it is common. (Boethius, *Commentaries on the Isagoge of Porphyry*, in *Medieval Philosophers*, 2 vols, ed. R. McKeen, New York, Charles Scribner's Sons, 1929)

Boethius speaks here of a 'genus', but we shall take as our example an essential property, namely, the property of being human (of being a human being). Now, according to the argument, there are three and only three ways in which this essence could possibly be related to different people. Firstly, it may be so split up into a number of parts that every human being contains one of these parts. Perhaps an analogy will be of some help. Think of the essence as a pizza pie. This pie may belong to several people in the sense that every one has a slice of it. They all 'participate in the pizza' by each one having a piece of it. But it is clear that the essence cannot belong to human beings in this way, for every person is a full human being, so that the whole essence must belong to everyone. For, properly speaking, the pizza does not really belong to any one of the persons involved; only individual slices do.

Secondly, the essence may belong as a whole to different people, but only to one person at a given time. In our analogy, the whole pizza may belong first to David, who bought it, then to Susan, to whom he gave it as a present, and finally to Tom, who talked Susan out of it. But again, this cannot be the correct relation between the essence and human beings; for many persons are human beings simultaneously.

Thirdly, the essence may belong to human beings in the way in which an audience participates in a play. It may be related to different persons in the manner in which the pizza is related to all the people who see it, who have a look at it. But this cannot be the way in which the essence of being human is related to Socrates and to Plato, because this essence is supposed to be a part of Socrates and of Plato, *a part of their substances*. An accidental property may perhaps be related to a substance in this superficial fashion, but never an essence.

Since there are only these three ways in which an essence could possibly belong to several individual things, one argues, and since it does not belong tó them in any one of these ways, it cannot belong to *several* individual things, but must belong to just *one*. Thus Plato must have *his essence humanity, and Socrates must have his*. There cannot be just one essence, *humanity*, which belongs to all people. Rather, there must be as many different essences humanity as there are people. If we call Plato's humanity 'humanity$_1$', we can distinguish it from Socrates' humanity by another subscript: 'humanity$_2$'. Instead of one essence humanity, we have billions of individual essences. There is no such single entity at all. All there is are the various essences humanity$_1$, humanity$_2$, . . . humanity$_{203}$, etc. And these essences are truly parts of their respective substances. They are located in space and time. They are particulars rather than universals.

This argument rests on the assumption that the relationship in question must be a part-whole relation. The third alternative is rejected because of this assumption. The first two alternatives give expression to it. These two alternatives show that the part-whole relation is, moreover, conceived of as a spatial part-whole relation. The essence is treated as if it were a spatial thing, a sort of pizza pie. Otherwise, there would be another possibility. The essence could belong simultaneously and wholly to several individual things. Humanity would be as a whole a part of Socrates, of Plato, and of Aristotle. Thus we can easily avoid the thrust of the argument if we insist that there are part-whole relations other than the spatial one. We can avoid the conclusion, in other words, if we maintain that a human being is not a spatial whole which contains a spatial part humanity. More distinctly put, we hold that an essence is not a spatial thing at all, and therefore, could not be a spatial part of anything.

But there is obviously still another way out. We could reject the very idea that exemplification must be a part-whole relation. And this is indeed what I shall do. The property of being human or being a human being belongs to Socrates, not as a part belongs to a whole, but in a unique and indefinable way. The best we can do is to describe this relation as the relation which everything has to its properties. Exemplification, in our view, is unlike any other relation. It is not a part-whole relation of any sort, spatial or otherwise. Nor is it like the intentional nexus, as the third alternative suggests. We must be clear, however, that in rejecting the basic assumption of the argument, we reject a fundamental thesis of the Aristotelian tradition, namely, the thesis that the essence of a substance is *part* of the substance. And this implies that we abandon the basic distinction between essence and accident. Thus we are adopting a Platonic rather than Aristotelian stance in regard to properties. All properties dwell in the realm of being, the so-called essential ones just as much as the accidental ones.

We must not make light, however, of a powerful and profound motive for the Aristotelian's insistence that essential properties are part and parcel of their respective substances. In this way, one averts a catastrophe which permanently threatens the Platonic system. This catastrophe consists in the complete isolation of the world of being from the world of becoming. If the essential properties are parts of substances, then they are firmly tied to the world of becoming. They are a part of it. Properly speaking, there are not two worlds, but only one. And in this one, matter and essence are wedded to each other.

Our task is therefore clear: we must avoid the Platonic catastrophe by non-Aristotelian means. We must securely tie properties to individuals without making the former parts of the latter. One half of this task has already been accomplished. Properties and individuals, in our view, are inseparably conjoined by the nexus of exemplification. Properties, in our view, are not *parts* of individual things, but they do not stand aloof from them either. They are as intimately connected with individuals as they possibly can be without being parts of them. Thus we, too, know of only one world, a world in which individuals, conceived of as particulars, and properties, conceived of as universals, dwell side by side in perfect harmony.

The other half of the task concerns the theory of knowledge. Not only does the Platonic world threaten to split into two unconnected realms, but the Platonic mind does as well.

(3) *Perception versus reflection*

According to the Platonic tradition, we are acquainted with the world of becoming, the world of changing individual things, by means of *perception*. The senses inform us about the goings on in this realm. But perception is a matter of the sense organs, of eyes, ears, nose, etc. It is therefore said to be not a purely intellectual activity. It consists, in a manner of speaking, of an interaction between different parts of the realm of becoming. Universals, which float in the realm of being, cannot interact with the senses. They cannot be known to the senses. They cannot be perceived. *Perception is of the particular and only of the particular*. This conclusion is so important that I shall give it a special name. I shall call it 'the Platonic dogma'.

Granted the Platonic dogma and assuming that we are acquainted with universals, it follows immediately that there must be a mental faculty other than perception which informs us about the world of being. According to the Platonic tradition, we know universals by means of what I shall call '*reflection*'. Reflection is conceived of as a purely mental activity, independent of all sense organs, by means of which we gain knowledge about the world of being. Thus the Platonic mind is split into two parts, corresponding to the two realms of being and of becoming: there is reflection of the world of being, and there is perception of the world of becoming.

Some of the age-old prejudice against universals derives from the conviction that there is no special mental faculty of reflection. One of the main nominalistic arguments has always been of the following sort. If there were universals, then, according to realism, they could not be known by the senses. Thus there has to be a special kind of mental act whose objects they are. But no realist has ever been able to describe this kind of act or to point it out to us. We have nothing but his assurance that there must be such a faculty. Since this alleged ability to reflect upon universals remains mysterious, we may justifiedly be suspicious of the whole realm of universals, that is, of a world which presumably lies beyond the reach of the senses.

The Aristotelian tradition tries to bridge the gap between the two halves of the Platonic mind just as it tries to bridge the schism between the two Platonic worlds. In perception, as we saw, the essential property of the perceived object is thought to exist mentally in the perceiving mind. This means that essences are presented to us in perception, that we are acquainted with them through the senses. No special faculty of the mind is required. Of course, the process by means of which these essences arrive in the mind is rather complicated and involves more than the mere stimulation of the sense-organs. But, nevertheless, it is a process of perception.

We, too, must beware of postulating an obscure faculty of the mind in order to safeguard access to the world of being. Universals and particulars, I said, dwell in the same world, side by side, inseparably joined together like Siamese twins. Whatever mental faculty acquaints us with one, cannot help but acquaint us with the other. What could be plainer than that perception acquaints us, not only with apples and billiard balls, but also with their colors and shapes. Perception, and only perception, contrary to the Platonic tradition, is the window onto the (outside) world. The senses do not acquaint us with particulars all by themselves, but with particulars and their universals. We must reject the Platonic dogma!

In terms of this very sketchy outline of the Platonic tradition, we can give a tentative description of Husserl's Phenomenology. Phenomenology is largely a theory of how we know universals and particulars. It accepts the Platonic distinction between these two kinds of entity, and it also embraces the Platonic dogma. Thus its main task is to elucidate the nature of reflection. This task, as we saw, is not new. But Phenomenology approaches it with an amount of sophistication hithero unknown. The sophistication is a gift from Brentano's theory of intentionality. In one sentence: phenomenology attempts to explain the nature of reflection and the nature of perception within the framework of an intentional theory of the mind.

5. Husserl's early view on numbers

(1) *The historical background*

Edmund Husserl, the founder of Phenomenology, studied mathematics at the universities of Leipzig and Berlin. In 1881, he moved to Vienna where he got his Ph.D in 1883 with a thesis on a topic in mathematics. During the years from 1884 to 1886, he studied philosophy with Brentano at Vienna. These facts about Husserl's academic career are important for an understanding of his philosophical views about the nature of mind. It is likely that he will apply his philosophical tools to a problem about the foundations of mathematics. And this is precisely what happened. The result was Husserl's first major work, *Philosophie der Arithmetik* (*Husserliana*, vol. xii, The Hague, Martinus Nijhoff, 1970), which he dedicated to his teacher Brentano.

According to the Platonic tradition, there are two basic categories of things, namely, particulars and universals. Now, recall that earlier we pointed out that the Aristotelian division between substances, essences, and accidents is not complete. There are also relations and structures. The same must be said about the Platonic assay of what there is. It is not complete. We must add, at least, relations and structures to the two categories of particular and universal. But notice that this addition to the

Edmund Husserl: the problem of knowledge

Platonic inventory must be done carefully. As we described particulars and universals, they form mutually exclusive and exhaustive classes of things. Any entity whatsoever either is located in space and/or time or it is not so located. There is no third possibility. Thus relations, for example, must be either particulars or they must be universals. Of course, if you are a nominalist and deny the existence of universals, then you have no choice: if there are relations at all, they must be particulars. A Platonist, on the other hand, though he has a choice, will undoubtedly put relations together with properties rather than with individual things. What you get, therefore, is the following picture of the Platonic world. There are particulars and universals. But universals are of two kinds. There are properties of individual things, on the one hand, and there are relations between individual things, on the other. Neither the property round nor the relationship of being taller than exists anywhere in space or time.

What about structures, how do they fit into the Platonic scheme of things? Well, there are all kinds of structure, as we saw earlier. The squares of a chess board form a spatial structure; the positive natural numbers, arranged by size, form a non-spatial series. Thus there are structures which are universals and there are structures which are particulars. As a matter of fact, the ordinary perceptual objects around us, the apple Oscar and the two billiard balls Max and Moritz, are spatio-temporal structures. They are spatio-temporal wholes which have spatial and temporal parts. Among universals, therefore, we find properties, relations, and structures. Among particulars, we find spatio-temporal structures in the form of ordinary perceptual objects.

How can numbers be accommodated? Are they particulars or are they universals? If they are universals, do they belong to one of the three categories we just mentioned. If not, do they form a category of universals of their own? And if so, how is this category characterized? These questions loom very large in the philosophy of the last hundred years. Husserl, with his mathematical background and his philosophical training, was supremely qualified to answer them. And this is what he tried to do in the *Philosophie der Arithmetik*. Alas, his investigation was flawed. In order to get at the nature of numbers, he thought he

90

had to investigate the origin of our conceptions of numbers. And pretty soon, he was discussing these concepts, thinking all the while that he was still talking about the numbers themselves. (This, parenthetically, is a common philosophical mistake. One starts out with an inquiry into the nature of some sort of thing or other. Then one alleges that this inquiry can only succeed, if first one raises questions about the nature of the inquiry itself. Eventually, the original topic is completely forgotten, and instead of discussing the nature of some kind of thing or other, one talks about the nature of our knowledge of that kind of thing. This is, as we shall see, how Heidegger loses sight of the meaning of being and concentrates on the meaning of human being instead.) Instead of doing ontology, Husserl wound up doing psychology. Before we take a closer look at his mistake, let me briefly explain why it is important for the creation of Phenomenology.

Soon after his *Philosophie der Arithmetik* was published, Husserl realized that an inquiry into the origin of our concepts of numbers will tell us absolutely nothing about the nature of the numbers themselves. As to numbers, he now adopted the view that they are universals. As long as he did not sharply distinguish between numbers and their concepts in our minds, he could think of the former as part of the world of becoming, as part of the world of mental things. As soon as he made the distinction, however, numbers stood revealed as universals, as timeless, non-spatial entities. But he must also have noticed that numbers are not the only denizens of this world of being. All properties dwell in it, and so do all relations. There is a richness to this world, a variety and structure, which is overwhelming. The realization of the existence of this vast realm must have led Husserl almost immediately to another question, namely, to the question of how this realm is known to us. Having been educated in the spirit of Brentano's analysis of the mind, he must have asked himself: what kind of mental act acquaints us with universals? His problem now became: how can we reconcile the existence of a Platonic realm of being with the existence of an intentional mind? This problem is the main topic of Husserl's next and perhaps greatest work, the *Logical Investigations* (trans. J. N. Findley, 2 vols, New York, Humanities Press, 1970).

Two more historical remarks before we return to the philosophical discussion. It must be mentioned that Husserl's confusion between things and their concepts was quite common at the time. With very few exceptions, and one of great importance, his contemporaries supplanted ontological problems with epistemological ones. Some of us trace this epistemological bias back to the great German philosopher Immanuel Kant (1724–1804). But be that as it may, the important exception to the rule was the philosopher Gottlob Frege (1848–1925) who, in 1884, published a book on very much of the same topic as Husserl's. Frege's book is called *The Foundations of Arithmetic* (trans. J. L. Austin, Northwestern University Press, Evanston, Illinois, 1974). In this book, Frege sharply distinguished between a number, for example, the number three, and our idea or concept of it. That the two must be distinguished is obvious as soon as you realize that what is true of one is not necessarily true of the other. For example, the number three can be squared, but its idea cannot. It is the next number after one in the series of odd positive integers, but its idea is not. And so on. Frege argued convincingly that the acquisition of the idea of the number three, the formation of this concept in a given mind, is a topic for psychology and not for arithmetic. Nor does the pursuit of this topic shed any light on the nature of numbers. It was Frege, you should know, who wrote a very critical review of Husserl's *Philosophie der Arithmetik,* harking back to his own earlier work. We may speculate that it was this devastating review which contributed to Husserl's change of mind and, hence, to his discovery of the realm of essences.

The second remark is this. Brentano's theory of intentionality does not invite a psychological treatment of numbers or of any other kind of object. Quite the contrary. The three-fold distinction between a mental act, its content, and its object positively forbids any identification of, say, the number three with its idea or concept. The idea *of* the number three is, in our terminology, the content of a particular mental act of having an idea. It is a property of this particular mental act. This content, the idea or concept, stands in the intentional nexus to an object; in our example to the number three. Thus the idea of the number three is a certain property of a mental individual, of a mental act; and this idea is related to the number. The idea of a particular elephant is in precisely the same boat as the idea of the number three. It, too, is a content of mental acts, namely, of all of those mental acts which are acts of having the idea of this elephant. It, too, is related by means of the intentional nexus to the elephant in question. And it, too, must not be confused with the elephant itself. We may ride the elephant, climb on his back, feed him peanuts, but we cannot ride the idea of this elephant, climb on its back, or feed it peanuts. No, the reason for Husserl's original confusion between numbers and ideas of numbers cannot be laid at the doorstep of the theory of intentionality. It may be attributed, I suggest, in part to the Kantian temper of the times, in part to Brentano's own peculiar views about what is mental and what is physical. Brentano himself constantly and systematically substituted psychological investigations for philosophical ones. Here, therefore, we have one of those exciting ironies with which the history of ideas abounds: the very philosopher who, for the first time, sharply distinguished between mental acts, on the one hand, and their intentional objects, on the other, tended to deny the existence of these objects, unless they were themselves mental phenomena.

(2) *What are numbers?*

To what category of thing do numbers belong? What kind of entity, for example, is the number three? It is pretty clear that numbers are not particulars, for they are not located in space and/or time. You cannot go looking for the number three as you can search for the abominable snowman. Nor will you be able to place it somewhere in history. It did not come and go with the dinosaurs; nor will it survive the collapse of the sun. Most philosophers are pretty much agreed, therefore, that numbers are not particulars.

It follows that numbers must be universals. But what kind of universal? Are they properties of individual things? Is the number three a property of something, like roundness is a property of a billiard ball? There is much that speaks against this possibility. At this moment, there are *three* blue pens on the desk before me. Now, what could the number three here be a property of? It cannot be a property of each one of the three blue pens, for each pen is one in number and not three. None of these pens can be said to have the property of being three. Nor can the number three be a property of the bundle of pens, conceived of as a spatio-temporal structure. This bundle, too, is one in number–there is one bundle–and not three. Since the individual pens and the bundle of pens are the only two kinds of individual thing in the situation, and since we have seen that three is not a property of either, we must conclude that it is not a property of individual things at all.

It may have occurred to you at some earlier point that properties of individual things are not the only properties there are. Max, the billiard ball, is round; it has the property roundness. So roundness is a property of individual things. Max is also white. Therefore, whiteness is a property of individual things. But roundness and whiteness, these two properties of individual things, are distinguished from each other by having themselves different properties. Roundness is a *shape*, while whiteness is a *color*. Roundness has the property of being a shape, while whiteness has the property of being a color. Thus being a shape is a property of properties of individual things; and so is being a color. Hence there are also properties of properties of individual things. Properties themselves can have properties. Now, this discovery reveals another possible answer to the question of what kind of universal the number three is. Might it not be the case that three is, not a property of individuals, but a property of properties of individuals?

Let us return to the example of the three blue pens, and let us christen them. Let us call them 'Tom', 'Dick', and 'Harry'. Tom has the property of being a blue pen on my desk (at this time). He shares this property with Dick and Harry, but with nothing else in the world. Nothing else in the world has this property because nothing else in the world is (now) a blue pen on my desk. Here we have a unique property, shared by Tom, Dick, and Harry, but by nothing else. A brilliant philosopher may conclude that the number three is a property of this unique property; for this unique property has the property of being exemplified by exactly three things. Let us assume that there are also at the present three books on my desk. Then these books, and nothing else in the world, share the property of being a book on my desk at this moment. Since this property is shared by precisely three things, it, too, has the property which is the number three. In other words, the number three is a property which is shared by the property of being a blue pen on my desk and by the property of being a book on my desk at the present time. As a matter of fact, it is a property which is shared by all and only those properties which are ever exemplified by precisely three things. Just as the different color shades all share in the property of being colors, and all shapes share in the property of being shapes, so all properties that are exemplified by precisely three things share in a property which is the number three. Numbers, in general, are therefore *properties of properties*. The number two, for example, is a property of all of those properties which are exemplified by a couple of things.

I think that this view is extremely plausible. But it is not the most popular view. Instead, a different conception of numbers has been widely accepted. According to this view, numbers are *sets* of *sets*. In order to understand this view, you must know what a set is. Most likely, you are familiar with sets from your mathematics classes in high school. So I shall be brief and try to stress the philosophical point of view. Sets, you must realize, are a further addition to our ontological inventory of the world: they are neither individual things (particulars), nor are they properties (or properties of properties), nor are they relations, nor are they structures, nor are they facts. A set of things is a *group* of things, considered merely as things which belong to the group and without regard to any relations among the things of the group or to any properties these things may have. For example, all the left shoes that exist in the universe at this moment form a set. And so do the following three things: a hair on Richard Burton's head, the last pill which Marilyn Monroe swallowed, and the moon. It is important to distinguish between sets so conceived and structures, especially spatio-temporal structures. A *bunch* of grapes, for example is a structure rather than a set; for the individual grapes have to be arranged in a certain spatial fashion in order to form a bunch. If we think of these grapes as scattered all over the United States, we no longer have a bunch. But these scattered grapes would still form a set. The same consideration holds for a pack of wolves. To form a pack, the individual wolves have to live in close proximity; they must form a spatio-temporal structure.

This difference between sets and structures can be made most precise in terms of the different identity conditions which sets and structures have. You may recall what I said earlier about the identity of structures: three conditions must be fulfilled for structure T_1 to be the same as structure T_2: (1) the non-relational parts of T_1 must be the same as the non-relational parts of T_2; (2) the relations of T_1 must be the same as the relations of T_2; and (3) the same non-relational parts must stand in the same relations in both structures. For sets, the criterion is much simpler: a set S_1 is identical with a set S_2 if and only if they have the same members (elements). All that matters for the identity of sets is that they consist of the same things; no inner structure is presupposed. But this, of course, is just another way of saying that sets are not structures.

Consider now all the sets which have existed and will ever exist consisting of exactly three members. Among these sets will be the set of the blue pens which are now on my desk. Among them will also be the set of the books which are now lying on my desk. One may think that all of these sets have somthing in common: they are all triples, so to speak. What they have in common, one may reason, is a common property. They all share in a property. And this property, one may finally conclude, is the number three. In this fashion, one may come by the view that numbers are properties, not of properties, but of sets. I mention this further possibility because it lies halfway between the last view which we considered and the view which, as I mentioned, is the generally accepted one. All the sets which have exactly three members, of course, form a new set, namely, the set which consists of all of those sets which are triples. And fashionable wisdom has it that the number three is this set of triples. In short: numbers are *sets of sets*, namely, of all of those sets which have the same number of members. The number two, for example is the set of all couples, that is, of all sets which have two members.

Here, then, are three ontological possibilities. Firstly, the number three could turn out to be a property of the property of being a blue pen now on my desk. Secondly, it could turn out to be a property of the set consisting of the blue pens which are now on my desk. Thirdly, and most widely accepted, the number three may be the set consisting of all triples and, hence, include the set of blue pens on my desk. According to these possibilities, numbers are either properties or sets. They belong either to the category of property or to the category of set. I shall not hide from you my conviction that they are neither. I believe that all three views are mistaken, even the very popular one that numbers are sets of sets. Numbers, in my view, are of an entirely different sort. They belong to a category all of their own. I call this category 'quantifier'. Numbers are *quantifiers*. If you are interested in my reasons for rejecting these views and wish to learn more about quantifiers, let me refer you to another book of mine: *The Categorial Structure of the World* (Bloomington, Indiana University Press, 1983).

Our survey of views about the nature of numbers allows us to see Husserl's own analysis of the concept of number in the proper light. Let us then turn to Husserl's *Philosophie der Arithmetik*.

(3) *Husserl's analysis of the concept of number*

There is a classic definition of number which goes all the way back to Euclid:

> A unit is that by virtue of which each of the things that exist is called one. A number is a multitude composed of units. (Book IV, Euclid's *Elements*)

I think we don't go too far astray if we assume that what Euclid means by a 'multitude' is a set. A number, accordingly, is said to be a set of units. The number three, for example is a set of three units. Husserl starts his own analysis of the concept of number with Euclid's definition in mind. In effect, he offers a psychologically sophisticated rendition of Euclid's definition.

Husserl begins by considering what he calls a 'concrete multitude': the color red, the moon, and Napoleon. There exist quite a few such multitudes. For example there also exists the concrete multitude composed of a certain feeling of nausea, a particular angel, Italy, and the number three. Now, when we abstract from the particular things which compose these multitudes, so Hussetl claims, then we arrive at the notion of a *multitude of this sort* by reflecting on the characteristic relation which obtains between the members of every multitude, namely, the relation of 'collective connection'. In other words, Husserl maintains that if we pay attention to what all concrete multitudes have in common, we find out that it is a certain relation between their members. Notice two things. Firstly, Husserl explains here, not what a number is, but how we *arrive at the notion* of a set of this sort, namely, by abstraction from the particularities of its members. Secondly, Husserl holds that there exists a characteristic relation between the members of this sort of set, contrary to what we said in the last section.

By abstracting from the peculiar characteristics of the members of our particular concrete multitude, Husserl says, we arrive at the notion of a mere *something and something and something*. Every multitude of three things is a something and something and something, if we do not pay attention to the peculiarities of its members. But this notion, according to Husserl, is the notion of *one and one and one*. And this notion, in turn, is the notion of the number three. Thus we arrive at the notion of the number three by considering a concrete multitude of three things and abstracting from the peculiarities of its members.

What plausibility Husserl's analysis has, it derives from the fact that *one plus one plus one are three*: $1 + 1 + 1 = 3$. The left side of this equation may look, on first blush, like the abstracted notion of *something and something and something*. But a closer look reveals that the two notions are not at all the same. To begin with, the notion of the number one seems clearly to be quite different from the notion of something. The first is a notion of a number, but *something* is clearly not a number like two, three, and four. Of course, every something is one in number. But so is every fire engine, and nobody would conclude that the number one is a fire engine. Secondly the arithmetic sum relation cannot be the same as Husserl's collective connection. The latter relation is a most fragile bond, a mere will-o'-the-wisp. According to Husserl, it is created between the various items of a concrete multitude by the fact that these items are thought together by a mind. By the mere fact that you think in one thought of such diverse items as the color red, the moon, and Napoleon, you connect them in some way, so that they form a concrete multitude. If this is so, then it follows that this multitude does not exist if no one thinks of these three items in one thought. And what holds for this particular multitude, holds for all of them: none of them would exist if people would not think of various things together in one thought. And it follows further that the number three, the sum of one plus one plus one, would not exist if there were no thoughts of several items together. And this seems to me to be an unacceptable consequence of Husserl's view. Surely, I object, the fact that one plus one plus one are three does not depend on there being anyone who thinks of three things in one single thought. One plus one plus one would be three, even if no one had even formed the abstract notion of a something and something and something.

There is another decisive objection to Husserl's analysis. What we arrive at by abstraction is presumably the notion of *something and something and something*. But should this not really read: something and something *else* and something *else*? If we assume that the first something is the same as the second and the third, then there exists not a multitude (set) with three members, but rather a multitude (set) with just one member, namely, the certain something. A set that consists of the Eiffel Tower and the Eiffel Tower and the Eiffel Tower, consists just of the Eiffel Tower. It does not have three members, but only one. Thus in order to get an abstract multitude of *three* things, abstraction must have been carried just far enough to erase the differences between the color red, the moon, and Napoleon, without erasing the fact that they are different. The notion of the abstract multitude must therefore be the notion of something and something else and something else again. But then it becomes quite obvious that this notion is not the notion of one plus one plus one. In the latter, the number one does indeed occur identically the same three times. The first one is not different from the second and the third. What the formula 'one plus one plus one' represents can be expressed more perspicuously by 'the sum of one plus one, plus one'. In the familiar arithmetic symbols: '(1 + 1) + 1'. And the equation '(1 + 1) + 1 = 3' is a convenient abbreviation for: 'The number which is the sum of one and one (namely, the number two), plus one, is the number three. Put differently: 'The number which is the sum of the number which is the sum of one and one, and one, is the number three'. The sum relation as you can perhaps see, is a three-place relation. This becomes obvious if instead of the familiar '$m + n = p$' we always write '$+ (m, n, p,)$'. Instead of saying 'three plus five is eight', we could say 'the sum relation holds between three, five, and eight'. This part of our criticism of Husserl's analysis can be summed up by saying that the number three, though it is the *sum* of two and one, and though two is the *sum* of one and one, is not a *set* consisting of three (*different!*) ones.

So much for Husserl's analysis and our criticism of it. What we are interested in, primarily, is the fact that Husserl soon turned away from his psychological treatment of numbers, in terms of mental processes of collecting, and adopted a Platonic position, according to which numbers dwell in the realm of being together with other universals.

6.   Husserl's distinction between essences and their instances

(1) *The Platonic dogma and eidetic intuition*

Granted that numbers belong to the realm of being, let us consider anew such ordinary properties as colors and shapes. You will remember that I argued earlier, against rather stiff opposition, that roundness is not located in space. The mistaken impression that it is, say, over there, where the billiard ball Moritz is, arises because it is indeed Moritz rather than the book over here which *is* round. We are tempted to locate properties where, in reality, the individual things are located which have those properties. This is, at any rate, my view. But suppose someone keeps insisting that roundness is quite literally over there, that it is just as much and in the same sense located as Moritz is. What can I reply? All I can do is repeat myself: you are mistaken, you merely think that roundness is over there because something is over there which is round.

My opponent, on the other hand, has an ace in the hole, namely, the Platonic dogma. According to this dogma, whatever can be perceived, whatever comes through the senses, belongs to the world of becoming. The senses can only acquaint us with particulars; universals cannot be perceived. If this assertion were true, then it would follow that I must be mistaken. For it seems to be undeniable–and I shall not deny it–that I see, quite

101

literally and unequivocally, the roundness of Moritz with my eyes. But then it follows that this shape cannot be a universal. It must be a particular and, hence must be located in space and/or time.

Husserl never questioned the Platonic dogma. He therefore believed that Moritz's roundness and his color, as they are perceived, are particulars, located in space together with Moritz. If they are where Moritz is, then they must be *part of* Moritz. And since they are in space, since they are spatial, they must be spatial parts of Moritz. But, quite obviously, they are not. Moritz's shape is not a part of him in the same sense in which his left half is a part of him. We can split Moritz in half, take one half and hide it under the bed, and send the other half by airmail to Australia. But we cannot in like manner spatially separate his shape from the rest of him. While the left half of Moritz is a *separable* part of him, his shape is an *inseparable* part of him. This is the way Husserl puts it in the *Logical Investigations*; and he spends many pages discussing this difference. Notice that there is something strange about Husserl's view. Moritz's shape is (a) spatial and (b) a part of Moritz, and yet it is not a spatial part of Moritz. We wonder how something spatial can be a part of something else which is spatial, without being a spatial part of it.

But this is not the main point I wish to make. Assume that you are on Husserl's side and hold that Moritz's roundness is particular. Assume further that you are also convinced, on independent grounds, that there must exist a universal roundness as well. Then you will be faced once again with the question of how we are acquainted, not with Moritz's roundness, but with the universal roundness. And you will have no choice, being a victim of the Platonic dialectic, but to postulate a special faculty of the mind, other than perception, which acquaints us with the universal roundness. This is the unenviable position in which Husserl finds himself. Having convinced himself that there is a universal roundness, in addition to the particular roundnesses of round things, and relying on the Platonic dogma, he must explain how, by what means, we have access to the universal roundness. He responds with a bold move. Perception, he claims, is of two kinds. There is ordinary perception–what we usually call 'perception'–of particulars, including Moritz's roundness. And then there is a different kind of perception–Husserl calls it 'eidetic intuition'–of universals. What is bold about this move is the assertion that there is a *perception* of universals, that universals are presented to the mind just as immediately as ordinary individuals are in ordinary perception. The standard Platonic view has it, by contrast, that universals are somehow given to thought, to the understanding, as opposed to perception. Husserl, of course, does not deny that we can think of universals. But he also insists that they are given, in the first place, in a mental act which is very much like an act of perception.

There are some terminological matters to be attended to at this juncture: what I have called universals, Husserl calls–not too fortuitously, as you can perhaps see–'essences'. The universal roundness is an essence. What shall we call the particular roundness of Moritz? I shall say that it is an *instance* of the essence (or universal). Moritz's roundness, call it 'roundness$_1$', is an instance of (the essence) roundness. Max's roundness, we shall call 'roundness$_2$', is also an instance of this essence. And so is every particular roundness of every round individual thing. There are therefore many instances of the one essence roundness. All of these instances are located in space and time, but the essence is not. We perceive an instance of roundness in ordinary perception; the essence, on the other hand, is given to us in eidetic intuition. (Husserl's term uses the Greek word 'eidos' which was Plato's word for what I call 'universals', that is, for the inhabitants of the world of being. Eidetic intuition is thus the intuition (perception) of universals. Essences, in the Aristotelian sense, must of course be sharply distinguished from Platonic universals.) What perception is to the instances of roundness, eidetic intuition is to the universal roundness itself.

Husserl's world, like Plato's, constantly threatens to split into two unconnected halves, a world of instances and a world of essences. Perception, too, divides into two mutually exclusive faculties: the perception of instances and the intuition of essences. Knowledge is therefore of two kinds. There is knowledge of the world of becoming, gained through perception, and there is knowledge of the world of being, dependent on intuition. Is there any way of avoiding this rift? Can we make a case for the view that there is just one world, a world known through perception? I think so. But before we attempt to make it, let us take a look at Husserl's main argument for the existence of essences.

(2) *The argument for essences*

Consider again the two white billiard balls, Max and Moritz. According to Husserl's ontological assay, Max contains an instance of roundness, roundness$_1$, and Moritz contains a different instance of roundness, roundness$_2$. Compare Max and Moritz with a square Graham cracker; call it 'Graham' for short. Graham does not contain an instance of roundness, but contains instead an instance of squareness, call it 'squareness$_1$'. The three instances so far mentioned are all different from each other. Of course, this is just a fanciful way of saying that there are *three* instances. But it is a further fact that two of these instances are instances of roundness, while the third differs from them in being an instance, not of roundness, but *of squareness*. What is the nature of this fact? How shall we analyze it? A nominalist faces the following problem. He must account for the fact that two of the instances are different from the third in that they are instances of the same property, without invoking anything but particulars. Husserl claims that this cannot be done, and I agree with him. This is his main argument for the existence of essences. Here are some of the more popular nominalistic attempts to solve the problem.

It has been held that while there is the word 'roundness', there is no such thing as the universal *roundness*. Of course, there is roundness$_1$, roundness$_2$, etc., but these things are particulars rather than universals. Now, the fact that roundness$_1$ is an instance of roundness rather than an instance of squareness, it has been said, is nothing else but the fact that roundness$_1$ is somehow related to the word 'roundness' rather than to the word 'squareness'. The first instance, but not the second, *is called* 'roundness'. The fact that squareness$_1$ is an instance of squareness rather than of roundness is similarly explained as the fact that it is called 'squareness' rather than 'roundness'. A moment's reflection shows that this nominalistic explanation

Husserl's distinction between essences and their instances will not do. For one, it is clear that roundness$_1$ would be an instance of roundness even if there had never existed the English word 'roundness'. Max would be round, he would contain an instance of this sort, even if there were no language at all, neither English nor any other. Surely, the moon was round long before anyone talked about it. Secondly, it is also obvious that roundness$_1$ would still be an instance of roundness rather than squareness if we suddenly decided to call it something else. Max would continue to be round, he would continue to contain an instance of this kind, even if we suddenly called its shape, say, 'whiteness'. Thirdly, the word 'roundness' is itself a universal. We mean by this word, not a particular inscription on a particular piece of paper, but rather the design (shape, pattern) which this particular inscription shares with all other inscriptions of the word. On this page, the word 'roundness' occurs several times, that is, there are several different inscriptions of it. Each one of these inscriptions shares with all the others a certain design. But this means according to the view under discussion, that each inscription contains an instance of the design. What makes all of these instances instances of the design 'roundness' rather than of the design 'squareness'? You can see that the problem which we originally formulated in terms of instances of roundness and roundness recurs for instances of the design 'roundness ' and the design itself.

According to a slightly different nominalistic move, the fact that roundness$_1$ is an instance of roundness is really the fact that the word 'roundness' *is true* of roundness$_1$. But this view is open to the same objections as the previous one. In addition, there is the following consideration. The relationship of being true of cannot arbitrarily hold between the word and the instance, as our objections have indicated. Under what conditions, then, does it hold? What must be the case for 'roundness' to be true of roundness$_1$? According to the view we are considering, the relationship holds if and only if the sentence 'roundness$_1$ is an instance of roundness' is true. So, we have to ask next: under what conditions is this sentence true? We get the answer that this sentence is true if and only if roundness$_1$ is an instance of roundness. And here our questioning is supposed to end. And end it does, because we have come full circle. We started with the question of under what conditions the relation of being true of holds between 'roundness' and roundness$_1$. And we have just been told that it holds if and only if roundness$_1$ is an instance of roundness. But the sentence 'roundness$_1$ is an instance of roundness' is presumably just another sentence for the circumstance that 'roundness' is true of roundness$_1$. Thus we have in effect been told that 'roundness' is true of roundness$_1$ if and only if 'roundness' is true of roundness$_1$. And that is no explanation at all!

Finally, there is a view which tries to replace the universal roundness by a similarity relation between instances of roundness. According to this view, the fact that roundness$_1$ is an instance of roundness and not an instance of squareness is really the fact that roundness$_1$ stands in a certain relation of similarity to such instances as roundness$_2$, roundness$_3$, etc., but does not stand in this relation to such instances as squareness$_1$, squareness$_2$, etc. This view denies that there is, in addition to the various instances, the universal roundness, but assumes that there is instead a relation of similarity between these instances. But it is clear that roundness$_1$ is an instance of roundness cannot be the fact that roundness$_1$ stands in the similarity relation to some other instance, for the first fact would obtain even if there were no other instance to which roundness$_1$ is similar. Assume that near Mt St Helena there lies a piece of lava which has a very peculiar and complicated shape. We do not have a name in English for this kind of shape; nor does any other language. So we shall call it 'alpha'. It may well be the case that nowhere else has there ever existed nor will there ever exist a body with the shape alpha. But even then it would be true that the instance alpha$_1$ is an instance of alpha, that is, of that shape rather than any other.

Moreover, the question arises of whether the relation of similarity itself is universal or not. If it is universal, then the view under discussion does not succeed, for it merely replaces one universal entity, the universal roundness, by another universal entity, the similarity relation. There are then, after all, denizens of the world of being in the form of relations. No, a nominalist must maintain that there is no such thing as the universal relation, but merely a number of its instances, S_1, S_2, etc. This means that between roundness$_1$ and roundness$_2$, between these two instances, there holds an instance S_1, while between roundness$_3$ and roundness$_4$, these two different instances, there holds a different instance, say S_2. But it is, of course, a fact that S_1 and S_2 are both instances of similarity rather than instances of the father-of relation. And the question must be answered of how this fact can obtain without there being a universal similarity, of which S_1 and S_2 are instances. As you can see, the assumption that there are instances of this relation, but no universal relation, has merely raised our original problem anew; this time for S_1 and S_2 rather than for roundness$_1$ and roundness$_2$. We still have no answer to the question of how to assess the fact that an instance is an instance of one kind rather than another.

Nominalism, we agree with Husserl, does not get off the ground. There are universals. But are there also instances? I do not think so. Consider again the two billiard balls, Max and Moritz, and compare them with the square cracker, Graham. There are these three individual things. They belong to the category of particular since they are spatio-temporal entities. What about their shapes? Max is round, and so is Moritz; while Graham is square. The property roundness and the property squareness, I submit, are two universals. Furthermore, Max and Moritz exemplify one and the same shape, they both exemplify roundness. Graham exemplifies a different shape. But other square things exemplify the same shape as Graham does, namely, squareness. In each case, many particulars exemplify the same universal. Our assay of the situation thus encounters only three kinds of thing: the three particulars, two universal properties, and the universal nexus of exemplification which connects particulars with universal properties. Husserl's account, on the other hand, is quite complicated. The complication arises because of his belief in instances. Max, Moritz, and Graham are conceived of as structures of instances. Max, for example, consists of the instance roundness$_1$, the instance whiteness$_1$, etc.; Moritz consists of the instances roundness$_2$, whiteness$_2$, etc; and Graham consists of the instance squareness$_1$, the instance brownness$_1$, etc. Now, the fact that Max is round becomes rather complicated. First of all, Max contains the instance roundness$_1$. But this is not all. We must also take into account that roundness$_1$ is an instance of roundness rather than, say, squareness. So the fact that Max is round is really the complex fact that Max contains roundness$_1$ and that roundness$_1$ is an instance of roundness. This ontological analysis lists many more ingredients than ours. Firstly, there are the various instances (which belong to the category of particular). Secondly, there are the three structures, Max, Moritz, and Graham, (which belong also to the category of particular). Thirdly, there are the universals roundness, whiteness, and squareness. Fourthly, there is the relation between structures like Max, on the one hand, and the instances which they *contain*, on the other. This is a whole-part relation. Fifthly, there is the relation which obtains between an instance and the universal of which it is an instance. This is not a whole-part relation. It resembles, to some degree, our exemplification relation. Sixthly, there is a relation of conjunction, expressed by 'and', which connects the fact that Max contains roundness$_1$ with the fact that roundness$_1$ is an instance of roundness. Such is the complication introduced by Husserl's belief that there are instances.

Why does he believe that there are instances? Why would anyone believe that there are instances? As I have laid out the philosophical dialectic, there is only one reason: because he subscribes to the Platonic dogma! If it is true that we cannot perceive universals, then it follows that the shape of Max and Moritz, which I perceive, cannot be universal, but must be particular (or, rather, must be two particulars!). And then it follows that there are instances. Thus if we reject instances, we must reject the Platonic dogma. And this means that we must offer a different conception of the nature of perception.

(3) *The objects of perception*

The thesis which I wish to submit for your evaluation is this: every act of perception is propositional. I shall call this, tongue in cheek, Grossmann's dogma. We already know what perceptual acts are, namely, acts of seeing, hearing, smelling, tasting, and touching (feeling). Let us consider, as our paradigm, a case of seeing: I see that Max (the billiard ball) is round. What I see is *that Max is round*. I see, in other words, that *something is the case*. I express this by saying that seeing is *propositional*. What one sees, in this sense of the term, is a proposition, or a circumstance, or a state of affairs–these are all words for approximately the same thing–which is expressed by what follows after the 'that' in the sentence: 'I see that Max is round.' On another occasion, I see that Moritz is white. In this case, I see the state of affairs represented by 'Moritz is white'. Now, what I claim is that all perception is perception of states of affairs in this sense. I see *that* an elephant enters the circus ring; I see *that* the elephant lifts both of his front legs; I hear *that* the elephant tamer cracks his whip; I smell *that* my neighbor on the seat beside me eats popcorn; I taste *that* the peanuts I am eating are not salted enough; and I feel *that* the seats are much too hard for comfort.

Of course, someone may ask me after the show: 'Did you see the elephant?' And I may reply: 'Yes, I saw it.' The question and answer make it look as if the object of my perception was, not a state of affairs, but rather an individual thing, namely, an elephant. But I think this way of looking at the conversation is too superficial. What my friend was interested in was merely whether or not I had seen the elephant perform. He was not interested in what it precisely was that I saw. Otherwise, he might have asked: 'Did you see the elephant stand on its hindlegs?' Or he might have asked: 'Did you see the elephant dance in circles?' Very often, therefore, we report not precisely what it was we saw, but merely what the object was which we saw, or what the property was which we saw. The situation is similar to the one in which I report to my friend that I have been daydreaming about Venice. It is clear to him that I did not have before my mind, for some length of time, nothing but the city of Venice. Rather, he knows that what happened was that I remembered walking the streets of Venice, that I wished I were back, that I imagined taking the boat to the Lido beach, etc. A mental process of daydreaming took place, and this process consisted of many different acts of many different kinds, and these acts had as their objects, not the one thing, Venice, but various states of affairs. (I think that other kinds of mental act, not just perceptions, are propositional. But this is not of importance for our present point.)

When we look closely, I maintain, we will find that we always see some such thing as that Max is round, that the elephant is entering the ring, and that another elephant takes up his position to the left of the first. Now, when I see that Max is round, I see Max and I also see the property roundness. By seeing the fact that Max is round, I am automatically acquainted with Max and with roundness. To see Max, to put it differently is to see some circumstance about him. It is to see that he is round, or that he is white, or that he is moving across the billiard table, or that he lies to the left of Moritz. And to see roundness is to see that something or other is round. It is to see that Max is round, or that Moritz is round, or that the moon is round. In short, to see an individual thing is to see a circumstance about it; and to see a property, is to see that something has the property. Thus we can be said to perceive states of affairs, but also their constituents. And to see the former is to see the latter.

I am not saying that there are two kinds of seeing, the seeing of states of affairs and the seeing of their constituents. There is only one kind of mental act of seeing, and its object is always a state of affairs. But to see a state of affairs, is to see its constituents. Nothing more is required to see Max but that you see that Max is round. Of course, it also works the other way around: to see Max is to see some such thing as that Max is round. Nothing more is required. Let me state it again: when you see that an individual has a certain property, you see the individual as well as its property; you are acquainted with both the individual and the property.

This view about the propositional nature of perception, I want to impress on you, breaks with almost all previous views in the entire history of philosophy. According to what is perhaps the most widely accepted alternative view, perception is a matter of having sensations and of making judgments. For example, when you see that Max is white, you are said to experience certain visual sense-impressions and, on the basis of these sense-impressions, to make the judgment that Max is white. Precisely speaking, there is no such thing as a mental act of seeing. Perception involves only acts of sensing sense-impressions (of having certain sensations) and acts of judging. According to our view, on the other hand, an act of seeing–or any other perceptual act–does not consist of anything else. It is an unanalyzable mental phenomenon. It is as different from the experience of sense-impressions and from judgment as it is from desire and memory. This is a fundamental difference between the popular view and ours.

To say that an act of seeing does not *consist*, in whole or in part, of the experience of sense-impressions is not to say that it could occur without such an experience. When you see that Max is white, you do experience certain visual sensations; and you could not see anything without these sense-impressions. But the fact that perception is *causally dependent* on the experience of sense-impressions does not imply that the former consists, in whole or in part, of the latter. Nor does perception consist, in whole or in part, of judgments. To see, with your eyes wide open, that the moon is full is obviously quite a different mental phenomenon from judging that it is full by consulting a calender. We know quite well, under normal conditions, whether we have seen something or merely judged it to be so. But there is also a kernel of truth to the idea that perception involves judgment. Judgment, as traditionally conceived of, is *propositional*, in our sense of this word. You judge *that* something or other is the case; you cannot judge a thing. Since one noticed that a perception is often expressed in propositional form, one jumped to the conclusion that it must consist of judgment. The fundamental mistake of previous views has been their failure to realize that mental acts other than judgments can be propositional. While the popular view takes for granted that judgments and only judgments are propositional, we believe that all acts of perception are propositional. This is another fundamental difference between the two views.

From our perspective, to sum it up, the popular view realizes that perception involves the experience of sense-impressions. But it falls into error when it concludes that perception therefore consists of an act of experiencing sense-impressions. It also acknowledges that perception is in some sense propositional. But it infers erroneously that perception must consist of acts of judging. The truth is that perceptual acts themselves are propositional and that they causally depend on the experience of sensations.

What we perceive are states of affairs. What is a state of affairs? To what category does it belong? Is it particular or is it universal? By now, we automatically raise these questions for any new entity we encounter. And that shows how well we have learned to think philosophically. Unfortunately, we do not have the space to deal with these questions as fully as they deserve. I have to be brief and have to leave many of your questions unanswered. But a brief answer is better than none at all.

Are states of affairs particular or universal? Well, first of all, we must distinguish between states of affairs and facts. It is a fact, so we have assumed, that Max is round and white. It is not a fact that he is green. Yet, one may think or believe, one may even mistakenly see, that Max is green. The object of one's mental act of thinking, of believing, or of seeing is then not a fact. I call it a state of affairs which is not the case, which is not a fact. Thus, the way I use these terms, states of affairs are of two kinds, those that are the case, which I also call 'facts', and those that are not the case, for which I have no special term. Obviously, what we are interested in is the ontological category of fact. Since states of affairs which do not obtain do not exist at all, even though one can believe them, doubt them, even perceive them, they cannot belong to any category. (Recall in this connection our discussion of the problem of nonexistent objects.) We can categorize only things which exist. But by answering our question for facts, we gain an answer of sorts even for states of affairs which do not obtain. Obviously, we can say that such states of affairs *would* belong to the category to which facts belong, *if* they obtained. Similarly, if there were mermaids, they would be particulars; and being a mermaid would be a universal property.

Consider, then, the fact that Max is white. I think that it is rather evident that this fact is not a spatial entity. You cannot locate it somewhere south of the north pole; it has no shape or size. Of course, Max is spatial. But we are not talking about Max; we ar talking about the fact that Max is white. The case is not quite so clear in regard to time. Philosophers have been of two minds about the question whether or not facts are temporal. Assume that we paint Max green after a while, so that he is no longer white. Then it is true that Max is at one time white and at another time green. And we can interpret this fact in two different ways. Firstly, we may say that there is, properly speaking, no such fact as that Max is white or that Max is green, but that every presumed fact of this sort in reality contains a temporal indication. Thus it is a fact that Max at t_1 is white and it is also a fact that Max at t_2 is green. What is temporal, according to this interpretation, is Max. But the fact that Max at a certain time has a property, this fact is not itself temporal. It does not exist at a certain time, it has no duration, it does not cease to exist. The fact that Max at t_1 is white is atemporal, timeless, just as it is non-spatial, spaceless. Accordingly, facts are universals. They exist neither in space nor in time. I think that this is the correct view.

According to the second view, the fact that Max is white exists (obtains) at t_1, but does not exist (obtain) at t_2. This fact is therefore a temporal entity. It exists for some time, and then ceases to exist. If this were the correct view, then it would follow that facts are particulars; for even though they are not spatial, they are at least temporal. Or, more precisely, it follows that *some* facts are particulars. Consider the fact that two plus two is four, or the fact that midnight blue is darker than canary yellow. Neither one of these two facts can plausibly be said to have a duration; neither one can plausibly be dated. And if this is so, then these two facts are, not only not spatial, but also atemporal. Hence they are universal rather than particular. There are then two kinds of fact, facts which are particular and facts which are universal. Notice how, precisely, these two kinds of fact differ. The particular ones are all about individual things, that is, about particulars, while the universal facts concern universals. Max, since he is a particular, may at one time have one property, at another time, another; Max, in short, may change. But the number two, for example, cannot at one time be larger than one and at another time be smaller than one. It cannot change at all since it is a universal. Particular facts turn out to be exactly those facts which are about particulars, while universal facts are about universals. But this suggests, I submit, that all facts are really universal and, hence, that the first view is correct. It suggests that some facts may appear to be temporal simply because they are about temporal things. At any rate, I shall adopt the first view from now on.

It is time to pull the various strands of our discussion together. The Platonic tradition, of which Husserl is one of the most recent members, divorces the world of being from the world of becoming. And it divorces knowledge of the former from the perception of the latter. I have argued that there is only one world, a world in which universals and particulars dwell side by side in perfect harmony. We can now see what keeps this world together: it is the unity of the fact. There are particulars, and there are universals. The Platonist is not mistaken. But there exists also an entity which assures an over-arching unity that ties universals to particulars, and of which the early Platonists never even dreamed. The problem is, not how universals can be kept tied to particulars, but how facts are to be analyzed into their constituents. The unity of the world is not in danger. It is a fact. And so is the world. We analyze this unity, this fact, into its constituent parts. And in doing so, we find that it contains both particulars and universals.

The unity of the two realms is guaranteed by the existence of facts. The unity of our knowledge of the two realms is guaranteed by the propositional character of perception. Here, the Platonist is profoundly mistaken. There is no such thing as reflection on universals. There is no pure faculty of the mind which acquaints us with universals. Perception yields all. The basic unit of the world, the fact, is presented to us in a unitary act of the mind.

When you see that Max is white, you see Max and his color. But you can also see, literally with your eyes, that there are *two* billiard balls on the table. And if you do, you see the number two just as plainly as you see the color white when you see that Max is white. Therefore, not only properties are given to us in perception, but numbers are as well. And when you see that Max is to the left of Moritz, you see the relation of being to the left of. In this manner, Grossmann's dogma yields an answer to the question of how we know that there are all those kinds of universal which we have listed. The answer is that we know it by means of perception.

7. Husserl's distinction between individuals and their aspects

(1) *Aspects and partial bundles*

An essence, according to Husserl, can be presented to the mind wholly, in its totality, in one act of reflection. Perceptual objects, by contrast, can never be so presented. We can only perceive *aspects* of them. This is one of the fundamental differences between essences and certain individual things. In order to understand Husserl's view, we must be clear about the notion of an aspect. But this is easier said than done. It seems to me that at least two and, perhaps, even three such notions appear in his philosophy. Under these circumstances, we shall have to examine each one separately and compare it with the others.

Husserl's notion of an aspect is foreshadowed by a conception of Twardowski's (Twardowski, you may remember, was the Brentano student who held that the intentional nexus can connect a mental content with something that has no being.) Twardowski reasons as follows. A perceptual object, for example the apple Oscar, is a bundle of instances. It consists of instances of all the properties (what Husserl calls 'essences') which it has. But there are a gigantic number of such properties. Oscar has relational properties to everything else that now exists in the universe. He has the property of being so many miles

115

away from the sun, to mention just one. It follows, therefore, that Oscar is a tremendously complex bundle. But no content of an act of perception can be that complex. No idea of Oscar can be an idea of millions and millions of instances, of properties. Hence every idea of him, every perception, must be, as Twardowski puts it, 'inadequate' (*On the Content and Object of Presentations*, p. 79). The content of an act of perceiving Oscar can only intend certain instances of properties of his. For example, one may see Oscar's color, shape, and size in one glance, but one does not see all the different color nuances which a closer inspection would reveal. Oscar's properties (instances) can therefore be divided into two mutually exclusive groups, namely, into those which are perceived in a particular act and those which are not. And we may say that the former constitute an aspect of Oscar's, an aspect which is at that moment perceived.

Twardowski's view implies that we never perceive, in one act of perception, a perceptual object, but merely an aspect of it. If his view were correct, then we would have to be mistaken when we claim to have seen an elephant, heard an airplane, or tasted a pear. I look at Oscar and say: '*This* is an apple.' If Twardowski is right, then I must be mistaken. What I see, the *this* I am talking about, cannot possibly be an apple. It must be an aspect of an apple. And an aspect of an apple is definitely not an apple. But, surely, what I see is an apple. Hence, something must be wrong with Twardowski's theory. Any view which implies that we do not see, literally and unequivocally, perceptual objects must be false. Where does Twardowski's view go wrong? It is based on two essential assumptions. The first assumption is that a perceptual object is a bundle of a large number of instances of properties. The second assumption is that no content of an act of perception is sufficiently complex to be able to intend all of these instances. I think that we can put the matter more straight-forwardly by saying that, according to the second assumption, one can never perceive in one act of perception all of the instances of which a perceptual object consists. I believe that this second assumption is correct. When I see Oscar, I do not see *all* of his properties. I do not even see *most* of his properties. Another look at him reveals that he has properties which I had not seen before. And a really close inspection reveals even further properties. I see Oscar; there can be no doubt about that either. And from this I conclude that one (or both) of two things must be the case. Either Oscar is not a bundle of his properties (or a bundle of instances), or else to see such a bundle is not the same as to see all of its constituents. If Oscar is not a bundle of properties, but an individual thing, a particular, which has properties, but does not consist of them, then it is possible to see him without seeing all of his properties. And I think that this is indeed the correct assessment of the present difficulty. On the other hand, even if Oscar is a bundle, we can still see Oscar without seeing all of his properties, if it is possible to see a structure without seeing all of its parts. I shall leave it to you for a little while to evaluate this possibility.

Twardowski's view that every idea is inadequate resembles Husserl's theory of aspects. It resembles it, but it is clearly different from it. One notion of an aspect which is clearly explained in Husserl's book *Ideas* is that of a sense-impression. Things are really getting complicated now, as we shall see next.

(2) *Aspects as properties of sense-impressions*

Earlier, when we discussed Brentano's distinction between physical and mental phenomena, I distinguished between the properties of perceptual objects, on the one hand, and the properties of the sense-impressions, on the other, which we experience when we perceive the properties of perceptual objects. I wish to remind you briefly of this important distinction. When you look at Oscar through dark green glasses, for example, Oscar's color does not change, but the color of the visual sensation which you experience will be different from what it was earlier. The best example of the difference between property of perceptual object and property of visual sensation is that of true shape and shape from a perspective. A rectangular desk top, for example, will cause you to experience a trapezoidal sense-impression. So much for reminding you of the distinction. Let us now proceed to Husserl.

Husserl distinguishes between Oscar's color and the various colors of the sensations which we experience when we walk around Oscar, viewing him from different angles and with the light shining on him from different directions. But then he interprets this distinction quite differently from us:

> The perceived thing in general, and all its parts, aspects, and phases, whether the quality be primary or secondary, are necessarily transcendent to the perception, and on the same grounds everywhere. The color of the thing seen is not in principle a real phase of the consciousness of color; it appears, but even while it is appearing the appearance can and *must* be continually changing, as experience shows. The *same* color appears 'in' continuously varying patterns of *perspective color variations*. Similarly for every sensory quality and likewise for every spatial shape! (*Ideas. General Introduction to Pure Phenomenology*, trans. W. R. Boyce Gibson, New York, Collier Books, 1962, paragraph 41)

Oscar, with all of his properties and parts, is said to be *transcendent* to our perceptions of him. From the context, we may gather that this means that Oscar and his properties are not a part of the perceptual process. Oscar is not a part of the mental act which occurs when we see him. He transcends the mind, lies before it, and hence outside of it. We cannot but agree with this part of Husserl's view. But in the very same breath, Husserl also says something else, something with which we cannot at all agree. He says that Oscar's color appears to us *through or by means of* perspective color variations, that is, through the colors of our sense-impressions. Oscar's color is therefore 'transcendent' in another sense as well. It is not directly perceived, it is not immediately presented to us, but we know of it only through its appearances. What holds for Oscar's color, holds for his shape and for all his other properties as well. None of them is directly perceived. They are all known to us through their aspects. But this means, of course, that Oscar is not directly perceived. He, too, is only known through the aspects of his properties.

When I explained Twardowski's view, I simply took it for granted that we can perceive some of Oscar's properties, although we cannot perceive all of them in a single act of perception. We may perceive, say, Oscar's color. Now, if Husserl is to be believed, things are even more complicated than that. We cannot even directly perceive Oscar's color. What we perceive in a given act is only an aspect of Oscar's color. Oscar turns out to be twice removed from our perception of him. Firstly, we cannot see all of his properties but only some of them. Secondly, we cannot really see these few properties directly either, but can only see aspects of theirs. We can never see Oscar, but only aspects of some properties of his!

Let us assume, for the sake of illustration, that when you look at Oscar from a certain point of view, you experience a light green sense-impression, while when you look at him from another angle, you experience a yellow sense-impression. (Remember, Oscar is Berkeley's apple.) What color does Oscar have? (We assume, for the sake of simplicity, that his skin is uniformly colored.) The honest response is: 'How would I know?' He may be light green; he may be yellow; he may even be dark red. I think that you recognize the first steps of the skeptical argument which forced Descartes' contemporaries to conclude that color 'is only in the mind'. What lurks in the shadows is the argument that color is merely a sensation in the mind, and not a property of perceptual objects. If this argument is sound, then, applied to Husserl's view, it will lead to the skeptical conclusion that we cannot know Oscar's real color, or his real shape, or his real taste, etc. And since Oscar is conceived of as a bundle of such properties, it follows that we cannot know the real Oscar either. Since it has these devastating implications, we had better take a closer look at the skeptical argument.

The skeptic argues like this. If Husserl is correct in asserting that we know Oscar's color only through the colors of the sense-impressions which we experience, and do not know it directly, then it follows that we cannot know his color at all. For, in order to know Oscar's color, you must know some such thing as that the experience of a light green sense-impression, from a certain point of view, indicates that Oscar has the color F, where F is some definite color shade. You must know, in other words, some such thing as that, under certain circumstances, the experienced light green color *is an aspect of F*. Under different circumstances, from a different point of view, a yellow sense-impression may indicate that Oscar has the color F. Yellow may be an aspect of F. It all depends on the illumination, the angle of vision, the condition of the eyes, and other factors. But, now, how can we find out that light green, under conditions C, is an aspect of F? Obviously, there is only one way: we must *compare* the color of our sense-impression, under condition C, with the color of Oscar. We must 'look' at the sense-impression, noting its color, and we must 'look' at Oscar, noting his color. Comparing the two colors, we may formulate a law to the effect that things which have color F, like Oscar, will cause us to experience light green sense-impressions, given that condition C prevails. But if Husserl is correct, then we cannot compare the two colors; for we cannot take a 'look' at Oscar's color. We can only look at the color of our sense-impression. Oscar's color is allegedly known to us only *through* its aspects, that is, *through* the colors of our sense-impressions. But if we cannot compare the two colors, then we cannot know Oscar's true color.

In order to see just how powerful the skeptic's argument is, let us formulate it as generally as possible.

(1) We assume that we know the colors of our sense impressions. Thus we know that under condition C_1, we have a light green sense-impression; under condition C_2, a yellow sense-impression; etc.

(2) We know the color of Oscar only by means of the following description of it (Husserl's view): Oscar's color is *the color,* which under condition C_1, causes us to have a light green sense-impression; which under condition C_2 causes us to have a yellow sense-impression; etc. This amounts to: we know the color of Oscar as *the color* which stands in a certain relation R to light green (under C_1), to yellow (under C_2), etc.

(3) But to know Oscar's color only in this fashion is not to know what *particular color* he has. We do not know whether he is light green, or dark green, or yellow, or red, or any other specific color.

You can see that the argument rests on the principle that to know something only as the X which stands in relation R to A, is not to know what particular thing X is. You can easily verify that this principle holds quite generally. Assume that you want to know what particular person murdered the Dean of Women (assuming that just one person is involved). The obvious answer is: *the person* who murdered the Dean of Women. But this answer does not tell you who committed the crime. Or assume that you want to know how much money there is left in your bank account and the teller informs you that it is the sum which is left in your account.

I think that the skeptic's position is well taken. If we could know Oscar's color only as the color of which light green, yellow, etc., are aspects, then we could not possibly know what particular color he has. And what holds for his color, holds for all of his other perceptual properties. This, I think, is the inevitable consequence of Husserl's view. And Husserl seems to accept it without qualms when he concedes to the skeptic: 'no way of appearing claims to rank as giving its data absolutely, although a certain type, appearing as normal within the compass of my practical interest, has a certain advantage' (*Ideas*, paragraph 44). But we know better! We know that Oscar is, say, of a certain shade of yellow. He is so 'absolutely', whatever that may mean. That is his color. And since we know Oscar's color, we also know that objects with this particular color, not just Oscar, will cause us to experience a light green sense-impression under condition C_1. That we know his true color is incontrovertibly proven by the fact that we know how things of this particular color may appear under different conditions. Perhaps, our contention will be more persuasive when we turn to Oscar's shape. We know what shape he has since we know, *in a systematic fashion*, how things of this shape have to be drawn when viewed from different angles and distances. The whole art of drawing in perspective would be impossible if we could not know the true shape of perceptual objects.

We know Oscar's color, his shape, and some of his other properties. If Husserl's view were correct, we could not know that he has these properties. *Ergo*: Husserl's view must be incorrect. Oscar's color is known, not indirectly through its aspects, but directly. It is know to us, not through the colors of the sense-impressions which we experience when we look at him under different circumstances, but directly. It is known directly by means of perception. We *see* that Oscar is yellow! And we also *see* that he has a certain shape! Since we know, by looking at Oscar, what shape he has, we can compare this shape with the shape we have to produce on a sheet of paper, if we want to draw him realistically from a certain point of view. Since we know, by looking at him, what color he has, we can compare his true color with the color of the sense-impression which he causes in us when we look at him under a certain condition. Husserl's view is, in one sense, upside down. Far from being sure about the properties of our sense-impressions, we are actually quite sure about the properties of the perceptual objects around us. A child, as we know, *draws* a rectangular shape, because it *sees* that the desk top is rectangular. It will have to learn to draw, not what it sees, but rather the shape of its sense-impressions.

When you want to know the shape of the desk top, you take a look at it. When you want to know the shape of the sense-impression, you inspect the sense-impression. Comparing one with the other, you note that a rectangular top causes you to experience a trapezoidal sense-impression when you look at it from a certain distance and angle. These, I think, are the plain facts. But if they are plain, why does Husserl (and generations of earlier philosophers) not recognize them? A hallowed dogma stands in the way. What our view clearly implies is that an act of seeing, for example, is not to be analyzed into having sensations plus making judgments. Perception, to put it succinctly, is not a matter of *inference* from sensations. Rather, an act of seeing is a unique and unanalyzable mental phenomenon. I emphasized this point earlier when we discussed the Platonic dogma. But it is so important that I shall make it once again. Just as one cannot overcome the Platonic rift between perception and reflection unless one realizes the propositional nature of perception, so can one not overcome the skeptical attack on the efficacy of perception unless one sees that perception is not a matter of inference from sense-impressions. Husserl, of course, does not say that it is a matter of inference. But he does admit that it is indirect. Oscar's color is perceived only *through* its aspects. This part of the theory of aspects, it seems to me, is a modern, sophisticated version of the older inference theory.

(3) *Aspects as spatial parts*

There is another side to Husserl's theory of aspects. A perceptual object, he holds, can be presented to us only through its spatial parts. Here is how he puts it:

It is not an accidental caprice of the Thing nor an accident of 'our human constitution' that 'our' perceptions can reach the things themselves only and merely through their perspective modifications. On the contrary, it is evident, and it follows from the essential nature of spatial thinghood (and in the widest sense inclusive of 'visual illusion') that Being of this species can, in principle, be given in perception only by way of perspective manifestation; . . .

Where there is no Being in space, it is senseless to speak of seeing from different standpoints with a changing orientation, and under the different aspects thereby opened up, or through varying appearances and perspective shadings; on the other hand, it is an essential necessity to be apprehended as such with apodeictic insight that spatial Being in general can be perceived by an Ego actual or possible only when presented in the way described. (*Ibid.*, para. 42)

You have here a shining example of an essential insight, that is, of the knowledge we can gain, according to Husserl, if we reflect on essences. Presumably, a reflection on the essences *Ego* and *spatial being* will reveal to you that the former can perceive the latter only in perspective.

Now, whether or not you can gain this piece of knowledge through essential insight, it is at any rate true that we perceive perceptual objects always from a point of view. (Descartes mentions this fact and draws quite a different conclusion from it. Look up *Second Meditation* where he gives the example of people seen from above, so that only their hats and cloaks are visible.) For example, when we look at Oscar, only one side is turned toward us; we cannot see his back. When we look at a desk, we see its top side, but not its underside. Let us assume, for the moment, that Oscar is not uniformly yellow (as we had assumed before), but that he is light green on one side and yellow on the other. If we look at him from one side, we see that he is light green, but we do not see the other side and, hence, cannot tell what color it has. These are facts which cannot be disputed. But they are sometimes expressed in a manner which cannot but invite philosophical disaster. It is claimed that we can never see the *whole* apple from one point of view, but always only see a *part* of it. It follows, presumably, that *we can never see*

Oscar, but always only see part of him. Oscar is given to us always only through his spatial perspectives. He is never presented to us directly, as a whole. This seems to have been Husserl's line of reasoning.

How could it possibly be sound? When I look at Oscar, I see Oscar, this apple; I do not just see a part of Oscar. Of course, I may mistake a part of a perceptual object for the whole. I may think, for example, that I see a house when in reality there is before me merely the façade of a house on a movie set. Potemkin fooled a number of people in this fashion. But I may also not be mistaken: I may actually see the façade of a house. And this fact shows that there is a fundamental difference between seeing a house and seeing merely the façade of a house, between seeing Oscar and seeing merely a half of Oscar. When I look at Oscar, I may see that *this is an apple*. What I see, the *this*, quite clearly must be an apple, not a half of an apple; for otherwise, I would be mistaken: *this* would be a half of an apple, not an apple. What I see cannot be merely a spatial part of Oscar; for one of his spatial parts is not the same as Oscar, the apple; and I am seeing Oscar, the apple. If Husserl were correct, then it would follow that most of our perceptions would have to be mistaken. We would have to be mistaken every time we see that *this* is an apple or *that* is an elephant, when we see that *this* is an Oldsmobile or *that* is a rainbow, when we see that *this* is a billiard ball and *that* is a statue of Husserl. A view which has this consequence, you may wish to object, cannot possibly be true.

Yet, so convincing is Husserl's line of reasoning that few philosophers have been able to resist it. A case in point is the thoughtful British philosopher G. E. Moore (1873–1958). Taking as his example an inkstand rather than an apple, Moore says:

> Thus, when I judge, as now, that That is an inkstand, I have no difficulty whatever in picking out, from what, if you like, you can call my total field of presentation at the moment, an object, which is undoubtedly, in a sense in which nothing else is, *the* object about which I am making this judgment; and yet it seems to me quite certain that of *this* object I am not judging that it is a whole inkstand. (G. E. Moore, *Philosophical Studies*, Paterson, N. J., Littlefield, Adams, and Co., 1959, p. 229)

Moore here comes very close to contradicting himself. He comes close to saying that when he judges that *that* is an inkstand, he does not judge that *that*—the same *that*!—is an inkstand. Here is his reason:

> Nobody will suppose, for a moment, that when he judges such things as 'This is a sofa', or 'This is a tree', he is judging, with regard to the presented object about which his judgment plainly is, that it is a whole sofa or whole tree: he can, at most, suppose that he is judging it to be a part of the surface of a sofa or a part of the surface of a tree. (*Ibid.*, p. 230)

Well, I do suppose what Moore says nobody will suppose, namely, that I am judging, with regard to the presented object, about which my judgment plainly is, that it is a *whole* apple, not merely part of the surface of an apple.

The issue between Husserl and Moore, on the one hand, and me, on the other, is quite straightforward. While I claim that we see (whole) apples, inkstands, and sofas, they maintain that we see only (spatial) parts of them. What convinces them, I submit, is the conviction that one can only be said to have seen a (whole) perceptual object, if one has seen all of its spatial parts. What is at stake, therefore, is the truth of the following principle: *to perceive a perceptual object is to perceive all of its spatial parts.*

It cannot be denied that when I look at Oscar from a certain angle, I do not see his back. I cannot tell, for example, what color it has. In this sense, it is obviously true that I do not see all of Oscar's spatial parts when I look at him from one point of view. Having conceded this much, I shall have to embrace Husserl's view if I also grant the truth of the principle just formulated. Thus my course is clear: I must deny the principle. I must hold that to perceive a perceptual object is not to perceive all of its spatial parts. And so I shall. What plays a most important role in this dispute is the little, innocuous looking, word 'whole'. Moore emphasizes that I do not see a *whole* sofa or a *whole* tree. I think that his case would be far less plausible had he only spoken of seeing *a* sofa or *a* tree. It seems to me that the phrase 'a whole sofa' may in this context mean two quite different things. It may mean, firstly, something like 'all of the parts of the sofa'. If this is what Moore had in mind, then he is,

125

of course, correct in saying that he does not see the whole sofa. But then he still needs the principle mentioned at the end of the last paragraph to come to his conclusion. On the other hand, and secondly, 'a whole sofa' may have the connotation of something like 'not just part of a sofa'. And if it has this meaning, then, I think, I am plainly right in insisting that we do see a whole sofa.

I reject the principle that to perceive a perceptual object is to perceive all of its spatial parts. Earlier, we encountered a similar principle in connection with Twardowski's view of inadequate ideas, namely, the principle that to perceive a perceptual object is to perceive all of its properties. There is a common thread that connects these two principles. (As you can see, in philosophy we can always go still deeper into the matter!) What is this common thread? It could be the following general argument:

(1) Assume that you can perceive a perceptual object A.

(2) This perceptual object is (identical with) a structure, S, with certain parts p_1, p_2, p_3, etc.

(3) Hence, to perceive A is to perceive S.

(4) But you cannot perceive S.

(5) Hence, (1) must be false: you cannot perceive A.

I accept the first three steps, but want to know what justification there is for asserting (4). Why can I not perceive the structure S? It seems to be plain that I can; for that structure is A, and I know that I can perceive A. Perhaps, the following argument backs up (4):

(i) To perceive a structure S which has parts p_1, p_2, p_3, etc. is to perceive *that S has these parts*.

(ii) But you cannot perceive that S has all of these many parts.

(iii) Therefore, you cannot perceive S.

At long last, the culprit has been uncovered: it is assumption (i). Quite clearly, (i) is false. For example, when you see an apple which, as a matter of fact, has a small brown spot on one side, you need not see *that* the apple has this spot, nor need you see the spot at all. To see an inkstand which happens to be half full, is not to see *that* it is half full. To see a sofa which has a mahogany armrest is not to see *that* the sofa has a mahogany armrest. And so on. In short, to perceive a perceptual object which happens to have a certain property is not the same as to perceive *that* it has this property; and to perceive a perceptual object which has a certain spatial part is not the same as to perceive *that* it has this part.

I think, therefore, that Husserl is mistaken about both halves of his theory of aspects. The properties of perceptual objects are not given to us through sense-data aspects, and perceptual objects are not presented to us through their spatial aspects.

(4) *Aspects, descriptions, and noemata*

In order to understand fully the theory of aspects, we must attend to a distinction which is know to everyone, but whose philosophical importance was only recently fully appreciated. It was again Frege who first discussed the matter. The distinction I have in mind is the common distinction between a thing and its various descriptions. Frege gives as an illustration the example of the planet Venus which has been described as the morning star and also as the evening star. One and the same planet has these two different descriptions. I shall use, as our paradigm, the distinction between (the city of) Salzburg, on the one hand, and the two descriptions, *the birthplace of Mozart* and *the city at the site of the Roman Juvavum*, on the other.

As soon as you think about it, you realize that anything whatsoever can be described in different ways. Take Oscar. He can be described as the apple I have been talking about, or as the fruit which I have been calling 'Oscar', or as the apple which my daughter insisted on packing for my lunch, etc. But not only ordinary individual things can be described in different ways. Any entity whatsoever can be described. For example, the shape roundness can be described as the shape which Max and Moritz share. The number four can be described as the next number after three in the series of integers. And the description *the birthplace of Mozart* can be described as the description which relates Salzburg to the place of Mozart's birth. In general, we can talk about something either by naming it or by describing it. 'Salzburg' is a name of a certain city, 'the birthplace of Mozart' is a description expression (representing a description) which describes this very same city. Whenever we do not have a name for a certain entity, we cannot but use description expressions if we want to talk about it. Since most of the things in this world are not important enough for us to name them, we are forced to talk about them by means of description expressions. We give names to people, cities, rivers, etc. We do not name, ordinarily, such things as apples, billiard balls, typewriters, a hair on Napoleon's head, the left sock you are now wearing, etc. Nevertheless, I managed to talk about all of these things by describing them to you.

One thing needs special emphasis. As I use the word 'description', a description must not be confused with the expression that represents it. A description is not a linguistic entity. The *same* story can be told in different languages, that is, by means of different expressions. In the same sense, the *same* description can be given in different languages. Salzburg can be described as the birthplace of Mozart, and this very same description can also be represented by the German words: 'Der Geburtsort von Mozart'. Here we have two different expressions for the same description of the same thing. We must therefore distinguish between three quite different things, namely, between a description expression, the description which it represents, and the thing which it describes by means of the description. 'The birthplace of Mozart' is a different expression from 'Der Geburtsort von Mozart', but both *represent* the same description. The description *the birthplace of Mozart* is different from the description *the city at the site of the Roman Juvavum*, but both *describe* the same thing, Salzburg. It is important to realize that a description, unlike its expression, is not a linguistic entity. Precisely what kind of thing it is, is a very difficult philosophical question. It has been discussed rather vigorously ever since Frege first called our attention to the distinction between things and their descriptions. To try to answer it, would lead us too far astray from our main endeavor. But we shall connect descriptions with Husserl's notion of a *noema*.

This much is clear: a description involves properties which a thing has or relations in which it stands to other things. Take again the description *the birthplace of Mozart*. In this case a certain city is described by means of a relation in which it stands to a famous composer: it was his birthplace. Or take the description *the city at the site of the Roman Juvavum*. Here the same city is described in terms of a relation in which it stands to a Roman settlement. Finally, consider the description *the typewriter before me on my desk*. An object is described in terms of having a certain property, being a typewriter, and of having a certain relation to me and my desk. The property alone would not suffice to single out just this particular object. There are many typewriters in the world. Nor would the relation; for their are several things before me on my desk. It is the combination of property with relation which achieves the uniqueness necessary for a *definite* description. It may well be the case, that all descriptions, in order to be truly definite, must somehow involve relations to other specific entities.

Be that as it may, we are ready to return to Husserl. It may be tempting to identify Husserl's notion of an aspect of a thing with our notion of a description of a thing. Or, rather, it may be tempting to claim that in still another sense of aspect—in addition to the two senses mentioned in the last two sections—an aspect is simply a description. But I think that this would be a mistake. Before I can explain why, we have to take another, more careful look at our notion of an *object* of an idea.

Recall our previous distinction between a mental act, its kind, its content, and its object. Consider the act of seeing that the apple before me is yellow. This act is a mental individual; it occurs at a certain moment. It has two important properties. First of all, it is a seeing rather than, say, a believing. This is its kind. Secondly, it is a seeing of the circumstance that the apple before me is yellow rather than of some other state of affairs. The act has a property, its content, which relates it, by means of the intentional nexus, to this particular circumstance and to no other. As we noted, properly speaking, it is not the act—the individual thing—but its content which intends the respective object. Finally, there is the object of this act of seeing. According to our view, it is a certain state of affairs, namely, the fact that the apple before me is yellow.

Twardowski was one of the first philosophers who made the distinction between the content of an act and its object. He also noticed that one and the same thing has many descriptions. This gave him the idea to identify the description of an object with the content of an act which intends that object. In short, he tried to identify descriptions with ideas, and the described things with the objects of the ideas (*op. cit.*, p. 29). His terminology is

129

different from ours, though. In respect to the two expressions 'the birthplace of Mozart', and 'the city at the site of the Roman Juvavum', he says that they have different *meanings*, but *name* the same thing. In our terminology, we would say that they *represent* different descriptions, but *describe* the same thing. Next, he identifies these different meanings with different ideas (contents), and the thing named with the object of these ideas. What we have here, then, are two ideas with one and the same object, namely, Salzburg. But this, surely, must be wrong. What I think *of*, in the relevant sense of 'think *of*', when I think of the birthplace of Mozart is the birthplace of Mozart, *and not Salzburg*. Of course, since Salzburg happens to be the birthplace of Mozart, I may be said to think of Salzburg when I think of the birthplace of Mozart. But this is a different matter. Only because I think *of* the birthplace of Mozart, and since Salzburg *is* the birthplace of Mozart, can I be said, in another sense, to be thinking of Salzburg. If you think of the city at the site of the Roman Juvavum, then you do in one clear sense think *of* something else, namely, of the city at the site of the Roman Juvavum, and in another, equally clear, sense think *of* the same thing, namely, Salzburg.

What I am arguing is that the idea of the birthplace of Mozart is an idea of something different from the idea of the city at the site of the Roman Juvavum. These two ideas are not only different as ideas, but they also have different objects.

Twardowski comes very close to recognizing this fact when he remarks:

> For one conceives of something quite different when conceiving of the city which is located at the site of the Roman Juvavum from what one conceives of when conceiving of the birthplace of Mozart. These two presentations consist of very different parts. The first contains as parts the presentations of Romans and of an ancient city forming a fortified camp; the second presentation contains as parts the presentations of a composer and of the relation in which he stands to his native city, while the relation to an old settlement formerly occupying that site, which was presented by the first presentation, is absent. (*Ibid.*)

For 'presentation' you should read 'content'. If you do, then

Twardowski says in the last line that the relation to an old settlement is presented by the first content, but not by the second. But what is presented by a content is, by definition, its object. Clearly, therefore, the object of the first presentation cannot be the same as that of the second.

The notion of an *object* of a content (idea) must not be confused with the notion of an object of a description. Our terminology makes this perfectly clear. There is the *content* or *idea* of the birthplace of Mozart and the quite different *content* or *idea* of the city at the site of the Roman Juvavum. There is, furthermore, the *object* of the first idea, *the birthplace of Mozart*, and the object of the second idea, *the city at the site of the Roman Juvavum*. These objects are *descriptions* of Salzburg. There is therefore, lastly, the described *entity*, namely, Salzburg. The description *the birthplace of Mozart* is neither an idea nor is it a city. I think that it is, roughly, what Husserl calls a 'noema'.

Husserl's notion of a *noema* is one of his most important as well as one of the more obscure concepts. I cannot discuss here some of the more interesting interpretations of this part of Husserl's phenomenology. I shall simply state my own interpretation, assuming, as I do, that Husserl himself was not too clear about what he meant by a noema.

When, in the *Ideas*, Husserl first speaks of noema, he thinks of them, in the case of perception, as 'the perceived as such' (*Ideas*, paragraphs 88, 89). What distinguishes this perceived-as-such, for example, the tree just as it is perceived, from the real physical tree is the circumstance that even if there exists no physical tree, a tree-perception may still occur (*ibid.*, para. 90). Thus a noema appears to be the intentional object of a mental act, precisely as it is intended by the corresponding content. If you think of Salzburg by thinking of the birthplace of Mozart, the noema is, not Salzburg, but *the birthplace of Mozart*, that is, this particular description. And if you think of Salzburg by thinking of the city at the site of the Roman Juvavum, then your act of thinking has a different noema, namely, the description *the city at the site of the Roman Juvavum*. The noema is in each case the city in Austria *precisely as it is before your mind*, as it is intended by you, as it is meant by you. It is, as Husserl sometimes puts it, the *meaning* of your thought (*ibid.*, para. 90).

But Husserl also talks on occasion as if a noema consists not just of the intentional object, but rather of the object together with its content, and then he calls the content the *meaning*:

> We start from the ordinary equivocal phrase: the content of consciousness. Under content we understand the 'meaning' of which we say that in it or through it consciousness refers to an objective as its 'own'. As the superscription and the final end of our discussion, so to speak, we take the following proposition:
> Every noema has a 'content', namely, its 'meaning', and is related through it to 'its' object. (*Ibid.*, para. 129)

According to this explanation, the noema of your thought is, in the first instance, the idea (content) of the birthplace of Mozart and, through this idea, the birthplace of Mozart; and, in the second case, the idea of the city at the site of the Roman Juvavum and, through the idea, the city at the site of the Roman Juvavum. You see that Husserl in this context uses 'meaning' like Twardowski does, namely, for the content of a mental act. The intentional object, then, is not the meaning of the act, but rather the meant object. However, things become confused as soon as we also distinguish between a description and what it describes and, furthermore, call the former the 'meaning' of the description expression. I have carefully avoided this confusion by shunning the term 'meaning'. There is the *content* of a mental act and its (intentional) *object*. Its object may be (may involve) a description. If so, then we must further distinguish between the *description* and *what it describes*, its 'object'. To complicate things even further, what a description describes in the case of perception (according to Husserl's view) is never the perceptual object as a whole, but merely an aspect of it.

Noemata must not be confused with aspects. But they explain how aspects are related to the things of which they are aspects. Let us return to our earlier example. Oscar's color, according to Husserl, is given to us only indirectly through the colors of the sense-impressions which we experience when we look at Oscar in different ways. What we see is that Oscar has *the color which from this point of view causes a light green sense-impression*. Oscar's color is merely described. The italicized phrase represents a description of it. To be given or presented *through* an aspect means to be described by means of it. The description mentions an aspect, in order to describe the thing whose aspect it is. In our case, the aspect is the color of the sense-impression, light green. And the color of Oscar is related to this color by means of a causal relation: the apple has the color which causes us, under certain conditions, to have a light green sense-impression. In the case of spatial perspective, the aspect is a spatial part of the perceived object, and the object is described as the object which has this spatial part, that is, which stands in the spatial whole-part relation to this part.

Essences, according to Husserl, are not given to us through aspects. Reflection is direct. But, of course, there are descriptions of essences just as there are descriptions of individual things. I can describe the color yellow, assuming that Oscar is yellow, *as the color which Oscar has*. And I can describe the shape squareness as *the shape of a chess board*. The fact that there are descriptions of a given entity does not imply that that entity can only be known through aspects. A more specific argument is needed for that purpose. We have seen what Husserl's arguments are in the case of color and in the case of spatial objects.

(5) *The exaltation of consciousness*

According to Husserl, our knowledge of entities divides into direct and indirect knowledge, that is, into direct knowledge and knowledge through aspects. Essences are known directly, perceptual objects are known only through their aspects. But perceptual objects are not the only individual things of Husserl's world. It also contains mental acts and selves. How are these things known? Consciousness (mental acts) is known, like essences, directly. A mental act of seeing that Oscar is yellow, a desire to be in Venice, a remembrance of strolling down the beach in Acapulco, all these acts are given to us without aspects. Here, therefore, is a fundamental difference between the 'outside world' of perceptual things and the 'inside world' of consciousness: while the former are never presented to us wholly and completely in one mental act, the latter are fully given to us when we attend to them. But the self, the mental individual from which all mental acts issue, is only given to us indirectly, like a perceptual object. The realm of individual things thus divides into an 'immanent' part, consciousness, and two 'transcendent' parts, perceptual objects and the self. What we truly and directly know is consciousness. Every other individual thing is only known indirectly. This makes consciousness special. It invites a new characterization of the mind.

Descartes, we saw, defined the mind, the mental substance, in terms of mental acts. Brentano went one step further and characterized mental acts, in turn, as being intentional. Husserl now adds the opinion that mental acts are the only individual things which are known directly. Thus consciousness is not only essentially different from everything else in that it is intentional, but it is also essentially different from all other individuals in that it can be known directly. But this is not all. Husserl gets carried away. In his exaltation of consciousness, he makes an unprecedented claim. Consciousness, he maintains, has a different *kind of being* from other individuals:

> Between the meaning of consciousness and reality yawns a veritable abyss. Here a Being which manifests itself perspectively, never giving itself absolutely, merely contingently and relative; there a necessary and absolute being, fundamentally incapable of being given through appearance and perspective patterns. (*Ibid.*, para. 49)

But this is not the end of it. Not only has consciousness a being fundamentally different from other individual things, Husserl goes on to say that its being is superior:

> On the other side, the whole spatio-temporal world, to which man and the human Ego claim to belong as subordinate singular realities, is *according to its own meaning mere intentional Being*, a Being, therefore, which has the merely secondary, relative sense of a Being for a consciousness. (*Ibid.*)

With this claim that consciousness has a being different from all other things, a being, moreover, which is somehow more exalted, Husserl strikes a theme which becomes the central concern of Existentialism. Mind and body, to speak in Cartesian terms, are not just essentially different, but are existentially

Husserl's distinction between individuals and their aspects different. They do not just have different essences, they do not even exist in the same way. If Descartes had opened up a rift between mind and body, Husserl widened this rift until it became an unbridgeable abyss.

8.   The phenomenological method

(1) *The age of method-philosophizing*

I have treated Phenomenology as a theory of knowledge, as a theory which (1) emphasizes a distinction between perception and reflection, (2) holds that perceptual objects can be known only through aspects, and (3) exalts consciousness. But others often see it, not as a new view about old problems, but as a method of inquiry. Some philosophers seem to be drawn to Phenomenology with the expectation of learning *how* to solve philosophical problems, any problems. Treated with the phenomenological method, they believe, philosophical problems simply have to dissolve. Husserl is to be blamed in part for this unrealistic expectation. For he often talks, in his later writings, as if he had discovered a new science, the science of phenomenology, with its own method and characteristic subject matter.

Nor is he the only great philosopher of our century who stressed method over matter. Most of the philosophical movements of this century share this preoccupation with method. Usually, one does not claim to have solved certain traditional problems, but announces the discovery of a new way of doing philosophy. The Phenomenologists extolled the virtues of reflecting on laws about essences. The so-called 'Logical Positivists' thought of philosophy as an investigation of the logic and language of science. And the 'Ordinary Language Philosophers' claimed that philosophical problems were the product of inattention to the subtleties of ordinary discourse. All three movements share the conviction that philosophy in the old style, that metaphysics as practiced by Plato and Aristotle, by Descartes and Leibniz, is dead.

There are a number of reasons for this development. We cannot go into details, but a few remarks may provide you with an idea of the intellectual background of twentieth-century philosophy and may arouse your curiosity. On the philosophical side, there was the tremendous influence of the German philosopher Immanuel Kant. Kant had argued, at the end of the eighteenth century, that metaphysics is impossible. How effective his argument was, you can best judge from the fact that within a few short years after his death, there bloomed on the soil of Kantian philosophy, the most bewildering array of metaphysical flowers: the systems of Hegel (1770–1831), of Fichte (1776–1814), and of Schelling (1775–1854), to mention just three. But Kant cast enough doubt on the possibility of making progress in metaphysical matters that he created a crisis of philosophical self-confidence. This crisis was enhanced by the spectacular success of the natural sciences in the nineteenth century. One could hardly help comparing the rapid progress of science with the interminable clash of philosophical systems. In science, you seemed to have an orderly advance of knowledge and substantial agreement among scientists. In philosophy, you found a bewildering variety of views, ranging all the way from claims to have at long last found the ultimate metaphysical truths to denouncements of philosophy as pseudo-science.

The incredible success of the physical sciences quite naturally called attention to their method. And when some newcomers, psychology and sociology, claimed the status of science, they were invited to prove their legitimacy by defining their respective methods. What resulted were unending and tedious discussions of the true subject matters and appropriate methods of these new sciences. If you go back and read some of the numerous learned discussions of why there can or cannot be a science of psychology, since it has or lacks a proper method, you cannot but wonder what these sages would have said when faced with contemporary micro-biology, astro-physics, and physical bio-chemistry. No doubt, some would have proven, without getting up from their desks, that without a shadow of doubt, these disciplines are impossible.

Kant had cast doubt on the possibility of metaphysics. But here was a way of redemption: just as for any other science, one merely needed to show that philosophy has a well-defined subject matter and its own particular method. There followed, as in the case of the new sciences, a flood of meta-philosophical discussions. Husserl's claims in behalf of Phenomenology must be understood against the background of these discussions. He takes up the Kantian challenge. He tries to show that there is a genuine inquiry, distinguished both from the recognized sciences and from fruitless speculation, which deserves a place of its own. Philosophy, now renamed 'Phenomenology', Husserl argues, is at once the most fundamental and profound of all disciplines as well as the most precise of all sciences. His arguments are elaborate as well as frequently indirect. They are hard to pin down. But there are a number of specific doctrines, bearing on the topic of the phenomenological method, which we shall take up in the next few sections.

(2) *Eidetic reduction*

Eidetic reflection, that is, reflection on essences and their connections, is of course of the essence of Phenomenology. This reflection requires what Husserl calls 'eidetic reduction'. In perception, individual things and their properties are presented to us, but these properties, as we noted earlier, are instances rather than universals. (We know that the story is really more complicated than this, for the instances are only known through their aspects. But we must simplify in order to have manageable examples.) What you see when you see Oscar's color, is an instance of the essence yellow. Now, in order to get acquainted, not with an instance, but with the essence, you must perform a shift in mental attitude, you must perform what Husserl calls an 'eidetic reduction'. You must pay attention, not to the perceived instance, but to the essence of which it is an instance. After this shift has taken place, you will 'see' the essence yellow just as

The phenomenological method

directly as you earlier saw (the aspects of!) the instance yellow. But this is not all. With this mental set, through eidetic reflection, you also 'perceive' connections among essences. You discern, for example, that yellow is lighter than midnight blue, or that the essence triangle necessitates having inner angles adding up to two right angles, or that the essence mental act requires that all acts have objects. Eidetic reduction thus reveals to us truths about essences. Phenomenology, as we may now try to define it, inquires into the structures formed by essences. Its method, tentatively speaking, is eidetic reduction.

But Husserl also speaks of 'phenomenological reduction'. He claims that there is more to Phenomenology than the reflection on essences. At this point, the explanation gets to be rather murky. It is not hard to see why Husserl would make the claim. An inspection of connections among essences cannot be unique to Phenomenology, for it occurs presumably also in mathematics, geometry, and other fields. How, then, is Phenomenology distinguished from these other inquiries into the nature of essences? Husserl must answer this question. In answer, he points at phenomenological reduction.

(3) *Phenomenological reduction*

What Husserl says about phenomenological reduction divides, in my opinion, into two parts. One part consists of truisms. We are exhorted to look at things without prejudice, to go to the things themselves, to leave theoretical speculation behind, etc. Of course, we should adopt this attitude no matter what we do, in philosophy, in science, and in daily life. The second part is more specific. Here, Husserl shows his philosophic hand.

Phenomenological reduction consists, as a first step, in what Husserl calls 'the bracketing of the objective world'. We are supposed to suspend judgment about the existence of the things around us. The botanist takes for granted that there are trees and proceeds to tell us fascinating things about them. Now, when we adopt the phenomenological attitude, we do not deny that he is right. But we put his existence assumption in brackets, and try to describe the phenomena precisely as they present themselves to us. For example, we may study the object of a mental act of seeing a tree, the precise 'what' of what we are seeing at this moment, irrespective of whether our perception is correct, of whether there are trees, and of whether there are any perceptual objects at all. If you have a hallucination and see a tree, the object of your mental act, as an object, may be precisely the same as the object of a true perception. You realize, of course, what notion of an object is here at work: it is the notion of a noema!

We can shed some more light on this step of the phenomenological reduction, if we remember the problem of nonexistent objects. Some mental acts, we insisted, have objects which do not exist. Speaking somewhat loosely, if you see a pink elephant in your hallucination, your act of seeing has a nonexistent object, and this object can easily be distinguished from the nonexistent object of your imagination when you imagine a mermaid. If you study what is before your mind, just as it is before your mind, irrespective of its existential status, then you will have to study nonexistent objects just as much as real trees and elephants. From this point of view, phenomenological reduction is the royal road to the realm of nonexistent objects. While botany studies real plants, Phenomenology studies noemata in general, be they grounded in existents or not.

But can one really study nonexistent objects? The botanist, who studies trees, discovers what properties this particular birch tree has and also what properties it shares with all other birch trees. The hallucinated tree, on the other hand, since it does not exist, has no properties and cannot share properties with something else. And if it does not have any properties, what is there to study? What can one possibly discover about it? Any serious inquiry, any genuine investigation, must be concerned with existent things; for nonexistent objects have no properties, stand in no relations, and therefore have nothing that could be discovered.

To this, the phenomenologist could reply that we are simply mistaken: nonexistent objects have properties and relations just like existents. The hallucinated birch tree *is* a tree, it *has* leaves of a certain shape, the leaves *are* green, etc. Hamlet, to take another example, *was* a prince of Denmark and he *is* indecisive. Phenomenology studies the properties of nonexistent objects in the same way in which science studies the properties of existent objects. Thus there is a 'science' of objects in general, irrespective of their existential status, and this 'science' is Phenomenology.

I am not convinced. What, precisely, are these properties and relations which nonexistent objects are supposed to have? The hallucinated birch tree is supposedly a tree, and it has supposedly green leaves (we shall assume). But why is it not a birch tree whose leaves have come down, a birch tree in winter? Well, the answer is obvious: because it is hallucinated in this fashion and not as a bare tree. But what about other properties? How tall was the tree last year? Was it planted? If so, by whom? And so on. These questions make sense when we ask them about a real tree, but they do not make sense when we ask them about hallucinated trees. We can discover new properties which a real tree had earlier, but the hallucinated tree wears its properties on its trunk, so to speak. The properties which it supposedly *has* are precisely those which it *is hallucinated to have*. Does Hamlet have a mole on his left shoulder? If he were a real person, we could sensibly ask this question and be sure that there is an answer, even if we do not know it. But for Hamlet, there is no answer in principle.

But if the properties which an hallucinated object supposedly has are precisely those which it is hallucinated as having, then the suspicion lies near that it does not really have any properties, but is merely hallucinated to have them. Surely the usual distinction between what a thing is and what it merely is imagined to be (or believed to be, or envisaged to be, etc.) applies also to nonexistent objects. Someone may believe that the earth is flat, and he may imagine it to be flat. But this does not mean that the earth is flat. (To say that it is flat *for* him is just an atrocious way of saying that he believes it to be flat.) Similarly, someone may hallucinate a green birch tree. He may hallucinate that he is pursued through the woods and that he finally succeeds in hiding behind a birch tree. But this does not mean that he is running in the woods, that there is a birch tree, and that the tree is green. Thus while it is true that the tree is hallucinated to have green leaves, it is not true that it has green leaves. While it is true that Hamlet is imagined to be indecisive, it is not true that he is indecisive. Nonexisting objects can be conceived of as having all kinds of property, but they do not have any properties.

If this objection is decisive, then we cannot investigate nonexisting objects for their properties and relations. All we can study are the properties and relations which they are conceived of as having. I let you be the judge of how illuminating such a study would be.

In addition to the notion that nonexistent objects have properties and stand in relations, there is another idea which suggests that we can bracket the objective world and still retain a fascinating field of study. This is the idea that we can demonstrate the nature of a thing from its concept. Descartes makes this claim in the fifth *Meditation*:

> Thus, for example, when I imagine a triangle, even though there may perhaps be no such figure anywhere in the world outside of my thought, nor ever have been, nevertheless the figure cannot help having a certain determinate nature, or form, or essence, which is immutable and eternal, which I have not invented and which does not in any way depend upon my mind. This is evidenced by the fact that we can demonstrate various properties of this triangle, namely, that its three angles are equal to two right angles, that the greatest angle subtends the longest side, and other similar properties.

Descartes' example is not quite fortunate. After all, we do know that there are triangles. So, let us consider something which does not exist, a mermaid. We shall call her 'Lorelei'. We conceive of her as having a nude torso, long blond hair (which she constantly combs), and a fishtail. Can we, as Descartes claims, demonstrate various properties of Lorelei? If what I said just a moment ago is correct, then it follows that we cannot possibly show that she *has* certain properties. And if Descartes' triangle did not exist, then we could not possibly prove of *it* that its three angles add up to two right angles. But, of course, we may conclude something else, namely, that *if* Lorelei *existed*, *then* she would have long blond hair and a fishtail. *If* Descartes' triangle *existed*, *then* its angles would *be* equal to two right angles. Descartes is mistaken. From the concept (notion, idea) of a thing, we cannot demonstrate that the thing must have such-and-such properties; for there may not be such a thing at all. But we can demonstrate from the concept of a thing that if such a thing exists, then it has the properties intended by the concept. For example, assume that your concept of God is a concept of a being which, in addition to all other perfections, has the perfection of existing. Then it does not follow from your concept that God must exist. What follows is merely that if something corresponds to your concept, then that thing must exist. What follows, in plain English, is that if God exists, then He exists. Descartes' remark about the triangle occurs in the context of his second proof for the existence of God. This proof makes use of the notion of a most perfect being, just like my present example. If I am right, therefore, Descartes' proof fails for the reason just given.

Be that as it may, the example of Lorelei raises another important issue. Let us assume that persons who swim regularly for exercise have a lower incidence of heart attacks than other people do. Does this mean that there is some kind of connection between the property of being a regular swimmer and the property of having a relatively healthy heart? There is this kind of connection between the property of being a mermaid and the property of having a fishtail. We can tell in the latter case, just by knowing what is meant by a mermaid, that if there were mermaids, they would have to have fishtails. But we cannot tell, in the same fashion, that regular swimmers have to have better hearts. The answer must therefore be negative: there is no such connection between the two properties. No matter how closely we inspect the property of being a regular swimmer, we will not find that it somehow includes the property of having a healthy heart. And this raises the question of what connections, precisely, there are among essences. It is clear that Phenomenology as a study of essences is a study of relations among essences. Hence it must have a clear notion of how essences are related to each other. The essence *mermaid*, for example, *includes* the essence *fishtail*. Other essences may be connected by different relations. Two musical pitches, for example, stand in the relation of being equal or one being higher than the other. But what about laws like our presumed law connecting swimming with heart attacks? Do they rest on essential connections? If not, how are they different from essential laws? If they do rest on essential connections, what are

143

these connections in particular cases? Can we make a list of all the relations which obtain among essences?

(4) *Phenomenological reflection*

The phenomenological method enjoins us to study the intentions of our acts precisely as they are and irrespective of their existential status. But this is only the first step of the method, to be followed by a second and much more radical one. Husserl tells us that we must eventually turn away from the 'outside world' and concentrate our attention exclusively on conscious-ness. Here is how Husserl describes the proper attitude:

> At the phenomenological standpoint, acting on lines of general principle, we *tie up* the *performance* of all such cognitive theses, i.e., we 'place in brackets' what has been carried out, 'we do not associate these theses' with our new inquiries; instead of living *in* them and carrying *them* out, we carry out acts of *reflection* directed towards them, and these we apprehend as the absolute being which they are. We now live entirely in such acts of the second level, whose datum is the infinite field of absolute experience–the basic field of phenomenology. (*Ibid.*, para. 50)

On the deepest level, Phenomenology thus consists of a reflection on consciousness, that is, on ordinary mental acts of perception, experience, desire, fear, etc. This sets it quite clearly apart from the natural sciences. It has its own method, reflection on mental acts, and it has its own subject matter, consciousness. Of course, we are not really interested in particular mental acts, in the ebb and flow of mental processes, but must perform the eidetic reduction. According to Husserl, what we study is not this or that particular desire, but the essence of desire, of which the particular act is merely an instance. *Phenomenology*, we can finally sum up, *is the study of the essence of consciousness*.

Two objections have often been raised against this view of the nature of Husserl's 'exact philosophy'. The first objection is that Phenomenology, so conceived, is merely an introspective part of psychology, and not at all a new and independent philosophical discipline. I say 'a part' because psychology, of course, also does other things, like testing for intelligence and treating neuroses. But does it not also give us an inventory of the furniture of the mind? And does it not also try to discover the basic laws which hold for this furniture? Husserl, like Brentano's students, was acutely aware of this objection, and tried to answer it in various ways. For one, Phenomenology, in distinction to psychology, is said to be a science of essences like arithmetic or geometry. Its laws are, not empirical generalizations, but built on connections among essences. Of course, this leads us back to what we said at the end of the last section. We must ask: how, precisely, in individual cases, can we distinguish between these two kinds of law? Specifically, which psychological laws are grounded in essential connections and which are merely empirical generalizations?

The second objection goes to the philosophical heart of the matter. Philosophy, in Husserl's hands, takes on an idealistic form. The world fades into the background; consciousness reigns supreme. What there really is, in the fullest sense of being, we are told, is consciousness. All else pales into insignificance. Husserl can claim that this inward turn, this turn toward consciousness, does not neglect the rest of the world altogether, because he has convinced himself that consciousness 'constitutes' the world. Consciousness–we may say, although he would not put it this way–creates the world, so that one can read off what there is in way of a world by studying consciousness. Here is a quotation from Husserl:

> we direct the glance of apprehension and theoretical inquiry
> to *pure consciousness in its own absolute being*. It is this which
> remains over as the 'phenomenological residuum' we were in
> quest of: remains over, we say, although we have 'suspended'
> the whole world with all things, living creatures, men,
> ourselves included. We have literally lost nothing, but have
> won the whole Absolute Being, which, properly understood,
> conceals in itself all transcendences, 'constituting' them
> within itself. (*Ibid.*, para. 50)

Husserl's philosophy has been called 'transcendental idealism'. You can understand why. According to this philosophy, there

lies before the inner eye of reflective consciousness the proper
subject matter of Phenomenology: the realm of mental acts.
Every such act has two poles. There is the act itself and then
there is its object. But the object is a noema. Beyond these
noemata, *transcending them*, lies the non-mental world. This
world is forever beyond the direct grasp of consciousness. On
the other end, behind the world of mental acts, hides the 'pure
ego'. It, too, *transcends* the direct grasp of consciousness. Both
the self and the world are beyond our reach. But in the middle,
between the two, dwells consciousness in splendid lucidity.

Part III

Martin Heidegger: the meaning of being

9. Heidegger's project

(1) *The main question of philosophy*

Martin Heidegger, although he was not a student of Husserl's was influenced by Husserl's philosophy. He studied Husserl's major works and worked as his assistant from 1920 to 1923 at the University of Freiburg in Germany. Yet, if you compare Husserl's monumental work, *Logical Investigations*, with Heidegger's most important book, *Being and Time*, you will notice that they differ like day and night. Husserl writes in the style of the great philosophers from Plato to Descartes. Heidegger reads like nothing you have ever come across before. Husserl treats the history of philosophy with respect. Heidegger constantly complains that nobody else has seen the philosophical problems in the right light, that nobody has asked the really important questions, that philosophers have neglected the real issues, etc. There is the claim, in short, that for two thousand years or so, philosophers had lost their way. Heidegger, of course, will lead them back to the proper path. Much of Heidegger's fame and notoriety stems from this claim. We shall therefore begin by taking a look at Heidegger's conception of philosophy.

Being and Time (trans. John Macquarrie and Edward Robinson, New York, Harper & Row, 1962) starts out with the question: what do we mean by the word 'being'? According to Heidegger,

149

this is the most important question of philosophy, and his book sets out to elucidate it. Of course, in one sense, we all know what we mean by 'being'. We know what we mean when we say '*There are* elephants', or when we announce that mermaids do not *exist*, or when we quote: 'To *be* or not to *be*'. But in another sense, Heidegger maintains, the question has to arise anew for every generation of philosophers. What is this other, this philosophical sense? Heidegger never tells us. *Being and Time* was supposed to be the first installment of a two-part work. But the second part never appeared. It is this missing second part in which Heidegger promised to wrestle with the question of all questions, the question of the meaning of 'being'. (He does discuss this topic to some extent in his book, *The Basic Problems of Phenomenology*, trans. Albert Hofstadter, Bloomington, Indiana University Press, 1982.) In the first part, the part which we have, he is merely preparing the ground for this more important task. Heidegger's project thus turns into a magnificent failure. After he had unearthed the question, after he had claimed that it had been neglected by generations of philosophers, and after he had promised to answer it at long last, he does in the end no better than his precursors. Perhaps, the question cannot be answered. Or, perhaps, Heidegger could not find an answer. Or, perhaps, Heidegger's philosophical doctrines made an answer impossible. We shall see.

What kind of question is the question after the meaning of 'being'? I think that we can rephrase it and ask: what is the nature of being? And this is equivalent to asking: what kind of being is being? Well, what kind of being is Oscar? Oscar is an apple; that is the kind he belongs to. Since he is an apple, he is a fruit. He belongs to the wider kind fruit. And so on. When we reach the highest kinds, we deal with so-called *categories*. Oscar, as we have seen, belongs to the category individual thing, conceived of either as a material substance, in the spirit of Descartes, or else as a bundle, in the spirit of Berkeley. At any rate, he is not a property; he does not belong to the category property. Nor is he a relation. He is an individual thing. Thus there is a philosophical question: to what category does Oscar belong? And there is a philosophical answer: Oscar is an individual thing.

We have previously encountered a number of categories:

individual things, properties, relations, facts, sets, structures, and numbers. Precisely how many categories there are and what they are, is one of the most fascinating of all philosophical questions. In this book, we shall not be able to take it up. But as long as we can agree that there are at least several such categories, a further question arises: can we group these categories further? Are there 'super categories'? As soon as we contemplate this possibility, we seem to have an answer to our question concerning being. Since all of the categories contain things which have being, since the categories categorize nothing but existents, being is *the* 'super-category' which comprises all other categories. Being is a category, but it is a category which 'transcends' all other categories. It is the transcendental category. Everything there is belongs to this category. What belongs to this category can only be contrasted with what is not there at all.

But such is the nature of metaphysics, this most abstract (and, at the same time, concrete) of all intellectual inquiries, that we cannot rest content with the answer that being is the transcendental category. For we must press on and ask: what is a category? To which category does *category* belong? It is the task of metaphysics to categorize everything there is. There are categories of things. Hence we must raise the question of how to categorize *category*. Now, strange and difficult as this question may look, there is an obvious answer. All individuals share the feature, that is, category, of being individuals; all properties share the feature of being properties; all numbers have the characteristic of being numbers; and so on. It seems to be clear, therefore, that these categories are *properties*, that they belong to the category property. Oscar is an apple, he has the property of being an apple. Oscar is also a fruit; he has this 'higher' property as well. On the highest level, he has the property of being an individual thing. Oscar's color, on the other hand, does not have this property; it is not an individual thing. It belongs to the category of property. Oscar's color has the property of being a property.

Is being, then, like the 'lower' categories, a property? Is it *the* transcendent property? Is it a property which everything has? If it is, then we have answered Heidegger's question. We have given a philosophical answer to a philosophical question. I shall not show my hand just now. What I wanted you to see is what *kind* of question is the question after the meaning of 'being'.

(2) *The priority of human being*

Heidegger, as I said, never answers this question. Instead he embarks on a different investigation. He studies the nature of human being, that is, of the being which persons have. He believes that before he can attack the main question, he must first of all clarify what kind of being human beings have:

> All efforts of the existential analytic have one goal, to find a possibility of answering the question of the *meaning of being*. The elaboration of this *question* requires a definition of *that* phenomenon in which something like being becomes accessible, the *comprehension of being*. But this belongs to the state of being of human being. Only if this being has been sufficiently primordially interpreted, can one understand the comprehension of being which is contained in its state of being, and on this basis raise the question concerning the being which is comprehended by it and concerning the suppositions of this comprehension. (*Being and Time*, p. 424, see also p. 33. All translations are my own from the German edition.)

Heidegger's argument, in my words, seems to be this. In order to answer the question of the meaning of being, we must first look at that phenomenon through which being becomes accessible to us, namely, our *understanding* or *comprehension* of being. But this human capacity of understanding is a way in which human beings exist. It is a form of being which is unique to human beings. Thus in order to understand the capacity for understanding, we must first look at the kind of being which has understanding. Most concisely put, in order to understand being, we must first understand understanding; and in order to understand understanding, we must first understand the being which has understanding, namely, human beings.

If this is Heidegger's argument, then it is far from being sound. One may as well and with the same justification argue that in order to understand butterflies, one must first understand our capacity to understand; and in order to understand this capacity, one must first study the being which has this capacity. Therefore, before one can study butterflies, one must first study human beings. I dwell here on Heidegger's argument, because it commits a fallacy which is rather characteristic of much of nineteenth-century German philosophy, a philosophy greatly influenced, as I have pointed out, by Kant. I shall call it the 'epistemological fallacy'. It consists of arguing from the premise:

no understanding of any phenomenon is possible without human understanding,

to the conclusion:

no understanding of any phenomenon is possible without an understanding of human understanding.

Quite obviously, this conclusion does not follow from the premise. But can we not get the conclusion if we insert a further assumption, namely, the premise that human understanding somehow influences, shapes, determines, whatever it understands? I think that we can. It is this second premise which saves the argument. It is this second premise which is responsible for the recent turn away from ontology and toward epistemology. If I am correct, then Heidegger, at the very beginning of his inquiry into the nature of being, takes this Kantian turn.

But Heidegger does not stop there. He does not go on to study the nature of human understanding, the capacities of the human mind. If he had, he would have become another Phenomenologist. Rather, he proceeds to commit a second fallacy. This one shall remain nameless. It argues from the premise:

human understanding is part of what it means to be a human being,

to the conclusion:

in order to understand human understanding, one must study what it means to be a human being.

Heidegger argues that in order to understand part of human being, one must first understand the whole of it. Whatever else you may think of this argument, it does have the virtue of calling our attention to what it means to be a human being, rather than to the nature and limits of the understanding. It opens up to Heidegger's investigation a vast array of topics from the meaning of idle chatter to the significance of death, from the causes of anxiety to the function of guilt.

(3) *The unity and uniqueness of human beings*

Human beings, according to Heidegger, have their own unique mode of being which he calls 'existence'. I shall adopt his terminology but spell the word with a capital 'e' in order to mark Heidegger's special meaning. Human beings, to repeat, Exist. Nothing else Exists. The nature of the kind of being which human beings have is the nature of Existence.

Descartes, may I remind you, thought of a human being as a combination of a body and a mind. A person is a combination of two essentially different substances. But, and this is the point I wish to make, a person does not exist in any special way. Bodies and minds exist, and so does the third kind of substance, namely, God. There may be a problem about the kind of being which God has, since he is infinite and uncreated, but in regard to bodies and minds the case is clear: they both exist. We saw that Husserl abandons this evenhanded treatment of body and mind. According to him, the world around us has a 'mere intentional Being, a Being, therefore, which has the mere secondary, relative sense of Being *for* consciousness' (*Ideas*, para. 49). Heidegger carries this exaltation of the mind to extremes. Human Existence becomes the center of his philosophy. But we must also take note of some important differences between Husserl's and Heidegger's treatment of persons.

Firstly, there is the fact that the basic unit of interest for Heidegger is a person rather than a mind. In this respect, Heidegger sides with a great number of recent and contemporary philosophers who philosophize in the 'ordinary language' style, philosophers like Ludwig Wittgenstein (1889–1951) and, especially, Gilbert Ryle (1900–1976). These philosophers share Heidegger's belief that Descartes' division of a person into alien substances is fundamentally mistaken. Once you have broken up a person into these two essentially different pieces, they argue, there is, as in Humpty Dumpty's case, no way in which they can be put together again, so that they form a whole human being. As a result, you will eventually succumb to some form of idealism, either to Berkeley's immanent sort or to Husserl's transcendental kind. No, Descartes was mistaken. What is given to the unprejudiced phenomenological attitude is, not a self, a mind, a bunch of mental acts, but rather a piece of human Existence which is both 'embodied' and 'minded'. What Heidegger objects to in Descartes is Descartes' way of philosophizing from the inside out, so to speak: from the discovery of the self, of the mental substance, to the proof that there is an external world of bodies. Husserl is in this regard the quintessential Cartesian, except that he discovers consciousness rather than the self. Self and world, according to Husserl's philosophy, both transcend what is most intimately and with certainty given to us, namely, consciousness.

Secondly, even though Husserl exalts the being of consciousness, his whole philosophy centers around essences. Phenomenology tries to discover the eternal laws which govern essences and pays no attention to whether or not these essences are actually instantiated. The law that every mental act must have an object holds even if there had never been and never would be any mental acts. (Remember Descartes' claims that a triangle has inner angles adding up to two right angles, even if it does not exist.) Phenomenology thus turns away from the 'real world' and studies the realm of essences. Heidegger adopts quite a different attitude. Like Kierkegaard before him, he professes to be interested only in actually existing beings, for instance, in actual human beings. He analyzes, not the structure of the realm of essences, but the structure of the lives of human beings. He turns his back on the world of being and concentrates on the world of becoming. He stands Plato's theory of knowledge on its head. But what could it possibly mean to study a human being in its full individual existence? How can one possibly study anything without mentioning its properties, its features, its characteristics, its relations to other things? How can one describe an individual without mentioning essences in Husserl's sense of the term? It seems that Heidegger's approach is doomed from the start. Plato's view is correct: the only true objects of knowledge dwell in the realm of being. But Heidegger uses an ingenious move in order to avoid this objection. And this leads us to a third difference between Husserl and Heidegger.

Thirdly, Husserl claims that consciousness has quite a different being from everything else, but he does not make a further distinction between the different kinds of being of different consciousnesses. All minds have the same sort of being. What distinguishes one mind from another is, not that it exists in a different way, but that it consists of different mental acts, that it has different properties, etc. Assume, contrary to fact, that there are such things as the mind of the common man and the mind of the heroic man. According to Husserl, the former would differ from the latter in certain features, certain properties. For example, the mind of the common man would revolve around what other people think of him; what *one* eats, wears, reads, and thinks; and around how *one* behaves. The mind of the heroic man, on the other hand, is indifferent to these concerns. He despises the conventions and fashions of the day. Heidegger's ingenious move consists in turning such features of minds, or, rather, of human beings, into ways of being. Human beings do not only differ from other things in that they and they alone have Existence, they also differ from each other in having different kinds of Existence. The heroic person is not just different from the ordinary person, he also Exists in a different way. The poet Exists differently from the soldier. The philosopher Exists differently from the factory worker.

This claim that what appears to be differences in properties are really differences in ways of Existing saves Heidegger's approach, at least for a moment, from the Platonic objection. Heidegger simply turns essences, denizens of the world of being, into 'Existences', denizens of the world of becoming. In this way, essential differences are transformed into Existential ones. Knowledge of essences is supplanted by knowledge of 'Existences'. You find here one of the most original and radical views in modern metaphysics. We shall have to evaluate this view presently. For the moment, note that one of the cornerstones of Heidegger's philosophy is the thesis: 'All so-being of human beings is primarily being' (*Being and Time*, p. 67).

(4) *Being-in-the-world*

According to Heidegger, the fundamental state of Existence is being-in-the-world. It is a fundamental condition of being a person to have a world around you. We have here a traditional idea with a new twist. The traditional idea, of course, is that the mind is intentional. A mind is always related to something. A mind always comes with objects. Substitute for the mind (mental act) a person; for the intentional nexus, a mode of being called 'being in'; and for the objects, the world; and you get Heidegger's view. Just as we discussed in some detail the three parts of the intentional relationship, so Heidegger deals extensively with the three ingredients of a person's being-in-the-world. His philosophical originality, in my opinion, appears to a large extent in this analysis.

The world in which a person finds himself, Heidegger emphasizes, is not the abstract world of Cartesian material substances. It is the world around us as we experience it in daily living. It is not the world of the physicist; it does not consist of atoms or elementary particles. Rather, it contains apples, and shoe horns, and other people. What kind or kinds of being do the objects of this world have? Heidegger distinguishes between two main kinds: things with which we deal every day, which 'are at hand', which we use, and things which 'are merely there'. In addition, there are, of course, other people who 'are there with me'. The things we encounter are therefore of three kinds: those that are *at hand*, those that are *merely there*, and those that are *there with me*. Or, rather, I should have said that the things we encounter have three kinds of being: being at hand, being there, and being with me.

Other people have a kind of being called 'being there with me'. But do they not share Existence with me? Do they not also Exist? And if so, how is Existence related to being there with me? Existence, you must realize, is always conceived of by Heidegger as *one's own*. It is not something which several persons can share. We cannot talk about our Existence without using a word that functions like a predicate and, hence, without giving the appearance of talking about something that can be shared. But this appearance, according to Heidegger, is misleading. Existence consists of numerous individual pieces, each piece different from all others, and each piece characterized by the indefinable quality of being one's own. This is another fundamental tenet of Heidegger's philosophy to which we shall return later: 'The being, with which this kind of being is concerned, is always my own' (*Being and Time*, p.67).

How am I related to the things which are at hand, which are there, which are with me? I care, I am concerned. Heidegger maintains that the relation between a person and the world is one of *caring*. I think that a better translation of his term '*Sorge*' would be 'concern', but Heidegger makes so much of the connection of his notion with the Latin word 'cura' that I shall follow the usual practice and translate it by 'care'. Now, just as every important property is turned into a way of being, so also is every important relation turned into a way of being. The being of human beings, accordingly, is care. Existence and caring are equivalent forms of being.

There are a number of more specific ways in which we are related to the world. The two most important ones, according to Heidegger, are mood and understanding. By 'mood' Heidegger means, roughly, emotion as opposed to intellect. Fear, for example, is a possible mood. What he has in mind is that one may be related to the world, not just through understanding, judgment, thought, and reasoning, but also through one's feelings, emotions, affections, and moods. There is a fine balance of emphasis. Remember what I said earlier about a rough and ready distinction between Phenomenology and Existentialism: the former stresses the intellectual faculties of the mind, while the latter stresses the emotions. Heidegger tries to do justice to both, but there can hardly be any doubt that he is biased in favor of the emotions. This bias appears in several forms. For example, Heidegger neither understands nor appreciates the natural sciences. And he often waxes in a romantic mood. But be that as it may, he does say that emotions reveal the world to us: 'We must indeed *ontologically* in principle leave the primary discovery of the world to the "mere mood". A pure look, even if it penetrated to the innermost veins of the being of something, could never discover something like menace' (*Being and Time*, p. 177).

Fear and anxiety, as we should expect, make their appearance in *Being and Time*. Fear is a modus of the emotions. Anxiety is 'a fundamental mood which is a distinguished disclosure of human being' (*ibid.*, p. 228). Since we have discussed Kierkegaard's theory and a Freudian theory of anxiety, it is interesting to compare these with what Heidegger has to say about the matter. Let us briefly interrupt our exposition of being-in-the-world and pause for anxiety's sake.

Here are the four theses again which I attributed to Kierkegaard:

(1) Anxiety is only found in human beings.
(2) Anxiety is not the same as fear.
(3) The object of anxiety is nothingness.
(4) Anxiety reveals our freedom.

Heidegger, I believe, would agree with the first thesis. He adopts the second thesis in this form: the object of fear is always something which we encounter in the world, while the object of anxiety is our being-in-the-world as such (*ibid.*, p. 230). Anxiety, in other words, has no specific object; one does not know, specifically, what one is anxious about. Our Freudian interpretation agrees with this assessment, but the repressed object of anxiety is not being-in-the-world, as Heidegger holds. Heidegger also subscribes, in a fashion, to thesis (3). Here it is most interesting to observe how he gets from his claim that one is anxious about being-in-the-world to the view that it is nothing which one is anxious about. He seems to be saying that it is nothing, because the object of anxiety, in distinction to the object of fear, is nothing *in particular*. But this nothing-in-particular, he maintains, is grounded in a something, namely, in a something which is nothing in particular. And this something is the world as such. But the world enters into the being of persons as being-in-the-world. Hence it is this kind of being which is the ultimate object of anxiety. Here is how Heidegger expresses this convoluted train of thought:

> The nothing of what is at-hand is grounded in the most primordial 'something', in the *world*. The world, however, belongs ontologically essentially to the being of human beings as being-in-the-world. Accordingly, if the object of anxiety turns out to be nothingness, that is, the world as such, then this means: the object of anxiety is the being-in-the-world itself. (*Ibid.*, p. 232)

Anxiety, we agreed earlier, does not seem to have an object, contrary to what Brentano's thesis of intentionality maintains. In order to save the thesis, one must somehow find an object even for anxiety. Kierkegaard, as we saw, turns nothingness into an object. Heidegger's way out, as we can now see, is somewhat different, but no less ingenious. The object of anxiety, according to him, is nothing *in particular*. Since it is nothing in particular, he argues, it must be *everything*. And this everything is the world as a whole. So the object of anxiety is the world as a whole. But Heidegger also says that this object is being-in-the-world. When he stresses that it is the world as a whole, he maintains that anxiety, as a mood, discloses the world *as world*, that is, as the other term to which Existence is related. So it is not the world *simpliciter* which is the object of anxiety, but rather the world as being related to Existence, that is, the world as being-in-the-world. We could perhaps put it this way: the object of anxiety is not the world conceived of as an object of intentionality, but intentionality itself. How does this thought fit into our Freudian interpretation?

Recall the case of Anna. The object of Anna's fear is that she may act in accordance with her sexual desire for her father. We assumed that she succeeded in repressing this object, so that she experienced anxiety rather than fear. She is afraid, but she does not know what it is that she is afraid of. Perhaps she knows that she is afraid of doing something, or of saying something, or of hinting at something, or of showing something, but she does not know what it is that she may do, say, hint at, or show. We could therefore say that she is afraid of how she may deal with the world, of how she may conduct herself, of how she may relate to the world. In short, we may say that she is afraid of being-in-the-world. Of course, we know that her fear has a specific object. But this is not the way it seems to her. From Anna's point of view, she only knows that she is afraid of something or other concerning her relationship with the world.

Lastly, there is the fourth thesis, according to which anxiety reveals to us the possibility of our freedom. Heidegger's comments on this topic are in agreement with what we have said earlier. He states, for example, that 'anxiety reveals in human beings the *being* of the possibility of being one's own, that means, of *being free for* the freedom of choosing and defining

oneself. Anxiety confronts a human being with his being free for
. . . ' (*ibid.*, p. 232). But he also connects this view with another
line of thought. Anxiety, he says, *individuates*; it pulls us back
from the world of everyday living, where we are a part of what
one does, what *one* says, what *one* thinks (*ibid.* p. 235). Anxiety,
therefore, has a salutary function. We find in Heidegger the
same praise of anxiety which we observed in Kierkegaard. This
is decidedly not our attitude. Anxiety, as we conceive of it, is a
symptom of neurosis. It is the result of a successful attempt to
hide the truth from oneself and, hence, nothing to be exalted,
nothing to be praised, nothing to be proud of. Surely, it is
always better–better, in a moral sense–to face the truth about
one's wishes, desires, hopes, fears, dreams, disappointments,
etc., than to hide from it. We have here merely a special case of
the moral principle that we ought to face the truth and ought not
to lie to others and to ourselves. A neurotic is always slightly
reprehensible; and he is reprehensible precisely to the extent to
which he hides the truth about himself from himself.

This, as we noted, is not Heidegger's attitude. According to
his view, the 'normal', everyday life of the 'average', mentally
healthy person is an escape from the original state of being in
dread. First comes an impression of the strangeness of the
world, of its eerieness. In order to escape from this condition,
Heidegger tells us, we retreat into the world of the common
man, where we feel at home, familiar, comforted (*ibid.*, p. 234).
He offers us only two alternatives: the genuine existence of the
dreadful individual, or else the plastic life of the common man.
But these are not our only choices. One can share Heidegger's
distaste for 'mass culture' without having to glorify the so-called
heroic individual, alone and self-sufficient, aloof from society,
divorced from technology, conjoined to nature. 'Human *being* is
genuine', Heidegger says at one point, 'in the primordial
individuation of a silent resoluteness which dares to face
anxiety' (*ibid.*, p. 369). Whenever I think of Heidegger's hero, a
memory image appears in my mind. When I was a small boy, I
used to go mushroom hunting with my mother in the deep
forests of the Eastern part of Germany. Once, when we were all
alone in a magnificent forest of tall foliage trees, a forest-keeper,
like an apparition, appeared between the trees, silently crossing
a sun-drenched clearing. He wore a beautiful traditional green

outfit, with a green felt hat; his rifle was slung over his shoulder; and he was accompanied by a couple of dogs. He nodded at my mother and at me, but did not say a word. And he was gone silently before I could fully take in his majestic appearance. Of course, for several weeks afterwards, I told everyone that I was going to be a forest-keeper. Later on, when I was older, I tried to imagine how this splendid figure would have words with his wife, how he would drink, while playing cards, with his buddies in the local tavern, and how he would plan his next vacation on Mallorca. Needless to say, I did not succeed. So much for childhood heroes.

Let us now return to our main topic, namely, the three parts of the human condition of being-in-the-world. We have talked about Heidegger's conception of the world and of the ways in which we are in the world. But what is the I, the subject, that stands in these relations to the world? It is not the I of Descartes' 'I think'. It is not a mental substance whose essence is thought. Nor is it some other kind of mental individual, a self, an ego. No, *this I is a piece of naked Existence*. 'The substance of man', he declares, 'is Existence' (*ibid.*, p. 255 and p. 262). Heidegger, I said earlier, turns the essential properties of human beings into ways of Existing. Existence is of many kinds. But this is not all. We now learn that each of these kinds splinters further into many pieces. The true subject of the relationship of being-in-the-world is always such a piece of a kind of Existence.

In summary, here are the three cornerstones of Heidegger's philosophy which we shall have to discuss more thoroughly:

(1) The so-being of human beings is primarily being
(2) The substance of a human being is Existence.
(3) The Existence of a human being is completely individuated.

In our own words:

(1) Existence is of different kinds.
(2) Existence is the substance of man.
(3) Existence is individuated.

10. Modes of being

(1) *Heidegger's way of multiplying modes of being*

Husserl distinguishes between the kind of being which consciousness has and the kind which everything else has. Heidegger
turns all of the essential properties of human beings into ways of
Existing. But are there really these differences in the way in
which human beings exist? More generally, are there different
modes or kinds of being? This is the fundamental question
which we must try to answer.

But before we do, let us take a look at Heidegger's way of
multiplying modes of Existence. His view is that 'the essence of
human being lies in its existence. The discernible characteristics
of this being, therefore, are not properties of a something which
"looks to us" so or so, but are possible ways to be and only that'
(*ibid.*, p. 67). This view sees kinds of being everywhere. Let me
give you some examples. Consider how Heidegger conceives of
truth. As ordinarily understood, an assertion (judgment) is true
if and only if it corresponds to a fact. Since it is a fact that the
earth is round, the assertion that the earth is round is true. Since
it is not a fact that the earth is flat, the assertion that the earth is
flat is not true. Truth is thus conceived of as a relation between
two things, an assertion and a fact. Heidegger rejects this

standard view. Or, rather, he modifies it and gives it a typical Heideggerian twist. According to him, that an assertion is true means that it *discovers* a fact. A true assertion reveals (uncovers) a being as it truly is. To be, therefore, is to be discovering, revealing. But to be discovering, to be revealing, presupposes being-in-the-world. In fact, it is just one of the many possible ways of being in the world (*ibid.*, pp. 257–69). Hence it is one of the ways in which human beings are (have being). It follows, therefore, that to be true is a mode of being of human beings. In short, truth is a mode of being of human beings (*ibid.*, p. 270).

Heidegger's line of thought follows the familiar pattern. In a first step, a mental act is conceived of as property of human beings. The mental act of asserting something is thought of as a property of human beings. Since we assume that the assertion is true, this act is called a 'discovering'. When an assertion is true, it is a discovering of a fact. Now, this property of discovering facts is, in a second step, turned into a mode of being. To be a discoverer of truth is a way to be. In step one, a relation is turned into a property. In step two, this property is turned into a kind of being. As a result, we arrive at the rather implausible view that truth is a mode of being of human beings.

For our second example, we select one of the Existentialist's favorite topics, death. Death, of course, is the *end* of human life. It is the end of a human being. But this ending of a human life, according to Heidegger, is not like the ending of a rain shower. If one thinks that it is, one commits the serious philosophical mistake of conceiving of a human life as something which is merely there, as things are merely there, rather than as something which Exists. Thus we must not think of death as a human being's being 'no longer there', as we think of bread as being no longer there after we have eaten it (*ibid.*, pp. 288–90). No, death must not be conceived of as the end of a human being, but rather as a form of human being, namely, as a being towards the end of Existence. Therefore, 'death is a way of being which a human being takes on as soon as it is' (*ibid.*, p. 289).

Finally, look at what Heidegger has to say about science. Science consists in scientific investigations. Obviously, such investigations discover facts. But such discoveries, as we saw earlier, are a way to be. Hence science, too, is a way to be for human beings: 'The existential concept conceives of science as a

Modes of being

way of Existence and therewith as a mode of being-in-the-world which discovers beings or being' (*ibid.*, p. 408).

Truth, death, and science, are modes of Existence. Everything there is in or about human beings is in danger of being turned into a mode of being. One is quite tempted to parody Heidegger by developing an ontological (rather than an ontic!) analytic of sexual difference. Obviously, there is a biological difference between the two sexes. But we must go deeper! We must choose an ontological approach to the problematic of male-female difference. If we do, we shall find out, after a tortuous but profound inquiry, that being male or being female are existentials, that is ways of Existing. Can you imagine how this result will be received by those misguided persons who try to belittle, or even to deny, the obvious physiological differences between the sexes? On the other hand, would not this existentialistic view lend some plausibility to the suspicion that males simply do not understand females, and vice versa?

But an end to levity. I hope to have impressed you with the extent of Heidegger's practice of turning properties into modes of being. Modes of being have been introduced by earlier philosophers. But nobody went as far as Heidegger. The question before us is whether or not there are any modes of being at all. I do not think that there are. But to convince ourselves, we must look at the main reasons for the contrary view.

(2) *Existence and exemplification*

When we ascribe properties to things, we use (in English and some other languages) a form of 'to be'. We say: 'Jumbo *is* an elephant', 'Caesar *was* a Roman Emperor', and 'There *will be* no more revolutions in Poland'. This pervasive linguistic fact invites the following argument. To say that Socrates *exists* is just another way of saying that he *is*. But 'Socrates is' has to 'Socrates is a man' the relationship of the generic case to the more specific case. To be a man, in other words, is a specific case of being. To be a man, therefore, is a specific way of being. Just as a human and a canary are instances of animals, so *being a male* and *being a female* are instances of *being*. The relationship which the two

165

animals have to the property of being an animal is the same as the relationship between these two ways of being and being in general.

If you argue in this fashion, then you will eventually arrive at the view that all properties are ways of being. Every classification of things according to their properties becomes a classification according to their ways of being. The difference between an elephant and a mouse, consisting in their having different properties, becomes a difference in their modes of being. The elephant likes peanuts; the mouse likes cheese. But liking peanuts is a kind of being–just as a human is a kind of animal–and so is liking cheese. In having the former property, the elephant has a different kind of being from the mouse who has the latter property.

I do not know whether or not Heidegger ever explicitly used the argument which I have just outlined. I do know, though, that he often talks *as if* to be something or the other is a kind of existence. He says, for example, 'we think being just as often as, daily, on innumerable occasions, whether aloud or silently, we say "This *is* such and such", "That other *is not* so", "That *was*", "It will be". In each use of a verb we have already thought, and have always in some way understood, being'. (*The Basic Problems of Phenomenology*, p. 14). It is at any rate clear that Heidegger could not have made use of the argument in its full generality. For, if he had, then he would have arrived at the unwelcome conclusion that any two things, as long as they differ in a property, have different modes of being. I call this conclusion unwelcome because it would completely trivialize Heidegger's laborious sorting out of modes of being.

Whether or not Heidegger actually thought of the argument, does it have merit? Well, it is certainly seductive; as seductive as the assertion that to be a man is a way to be. However, I think that the argument breaks down at two crucial points. Firstly to be a man, it seems to me, is not a way *to be*, but, rather, a way *to be something*. Just as a human being is an example of an animal, so being a man is an example, not of being, but of being *something or other*. But to be something or other is the same as *to have a property*. To be a man, therefore, is, not a case of being, but is a case of having a property.

As soon as we realize that to be a man is a case of being

something rather than of being, we also realize, secondly, how far removed this notion of being is from the notion of existence. In the sense in which we are now talking about being, nothing can just *be*: it must always be something. Being is here conceived of as a relation. It is, in our earlier terminology, the nexus of exemplification. Existence, on the other hand, is an entirely different kettle of fish. It is not a relation or, at least, not obviously so. Socrates exists. We do not believe that he exists something or other. To think of 'exists' in 'Socrates exists' as the 'is' of predication (as a form of to be), is as mistaken as to think of the 'is' in 'Socrates is a man' as existence. 'Socrates is' is as little an expression of the fact that Socrates exists as 'Socrates exists a man' is an expression of the fact that Socrates is a man.

Let us take another look at this argument for modes of being. It begins with the assertion that to say 'Socrates exists' is to say 'Socrates is'. This, as we now see, is clearly false. If the 'is' in the second expression is the 'is' of predication (the 'is' which signifies a form of to be), then the expression, as it stands, does not even make sense. It is not a complete sentence. We must add a word like 'something': 'Socrates is something (or other)'. But if we do, then it becomes obvious that 'Socrates exists' is no longer the same as the new sentence, namely, the sentence 'Socrates is something'. Of course, we are not denying that if Socrates exists, then he has some property or other, and conversely. What I claim is merely that to say that he exists *is not the same* as to say that he has some property or other. We are dealing here with two distinct though connected facts, and not with just one fact expressed in two different ways. Hence, while it may be argued that to be a man is an example of being something (of having a property), it cannot be argued that to be a man is an example of existence. In order to mark the fundamental difference between being, in the sense of being something, on the one hand, and existence, on the other, we shall from now on avoid the term 'being' altogether. Instead, we shall speak of exemplification, on the one hand, and existence, on the other. To be something or other is the same as to exemplify some property or other. Nothing can just be, just as nothing can just exemplify. But something can just exist. Existence, we may note for future reference, does not appear to be a relation.

The view that there are many modes of being, we sum up, may arise from a confusion of exemplification with existence. I shall let you be the judge of whether or not Heidegger is guilty of this confusion.

(3) *Existence and the categories*

We have seen that Plato's world divides into two realms: the realm of being and the realm of becoming. It has often been claimed that the entities of these two realms exist in two different ways. Particulars are said to be *real*. They exist in the mode of reality. Universals, on the other hand, are not real. They exist, but they exist in another mode. Real *versus* non-real entities: here we have a distinction that rivals Heidegger's fundamental dichotomy between Existents and non-Existents. Whatever argument speaks for the former may conceivably also support the latter. What arguments show that particulars exist in a different way from universals?

Well, there is a hint from the English language. Instead of 'Crocodiles exist' we say 'There are crocodiles'. (But notice that we won't say 'There is Socrates' instead of 'Socrates exists'.) One may infer from this slender clue that to *exist* is to be *here or there*, that is, to be somewhere (in space). And one may further conclude that if anything else has being, it must have a being other than existence. Since we hold that universals have being, for example, we might conclude that they do not exist, but have another kind of being. Or, to use our less confusing terminology, we may conclude that universals exist but are not real. Among all existents, some are *there* and these are called 'real'; others are not there and they are not called 'real'.

Before we take a critical look at this line of reasoning, let us note that the German word used by Heidegger to talk about the peculiar form of being of human beings is the word 'Dasein'. This ordinary term translates into the English 'there-being' or 'being-there'. Heidegger sees a vast amount of significance in the fact that 'Dasein' divides into two words indicated by my translation. He even writes the German word on occasion with a hyphen: 'Da-sein'. And he says such things as: 'A mood reveals "how one is and will be" In this "how one is" being-in-a-mood brings being into its "there"' (*Being and Time*, p. 173). Needless to say, our interpretation of being-there does not agree with Heidegger's. We are tentatively separating the real from the non-real, while Heidegger distinguishes between human being and all other being. But this discrepancy raises an interesting point. Why did Heidegger, who puts so much stress on etymological connections, pick up this particular word for the being of *human* beings, when it so clearly indicates the being of all *spatial* beings? It is true, of course, that human beings are spatial; they are particulars rather than univerals. It may even be true that their spatiality is an essential feature. (Remember Husserl's doctrine of the perspectival aspect of all perception.) But it is equally true that the world is full of other spatial things as well, so that 'spatial being' is shared by human beings and many other particulars. 'Spatial being' is therefore not a defining characteristic of human beings.

Back to the argument under scrutiny. These last considerations clearly show that the argument from the phrase '*there* are' does not yield the desired division into real and non-real entities, into particulars and universals. Instead, it divides entities into those that are *spatial* and those that are not. Temporal particulars would have to be classified as unreal. A mental act of desiring, for example, would not be *there*, even though it would be *now* or *then*, and, hence, would have to have a different mode of being. Contrary to our intention, it would have to be categorized as non-real. Besides, there is the minor point that the English phrase 'there are' translates into the German '*Es gibt*', which literally translated, amounts to 'It gives'. '*Es gibt*', therefore, does not contain the slightest whiff of spatiality.

More important, though, is the following consideration. Let us grant that there is a profound difference between particulars and universals, a difference much deeper than that between a mouse and an elephant, much deeper even than that between a human being and a stone. In philosophy, we call such a difference a '*categorial* difference'. Particulars and universals, accordingly, are the two categories of the Platonic system. Now, what we must clearly fix in our minds is the fact that the existence of a categorial difference does not imply the existence of a difference in kind of existence. From the fact that two entities belong to different categories, it does not follow that they must exist in different ways. From the fact that Socrates belongs to a different category from the universal wisdom, it does not follow that he exists in a way which is different from the way in which wisdom exists. This follows no more in the categorial case than in the case of a mouse and an elephant. A mouse is quite different from an elephant, but this does not mean that a mouse has a kind of existence which an elephant does not have, and conversely. Socrates, who is a temporal being, is quite a different entity from the universal wisdom which dwells in the realm of being. But this does not imply that he has a mode of existence which is different from the one which wisdom enjoys. In short, from the fact that two entities differ in their properties, even in their categorial properties, it never follows that they must differ in their modes of existence.

What holds for particulars and universals holds also for mental and non-mental particulars. Assume that Brentano were correct–which he is not–that all mental and only mental things are intentional. The realm of particulars (Plato's realm of becoming) could then be divided into intentional and non-intentional things. But from the existence of this division we could not conclude that some particulars have one sort of existence, while others have a different sort. (Look at this revealing quotation from Heidegger: 'A distinguishing feature between the existent [what has being in the sense of Existence] and the extant [what has being in the mode of being at hand] is found precisely in intentionality . . . A window, a chair, in general anything extant in the broadest sense, does not exist, because it cannot comport toward extant entities in the manner of intentional self-directedness-toward-them' (*The Basic Problems of Phenomenology*, p. 64).) Nor can we arrive at this conclusion from Heidegger's distinction between human beings, on the one hand, and all other beings on the other. All human beings and only human beings may indeed share the feature of being-in-the-world. But this fact does not imply that human beings exist differently from other things. All human beings and only human beings may indeed be characterized by the fact that they can raise the question of the meaning of being. But this does not imply that they exist differently from other things. All human beings and only human beings may indeed live in the anticipation of death. But this does not mean that they exist differently from other beings.

Of course, we get a valid argument for modes of existence if we add a further assumption, namely, the assumption that a difference in fundamental properties always implies a difference in modes of existence. For example, if we assume that an existent which can raise questions about the nature of existence must have a different mode of being from all other existents, then it follows that human beings must exist differently from everything else. But then we must ask: what justifies this assumption? What consideration speaks for the principle that a difference in properties implies a difference in existence? As far as I know, Heidegger never raises this question. Nor do I know of anyone else who has argued for the principle. It is simply one of the basic axioms of Heidegger's philosophy that where everyone else sees qualitative differences, existential differences obtain.

There is something ironic about Heidegger's approach to ontology. His most important, most fundamental, distinction is the distinction between Existence and being at hand. This is a distinction between human beings and other kinds of individual thing. It is a distinction *within* the category of individual thing. But ontology, I would urge, becomes a unique philosophical enterprise only after a distinction has been made between individual things, on the one hand, and all other kinds of entity–properties, relations, facts, etc.–on the other. When the Greek philosopher Anaximander (610–546 B.C.) speculated that everything consists of the four elements, fire, earth, air, and water, he proposed in effect a rudimentary theory of chemistry. Ontology was only born when someone realized that any such view presupposes a distinction between individual things–a table, a mountain, a bucket of water–and their properties–a degree of warmth, wetness, etc. Ontology was only born when someone saw that there are not only different kinds of individual thing, but also different kinds of entity. This is precisely what distinguishes ontology from all of the sciences: the sciences are interested in what kinds of individual thing there are and how these kinds behave, while ontology inquires into what kinds of entity there are and what the laws are that govern them. The physicist wants to know what kinds of elementary particles there are and how they interact; the chemist inquires into what kinds of element there are and how they combine; the botanist asks what kinds of plant there are and how they grow; and so on. By contrast, the ontologist asks what the categories of the world are and how they hang together.

When Descartes distinguished between mental and material substances, his purpose was, not to give an ontological inventory, but to emphasize the substantial nature of mind. Descartes simply accepted the Aristotelian ontology of substance, essence, and accident. He worked within the Aristotelian framework. He merely tried to correct what he conceived to be a minor mistake in the classificatory scheme of the tradition: minds are not essences of bodies, but are substances in their own right. Heidegger's distinction between human beings and other kinds of individual thing runs parallel to Descartes' distinction between minds and mere bodies. But Heidegger, in distinction to Descartes, sets out to overthrow all previous ontology and to create an entirely new ontological system. His aim is lofty; the scope of his intended inquiry, vast. Yet when he starts to fill in the details of his imposing project, his horizon narrows, his treatment of the basic problems becomes sketchy, and his ontological reach remains limited. This is what I meant when I said that Heidegger's approach to ontology is ironic.

There is an obvious reason for this ontological narrow-mindedness. If you start out by distinguishing between human beings, on the one hand, and everything else, on the other, all kinds of non-human entity will pale into insignificance. What does it matter then that properties are different from individual things? That in addition to properties, there are relations? That relations must be distinguished from the structures which they create? That structures must be distinguished from mere sets? That there are also numbers? And that these numbers are not sets? All of these profoundly different categories will be thrown into the same pot, the pot which contains everything other than human beings. Ontology is supplanted by anthropology. Call it *philosophical* anthropology, if you wish, but the fact remains that Heidegger's ontology bears little resemblance to the monumental ontologies of the past–to Plato's and Aristotle's systems–or of the present–for example, to Frege's philosophy.

Heidegger promises to deal with the most profound and most general problems of ontology. He stakes out a claim to the most distant horizons of ontology. But he seldom succeeds in seeing farther than the end of his human nose.

(4) *Existence and being an object*

We now return to a theme which we have already mentioned. The problem of nonexistent objects of mental acts, as we saw, led some philosophers to distinguish between being, on the one hand, and existence, on the other. Everything, according to this view, has being, even the wildest creations of the imagination, like unicorns and golden mountains, and even contradictory objects, like round squares. But among all the objects which have being, a few actually exist. Mt Everest exists, the golden mountain merely has being. Julius Caesar exists, Hamlet merely has being. This was at one time Bertrand Russell's view. I do not think that it is correct. I told you earlier that I do not believe that *there are* all of these nonexistent objects like the golden mountain, unicorns, Hamlet, the round square, etc. But we must try to go a little deeper into this matter.

Strictly speaking, we must distinguish between two different versions of Russell's view. One may hold that everything has being, but that some things *in addition* have existence. Or else one may hold that everything has Being (with a capital 'b'), but that Being comes in two kinds, being (with a small 'b') and existence. Thus Mt Everest and the golden mountain have Being, but the former has a sort of Being called 'existence', while the latter has a sort of Being called 'being'. It does not matter greatly which of these two views we consider; for in the long run, they come down to very much the same thing. I shall discuss the second version, the view that the golden mountain has some kind of Being different from Mt Everest. There are at least two profound arguments for this view. Both of them can already be found in Plato's *Sophist* (237B–239C).

The first argument goes like this: some kind of Being must belong to everything, since Being must belong to whatever can be counted. For, if A is anything that can be counted as one, then A is something and, hence, A is.

This is the second argument: the assertion 'A is not' must either be meaningless or false, no matter what A may be. But it is clearly not meaningless. If it is not meaningless, then it is about A. But if it is about A, then A must be. Hence the assertion 'A is not' must be false. Therefore, A must have Being, no matter what A is.

The first argument makes two important assumptions. The first assumption is that if A is one, then it must be one *something or other*, that is, A must have *some property or other*. The second assumption is that if anything has a property, it must have Being. Together, these two premises yield the conclusion that everything has Being. If you cannot accept the conclusion, if you cannot convince yourself that the golden mountain has Being, you must find reasons to reject one or both of these premises. You already know where I stand: I cannot believe that there is a golden mountain, in any reasonable sense of 'there is'. I mentioned earlier that I accepted the ontological principle that if anything has a property, then it exists. Thus I have no choice. I must argue against the first premise. But this premise is extremely plausible. If Hamlet is *one* person, then surely Hamlet is *a person*. If the brothers Karamasov are *three*, then it seems obvious that they are the brothers which are called 'Karamasov'. In general, whatever one counts as so many so-and-so's, must be so-and-so's. And since one cannot count anything without counting it as a so-and-so, anything which one can count must be a so-and-so. Recall in this connection our discussion of the nature of numbers as quantifiers.

I must explain how we can count Hamlet as one person and the brothers Karamasov as three brothers, even though Hamlet is not a person and the Karamasovs are not brothers. Since Hamlet does not exist, I hold, he cannot have any properties and, hence, cannot have the property of being a person. Since the brothers Karamasov do not exist, they cannot have any properties and, hence, cannot have the property of being brothers. Since Hamlet does not exist, he cannot even have the categorial property of being an individual thing, or of being an entity. Hence I must go so far as to deny that he can be counted as one individual thing or as one entity. But, and this is the crucial insight, Hamlet is indeed an *object* of Shakespeare's imagination, an *object* of our fancy, in short, an *object* of thought.

The golden mountain is not a mountain; it is not even an individual thing or an entity. But it is an object of thought; it is something we can conceive of; it is something we can imagine. We can even conceive of a round square, although we cannot imagine it. This makes the round square an object of thought (though not an object of imagination). Anything that can occur before a mind, no matter how crazy or even contradictory it may be, is in this sense an object of thought. Obviously, I cannot give you examples of things which cannot be objects of thought; for if they cannot be objects of thought, I cannot think of them and, hence, describe them to you. Now, it is true that everything that can be counted must be an object of thought; for in order to be counted, it must occur before the mind. But this does not mean that it must have a certain *property*, the property of being an object of thought. There is no such property. To be an object of thought is not to have a certain property, but to stand in the intentional nexus to a mind. And this nexus, we conceded a long time ago, is abnormal in that it can connect existents with nonexistents. It is indeed true of the golden mountain or of Hamlet that they can be related by means of the intentional nexus to a mind. But this feature of the golden mountain and of Hamlet is not a property, in the relevant sense of the term, of the golden mountain and of Hamlet. I conclude, therefore, that we cannot infer that the golden mountain has Being from the fact that it can be an object of the mind.

But what we are really after is an explanation of how we can count Hamlet as one *person* and the brothers Karamasov as three *brothers*, even though Hamlet is not a person and the Karamasovs are not brothers. Hamlet is not a person, but he is *imagined to be* a person (rather than, say, to be a horse). The brothers Karamasov are not brothers, but they *are imagined to be* brothers. The golden mountain is not a mountain, but it is *thought to be* a mountain. The round square is not round and it is not a square, but it is conceived of as round and square. And the same holds for numbers: Hamlet is not one person, but he is conceived of as one person; the brothers Karamasov are not three brothers, but they are imagined to be three brothers. We can count the objects of our and other people's imagination, not because they have certain properties like being a person or being brothers, but because they are imagined to have these properties. Just as we can imagine there to be a person who is indecisive, so can we imagine there to be *one* person who is indecisive. Just as we can imagine there to be brothers called 'Karamasov', so can we imagine there to be precisely three brothers called 'Karamasov'. And as little as it is true that *there are* these *brothers* called 'Karamasov', just as little is it true that *there are three* such brothers. As little as it is true that Hamlet is indecisive, just as little is it true that he is *one* person.

One may object that being imagined to be one person is a property of Hamlet's. Hence Hamlet has a property after all. Therefore, Hamlet must have Being. But remember what I just said about the alleged property of being an object of thought. The same holds for the alleged property of being imagined to be one person. There is no such property! There is merely the fact that Hamlet is related by means of the intentional nexus to certain mental acts of imagining. And the feature of being so related to minds does not count as a property when we accept the principle that everything that has a property must exist.

The crucial assumption of the second argument for the Being of nonexistent objects is that if an assertion *is about A*, then *A* must have (at least) Being. Consider the statement: Hamlet does not exist. It is clearly not a meaningless jumble of words. To the contrary, we believe that this is a perfectly good assertion which, moreover, is true. We believe that it is a true assertion *about* Hamlet. But if so, then it follows presumably that Hamlet must have Being. Given our philosophical way of thinking, it is assumed that the *aboutness relation*, which holds between an assertion and its subject, is not abnormal! But this aboutness relation is nothing else but the intentional nexus in disguise. When there occurs a mental act of asserting that Hamlet does not exist, this act stands in the intentional nexus to a certain state of affairs involving Hamlet. But we have insisted before and shall now emphasize anew that in this clear sense, an assertion can be *about* something that has no being whatsoever. The crucial assumption of the second argument, from our point of view, is simply false: an assertion can be about what has no being at all. (And, consequently, a sentence can be about something which has no being at all.)

I conclude then that these two arguments do not prove that nonexistent objects must have a kind of being different from existence. But if this is true, then we have succeeded in turning back all three attempts to justify the view that being has modes, that there are kinds of it, that it is a genus with several species. We have successfully defended our position that all there is, is existence. An object either exists or it does not exist. It cannot have some sort of existence and lack another. And if this view is correct, then Heidegger must be mistaken. There is no special kind of being, 'Existence' spelled with a capital 'e', which only human beings have. As far as existence is concerned, Caesar exists in precisely the same manner in which Mt Everest exists. Nor are there different kinds of human Existence. Caesar does not exist any differently from Hitler; Mozart does not exist any differently from Heidegger. Whatever differences there are between human beings, on the one hand, and dogs, sticks, and stones, on the other, are a matter of quality, of properties. And whatever differences there are among people, they too are a matter of quality, of properties. We confront Heidegger's thesis of modes of being with a fundamental metaphysical principle of our own: whatever differences and similarities there are in the world, they are all due to properties and relations.

11. The nature of existence

(1) *Existence as a property*

Heidegger says repeatedly that the problem of the nature of being had been forgotten by traditional philosophy. But this is not correct. It is true that you will not find many discussions of it. But this is due to the fact that the Aristotelian tradition had more or less settled on a particular solution of the problem. There was a standard view which was widely accepted. According to this view, being is a transcendental genus, a most general property. It is a property which everything has. It is a property which all *entities* have, since the term 'entity' means 'a being'. To be an entity and to have being are one and the same thing. Perhaps you can sense that we are up against another ontological puzzle: how can we possibly claim that *everything* has being without either saying something that is trivially true or else saying something that is false? If by 'everything' we mean 'every entity', then we assert that everything that has being has being, and that is trivial. But if we mean by 'everything' something like 'every object of thought', then we assert something false; for the golden mountain is an object of thought, but it does not have being. We shall return to this difficulty later on.

The notion that being is a property ties in with a traditional proof for the existence of God. This proof is called 'the ontological proof for the existence of God'. Much of the discussion of the nature of being (of existence) centers around this proof. You find a version of the proof in Descartes' *Fifth Meditation*. I shall here merely give an outline of it, in order to call your attention to the particular notion of existence which it employs.

Recall, please, our earlier discussion of Descartes' claim that:

> when I imagine a triangle, even though there may perhaps be
> no such figure anywhere in the world outside of my thought,
> nor ever have been, nevertheless the figure cannot help
> having a certain determinate nature, or form, or essence,
> which is immutable and eternal, which I have not invented
> and which does not in any way depend upon my mind. This
> is evidenced by the fact that we can demonstrate various
> properties of this triangle, namely, that its three angles are
> equal to two right angles. (*Fifth Meditation*)

The ontological argument rests on this claim. Instead of the notion of a triangle, we consider the notion of God. The notion of God is the notion of a most perfect being. We do not as yet know, just as in the case of the triangle, whether or not there exists such a most perfect being; we merely know that we have a notion of it. Now, just as in the case of the triangle, we can presumably demonstrate that such a being must have certain properties; for example, that it must be perfectly just and totally kind. That we can demonstrate these particular properties of God follows from the fact that our notion of Him is a notion of a most *perfect* being. At this point, existence makes its appearance. One assumes that *existence is a perfection* like being perfectly just and being totally kind. Existence is treated like one of these properties. Moreover, it is treated like a property which is such that, if a thing has it, it is more perfect than it otherwise would be. (You may want to object at this point that it makes no sense to compare two things in regard to how perfect they are when it is assumed that one of them does not exist. You may want to object, in other words, that it makes no sense to compare objects of thought in this way; it only makes sense to compare entities. But we cannot pursue this valid criticism.)

The rest of the proof is obvious. Since existence is a perfection, it follows from the very notion of a perfect being that this being must have this perfection, that is, that it must exist; just as it follows from this very notion that the being must be perfectly just and totally kind. And this follows *as surely as* that Descartes' triangle must have inner angles that add up to two right angles. Hence, the most perfect being exists, that is, God exists.

There are two standard objections to this proof. We have already mentioned one of these in connection with our discussion of the triangle example. From Descartes' notion of a triangle, we said, one cannot infer that *this triangle* must have inner angles that add up to two right angles, but only that if there exists such a triangle, then it must have this property. From the notion it follows that *if there is something* corresponding to the notion, then this thing must have the properties represented by the notion. From my notion of a mermaid, for example, it follows, not that *this or that* mermaid has long blond hair, but merely that if something corresponds to the notion, that is, if there is a mermaid, then it will have long blond hair. From the notion of a perfect being it does not follow that *this* being is perfectly just, but only that if there is such a being, then it is perfectly just. Assuming that existence is indeed a perfection, what follows is, not that *this* perfect being must exist, but only that *if there is* such a being, *then it exists*.

The second standard object to the proof denies that existence is a property like other properties. You can see that the proof breaks down if existence is not a property; for then we cannot treat it like the property of being perfectly just or the property of being totally kind. Sometimes, this second objection is expressed by saying that existence is not a part of the nature, form, or essence of a thing. We must be a little careful at this point, however, and distinguish between the Aristotelian notion of an essence and the notion of a nature which we introduced in connection with Leibniz's story of the creation of Adam. For our purpose, it is best to consider the latter. The nature of a thing, so conceived, consists of all the properties which a thing has (during the course of its existence). To say that existence is not part of the nature of a thing then amounts to saying that it is not a property of a thing. We are faced with a difficult question: is existence a property of things or not?

I do not think that language provides us with unambiguous clues. On the one hand, in a sentence like 'Socrates exists', 'exists' seems to function as some sort of predicate, indicating that what it represents may be a property. On the other hand, there is no 'is' of predication present, as in most sentences which attribute properties to things. 'Socrates exists' is quite different from 'Socrates is tall' and 'Crocodiles exist' is quite different in this regard from 'Crocodiles are reptiles'. We may take this as a sign that existence is not exemplified, that it does not stand in the nexus of exemplification to the entity which exists. If we further assume that every property stands in this nexus to the entity which has the property, then it follows that existence cannot be a property. I am inclined to put some stock in this line of reasoning. Furthermore, there are also such expressions as *'There are* crocodiles' and *'There is* no Santa Claus', and here the crucial phrases 'there are' and 'there is' clearly do not function as predicates.

Kant is one of many philosophers who have claimed that the ontological proof fails because existence is not a property, and he gives an argument for this contention:

> By whatever and by however many predicates we may think a thing–even if we completely determine it–we do not make the least addition to the thing when we further declare that this thing *is*. Otherwise, it would not be exactly the same thing that exists, but something more than we had thought in the concept; and we could not, therefore, say that the exact object of my concept exists. (Immanuel Kant, *Critique of Pure Reason*, trans. Norman Kempt Smith, New York, St. Martin's Press, 1965, p. 505)

Kant argues here that existence cannot belong to the nature of a thing. Let the individual thing in question be the Loch Ness monster, and let us ask whether or not this monster exists. Assume, furthermore, that we think of the Loch Ness monster as *the thing which is F, G, H, . . .*, where *F, G, H*, etc. are certain properties. Kant claims that existence cannot be one of these properties, even if this list of properties includes every property which the Loch Ness monster has. Consider, first, the case where the list contains only a few properties. Why could we not ask ourselves: does the thing with properties F, G, and H have the further property of existence? We surely can ask ourselves whether or not the thing with F, G, and H has the further property, say, of being over fifty feet long. If we answer this last question positively, we assert that the thing we thought of as having F, G, and H has the additional property of being over fifty feet long. Does this mean, as Kant seems to argue, that it would not be exactly the thing we questioned that is over fifty feet long, but some other thing? Yes and no. It is true that when we thought of the monster as having F, G, and H, we did not think of it *as* having the property of being over fifty feet long. But this does not mean, as Kant seems to believe that when we think *of* the monster as being, among other things, over fifty feet long we do not think *of* the same thing as when we think of the thing which is F, G, and H.

We must clearly distinguish between *how* we think of something and *what* it is that we are thinking of. When I think of Salzburg as the birthplace of Mozart, I think of the same thing (city) as when I think of it as the city at the site of the Roman Juvavum. But I do not think of it in the same way. There is an ambiguity in the Kantian expression 'exact object of my concept'. It may mean: 'an object which indeed has the properties which I ascribe to it when I think of it'. Or it could mean: 'an object which has *no other properties* than the ones I ascribe to it when I think of it'. If we decide that the Loch Ness monster is over fifty feet long, we can say that the 'exact object of our concept' is over fifty feet long, using this phrase with the first meaning. We cannot say that *it* is over fifty feet long with the second meaning. But nobody would have this second meaning in mind under the circumstances. The very fact that we are asking ourselves whether or not the Loch Ness monster is over fifty feet long eliminates the second meaning. And what holds for the property of being over fifty feet long, also holds for existence. When we ask whether the thing which is F, G, and H exists, we are asking whether the thing which has the properties F, G, and H also has the feature of existence. We are not asking whether the thing which has no other property, feature, characteristic, or what-have-you, then *F*, *G*, and *H* has the further feature of existence. Thus I conclude that Kant's argument is not sound for the limited case.

But what happens when we turn to the unrealistic case when the description of the contemplated thing is complete, that is, contains all of its properties? Obviously, we would not ask whether or not this thing has the further property of being over fifty feet long. That would be like asking whether or not the birthplace of Mozart is the birthplace of Mozart. Could we ask whether or not the thing exists? That depends on whether a *complete* description of the thing includes existence, that is, on whether or not we include its existence among its properties. Someone who holds that existence is a property will claim that a complete description of a thing includes this property of existence. We cannot make any progress along this line. Let us then ask whether we may conclude that the thing which is *F*, *G*, and *H* also exists–assuming that *F*, *G*, and *H*, are all of the 'ordinary' properties of the thing–and hold simultaneously that existence is a property of sorts. I see no reason why we may not, as long as we sharply distinguish between the two meanings of 'exact object of our concept' and employ the reasonable first meaning. Hence I conclude that Kant's argument also fails for the unlimited case when we consider a 'complete' description of the thing.

But even though Kant's argument does not succeed in showing that existence is not a property, it is clear that existence cannot be an 'ordinary' property. (And perhaps this is all that Kant's argument was intended to prove.) Every ordinary property divides all entities into two mutually exclusive classes, the set of things which have the property and the group of things which do not have the property. But this is clearly not true for existence: every entity has existence and, hence, there is no such thing as a group of entities which do not exist. To put it differently, every property is such that there is at least one entity which has the property and at least one entity which does not have the property. And this even holds for categorial properties. But it does not hold for existence; for there is no entity which does not exist. This is precisely the reason why Aristotelians spoke of existence as a transcendental category.

I know of no further arguments that existence is not a

property. I am convinced that it is not a property, but find it hard to sound convincing. Existence is not a property, I believe, because it is not exemplified. But I do not really know how to argue for this contention. It seems to me that for everything, we can distinguish between the thing, on the one hand, and any one of its properties, on the other. There is the pen on my desk, and then there is its color; there is the color shade midnight blue, and then there is the property of being a color; there is the number seven, and then there is the property of being a number. But this distinction seems to me to break down when we turn to existence. When I try to distinguish between the pen on my desk and its existence, I cannot divorce the one from the other. Without its existence, there is no pen left. Somehow, the pen seems to *consist* of its existence. It appears to be one and the same with it. I apologize for being so vague, but I find it impossible to be more precise at this point.

Of course, an entity cannot be identical with existence in general. If it were, then all entities would have to be identical with each other, since every one of them would be identical with existence. As a result, there would only exist one entity (God?). Now some philosophers may embrace this conclusion with open arms, but we shall not. We shall distinguish between existence in general, existence as a feature which every entity has, and the existence of a particular entity. But this distinction, too, must be made more precise later on. Taking it for granted for the moment, let me sum up my intuition about the relationship between an entity and its existence by saying that an entity does not exemplify its existence, but somehow *consists* of it.

(2) *Existence as a property of properties*

As we have seen, there is a traditional view of existence as a transcendental genus or category. But there is also a more recent view, widely accepted by contemporary philosophers, which Heidegger completely overlooks. This view goes back to Gottlob Frege, the same German philosopher whom we have mentioned on several previous occasions. It will take me a little while to explain this ingenious view to you.

In Aristotelian logic, certain arguments, called 'syllogisms', play a crucial role. Such syllogisms consist of sentences which have one of the four forms: All F are G, no F are G, some F are G, and some F are not G.

The following sentences are of these forms: all politicians are liars, no politicians are liars, some politicians are liars, and some politicians are not liars. Here is a syllogism which consists only of the first type of sentence:

All men are mortal

All Greeks are men

Therefore: All Greeks are mortal.

This argument is *valid*, that is, the conclusion follows logically from the two premises. Here is an example which is not valid:

Some men are Greeks

Some Greeks are wise

Therefore: Some men are wise.

Now, Frege proposed a certain interpretation of these and similar sentences, an interpretation which promises to enhance our understanding of logical reasoning. The four sentence forms are interpreted to mean:

(1) all things are such that: if they are F, then they are G;

(2) no things are such that: if they are F, then they are G;

(3) some things are such that: they are F and they are G;

(4) some things are such that: they are F and they are not G.

For example, the assertion that some politicians are liars becomes the assertion that some things are both politicians and liars. Admittedly, this reading is clumsy and not the best of English, but it is more perspicuous for philosophical (logical) purposes. What this assertion amounts to, according to Frege's theory, is that some things in the universe, some entities, have the property of being a politician and the property of being a liar.

These readings of the four forms (and of similar, more complicated, ones) are now accepted by practically all logicians and philosophers. And Frege's theory is generally hailed as one of the most important advances in the history of logic. But this is only the first step to Frege's view on the nature of existence. The second step consists in transforming the sentence form

(3) some things are such that: they are F and they are G

into: (5) *there are* things which are F and G.

For example, the assertion that some politicians are liars becomes the assertion that *there are* things which are politicians and liars. This is how existence enters into the picture!

Next, consider the assertion:

(6) Tigers exist.

We take this to be another way of saying:

(7) There are tigers.

And this turns into:

(8) There are things which are tigers (which is the same as: some things are tigers).

As the third and last step in his analysis of existence, Frege claims now that (8) attributes a certain property to the property of being a tiger, namely, the property of *not being empty*. He claims that (8) says that the property of being a tiger is not empty, that is, *that it is exemplified*. To say that tigers exist is to say that the property of being a tiger is not empty. Existence, therefore, consists in the property of properties of not being empty. *Existence is a property of properties.* The property of being a tiger has this property, that is, tigers exist; the property of being a mermaid, by contrast, does not have this property, that is, mermaids do not exist. Some properties have this peculiar property, while others do not.

Before we try to evaluate Frege's theory, I must briefly mention two points; one by way of illustration, the other, because it will become important later on. First, the minor point. It is clear that if Frege's analysis of existence is correct, then the ontological proof for the existence of God must fail. If existence is a property of properties, then it cannot be a property of individual things and, in particular, it cannot be a property of God. Thus existence cannot be among God's perfections. But, by the same token, what sense could it then possibly make, if we adopt Frege's point of view, to say that God exists or that Caesar exists? We shall return to this objection to Frege's view in a moment.

The second remark concerns the unfortunate practice of logicians and philosophers to speak of 'the existential quantifier'. They usually translate the sentence 'Tigers exist' into the more perspicuous '*There are things* which are tigers'. So far, so good.

But then they go on to call the phrase which I have italicized the 'existential quantifier' and *claim that existence is represented by the existential quantifier*. This practice confuses the true state of affairs. For, notice that the phrase 'there are things' fulfills two quite distinct functions. It gives you the *quantity* of the things involved and it also touches upon *existence*. What I have in mind becomes clear if we change

      (8) There are things which are tigers

into: (9) *Some things which there are*, are tigers,

and compare (9) with

      (10) *All things which there are*, are tigers,

and (11) *No things which there are*, are tigers.

In the italicized phrases of (9), (10), and (11) we can distinguish two parts, a part in which the three sentences differ, and a part which they share. (9) talks about *some* things which there are, while (10) talks about *all* things which there are, and (11) about *no* things which there are. But all three sentences talk about *things which there are*, that is about *entities*. You see now that the so-called existential quantifier 'There are things', which we have changed for reasons of perspicuity into 'Some things which there are', has two parts. There is a word that indicates the *quantity* of the things, and there is a phrase or word for existing things. What distinguishes among (9), (10), and (11) is the first word, the word that indicates the quantity: In (9), it is 'Some'; in (10), it is 'All'; and in (11), it is 'No'. I shall say that this word *represents* a quantifier; it is a word for a quantifier. You may recall that at one point I voiced the opinion that numbers are quantifiers. Well, the number four, for example, behaves in my opinion very much like the quantifier *all* or the quantifier *some* (which is usually taken to mean: at least one). For example, the assertion that there are four pens on my desk means: *four* things which there are, are pens on my desk.

But this is not the point I wish to make. Rather, what I want you to realize, firstly, is that only part of what is usually called 'the existential quantifier' is really an expression for a quantifier, namely, the part 'some' (or: at least one). The rest is a word for *entity*. Secondly, there are other words for other quantifiers: for example, 'no', 'all', 'almost all', 'quite a few', etc., plus all the numerals. Thirdly, the existential burden in (9) is carried, not by the quantifier word, but by the phrase 'things which there are' or, for short, by the word 'entity'. And this phrase also occurs in (10) and (11) which do not begin with the so-called *existential* quantifier. In my view, therefore, the so-called existential quantifier is doubly misnamed (aside from the fact that it is not the expression, but what the expression represents that is at stake). Firstly, only a part of the expression 'Some things which there are' is really an expression for a quantifier; and, secondly, the whole expression has no more to do with existence than other so-called quantifiers like 'All things which there are', 'No things which there are', 'Four things which there are', etc. I had to dwell on this apparently tedious point to some length because it is so important for your understanding of the view of existence which I shall later propose.

Let us return to Frege's view on existence. According to him, existence resides in the so-called existential quantifier, and this quantifier is said to represent a property of properties, namely, the property of not being empty. I have two main objections to his view. The first is that I do not know what to make of the alleged property of being empty. When I first mentioned this property, I explained it by saying that the property of being a tiger is not empty because it is *exemplified*. My problem with Frege's view is that I can only make sense of talk about a property which is not 'empty', if I take it to be a picturesque way of talking about a property which is exemplified. But to say of a property that it is exemplified is to say that *some thing which is there* has the property or, better, that some *entity* has the property. And this, of course, brings us back to the notion of existence.

I anticipated the second objection when I mentioned Frege's criticism of the ontological argument. If existence is a property of properties, then it cannot belong to individual things. Nor can it belong to sets, nor to facts, nor to numbers. But here we must be careful. Frege's view does not really state that existence is a property of properties. Rather, it holds that when we assert that something exists, we attribute a property to a property. To say that tigers exist, is to say that the property of being a tiger is not empty; to say that numbers exist, is to say that the property of being a number is not empty; to say that facts exist, is to say that the property of being a fact is not empty. And so on. So we can, after all, attribute existence to things other than properties.

But what we cannot do, and this is where my criticism is concentrated, is attribute existence to individual things. According to Frege's view, it makes no sense—it is literally nonsense—to say that Julius Caesar exists or that Hamlet does not exist. (Russell boldly claims, following in Frege's footsteps, that 'the individuals that there are in the world do not exist, or rather it is nonsense to say that they exist and nonsense to say that they do not exist') (B. Russell, *Logic and Knowledge*, ed., R. C. Marsh, London, Allen & Unwin, 1956, p. 252). It is easy to see why Frege (and Russell) must draw this absurd conclusion. To say that tigers exist is to say, according to his theory, that something has the property of being a tiger. To say that Caesar exists is to say that something has the property of being a Caesar. But this latter expression makes no sense, according to Frege (and Russell), because Caesar is not a property, but is an individual thing. (You must of course keep Caesar distinct from such properties as *being identical with Caesar* and *being a Caesar* in the sense of being an emperor of status.) It is therefore a direct consequence of Frege's view that it makes no sense to attribute existence to individual things. But since it quite obviously does make sense, Frege's view must be mistaken.

Existence, I claimed at the end of the last section, is not a property. It is much more intimately tied to what exists than are properties. An existent somehow consists of its existence. I shall now add a second characteristic of existence: existence is a feature that belongs to everything. It belongs to individual things no less than to properties, to numbers no less than to facts, to categories no less than to 'ordinary' properties. It makes sense to say of anything that it exists or that it does not exist. It even makes sense to say of existence that it exists! Not only does it make sense to say this, it must be true that existence exists. How could existence possibly not exist? If there were no such feature (whatever it may turn out to be) as existence, then nothing could have this feature. But this means that nothing would exist. Quite obviously, though, many things do exist. Hence existence must exist too.

(3) *Attempts to define existence*

If existence is neither a property nor a property of properties, what could it possibly be? When stumped, philosophers often resort to definitions. They proceed to define something as something else. One of the most ingenious attempts to define existence out of existence was proposed by Frege before he developed the theory which we have just discussed. (See his 'Dialog mit Pünjer über Existenz', in Gottlob Frege, *Schriften zur Logik und Sprachphilosophie*, Hamburg, Felix Meiner, 1971.) Frege starts out in this conversation with the idea that 'existence' is just an empty word, that to say of anything that it exists is completely uninformative. We learn nothing new about the entity *A*, when we realize that it exists. I think that Frege then asked himself what kind of statement has this character of being uninformative, and he noticed that statements of self-identity are of this sort. To say that *A* is identical with *A*, that *A* is self-identical, is to say something that (a) does not tell us what kind of thing *A* is, and (b) is true of everything. It is therefore like saying that *A* exists. Frege concluded that to assert *A*'s existence is nothing but to assert its being self-identical. He defined existence as self-identity. What he claimed was that there is really no such feature as existence, but only the fact that things are self-identical.

Frege's view implies, as you can easily see, that nonexistent objects, like the golden mountain, cannot be self-identical. Identity, he assumes, is a relation which can hold only between existents (and themselves). This assumption is not generally accepted. There are some philosophers who believe that everything is self-identical, every object of thought, whether it exists or not. Hamlet is identical with himself, according to this belief, just as Caesar is identical with himself. I agree with Frege on this point. Hamlet, I maintain, is not identical with himself, and the reason is the by now familiar one: just as Hamlet cannot be said to be indecisive, since he does not exist, so he cannot be said to be self-identical, since there is no such person. But, of course, once again, Hamlet can be *thought to be* indecisive and he can be *thought to be* self-identical. You are by now familiar with my line.

But even though I agree with Frege that identity only holds between entities, I do not agree with him that existence boils down to self-identity. It is true, of course, that every entity is self-identical, and that everything which is self-identical exists (is an entity), but this does not prove that one feature is the same as the other. My argument is not very strong. I just find it extremely implausible that I should be trying to convince you that werewolves are self-identical when I try to persuade you that they exist.

Another attempt to define existence away rests on the assumption that there are certain properties, 'existence-implying properties', which are such that object A exists if and only if it has at least one of these properties. To say of A that it exists is to say of it nothing more than that it has one of these properties. Precisely speaking, there is no such feature as existence, but only the fact that certain objects have certain properties. You know already that I think of all properties (and of all relations except the abnormal ones) as existence-implying: if Hamlet were indecisive, he would exist. I firmly believe in the ontological principle that every entity has (at least) a property and that everything that has a property is an entity. Still, I do not think that the fact that there are existence-implying properties can be used to define existence. And this for at least two decisive reasons. Firstly, I do not see how we could possibly distinguish between existence-implying properties and other properties without employing an independent notion of existence. Suppose we ask ourselves whether or not F is an existence-implying property. The only way in which we can decide this question is to ask whether or not something must *exist*, if it has the property F. But this question clearly uses a notion of existence other than the one in terms of existence-implying properties. If it did not, then the question would amount to asking whether or not something must have F or some other existence-implying property, if it has F. But clearly it does not. We are not asking whether or not something must have F, if it has F; for we know the answer to this question already. And we cannot be asking whether or not something must have some existence-implying property or other, say G, if it has F; for we cannot answer this question, unless we already know that certain properties are existence-implying.

The second reason is this one: to say that A exists, according to the proposed definition, is to say that A has some (at least one) existence implying property. But this is to say that *there is* an existence-implying property which A has. It is to say that one of the existents is an existence-implying property which A has. The expression which is used to define 'A exists' thus contains an expression for existence, either in the form of 'there is' or in the word 'existent' ('entity'). The definition is therefore worthless since it is circular.

Lastly, there is a rather widely accepted definition of existence in terms of the so-called existential quantifier. To say that an entity A exists, according to this definition, is to say that there is something which is identical with A. Let me write this down in a more formal manner:

(D) 'A exists' means 'There is a thing x such that: $x = A$'.

It seems to me to be quite obvious that this definition suffers the same shortcoming as the previous one: the notion of existence occurs in the defining condition–expressed by 'there is (a thing)'–so that the definition is circular. One may try to escape from this criticism by supplanting (D) by

(D') 'A exists' means 'Some (at least one) thing x is such that: $x = A$'.

But now we must recall our criticism of the logician's notion of the existential quantifier. The word 'some' ('at least one'), it is true, carries no existential commitment; it merely signifies the quantity in question. But the word 'thing' ('thing x') must here be understood to mean 'entity' rather than 'object'; for, only if it means the former can the definition be successful. Thus (D') must be changed into:

(D'') 'A exists' means 'some entity x is such that: $x = A$'.

And in (D'') the defining expression once again mentions existence in the form of entity and, hence, is circular.

(4) *Existence as the substance of the world*

You may be impatient by now. Do not tell us any more what existence is not, but tell us what it is, you may want to shout. Well, I am ready with my answer. Existence, I maintain, is an entity so unique that it does not fit into any known category. It is not even a category, as we have seen. For, if it were a category, it would have to be a property, and it is not a property. *Existence is the substance of the world.*

Existence appears in the world as that which is represented by the word (logicians speak here of 'variable') 'entity'. For example, the fact that all whales are mammals, if we believe in Frege's theory, is really the fact: all *entities* are such that: if they are whales, then they are mammals. Here existence occurs in the form of the entity *entity*, and we attribute the property of being a whale and attribute the property of being a mammal to it. (This is a little rough, but I think you know what I mean.) If we assert that some properties are exemplified, then we assert: some entities are such that: they are properties and they are exemplified. In this case, we attribute the property of being a property to the entity *entity*, and also the feature of being exemplified. In every fact which contains existence in the form of the entity *entity*, something is attributed to it. ('*Entity*' is, as a logician may put it, the *ultimate* variable.) On the other hand, the entity *entity* is never attributed to anything, not even to itself. Thus the entity *entity* is something to which one can attribute any property, but which cannot be attributed to anything. This is why I call it the *substance* of the world.

This conception of existence as a substance represented by the word 'entity', does not concur with the fact that 'existence' behaves grammatically somewhat like a predicate. From where I stand, therefore, I cannot but claim that in this case grammar is misleading. What we ordinarily express by

    (1) '*A* exists'

would, in my view, be more perspicuously represented by

    (2) 'Some (existent) *e* is such that: *e* = *A*'.

Put differently, (1) really means (2). (2) is the familiar definiens of the definition of existence in terms of the so-called existential quantifier. Note, though, that we do not think of (2) as *defining* existence. We do not claim that existence can somehow be eliminated in favor of the so-called existential quantifier. Rather, we are explicating that notion of existence, as it occurs in (1) by the entity existent (*e*), as it occurs in (2). We are claiming that to say of anything *A* that it exists is to say of *A* that it is an existent (an entity).

I think that this explication of the ontological nature of existence does justice to our earlier intuition that existence is somehow more intimately connected with the thing that exists than a property is. Existence I said, is not exemplified by an existent, but is part and parcel of it. Our explication implies that

193

an existent *A*, rather than *exemplifying* existence, *is identical with* an existent. The thing *A* is identical with its existence and is, therefore, most intimately connected with it. What could be more intimate in way of relationship than identity? Of course, I do not mean to say that *A* is identical with the entity *entity*. We do not have the following statement:

(3) $A = e$,

but rather the quite different assertion:

(4) Some *e* is such that: $e = A$.

And the difference between (3) and (4) points at the precise sense in which an entity *A* is and is not the same as its existence.

Existence, we agreed earlier, belongs to everything. Not only does Caesar exist, but so does the *color* midnight blue, the *number* three, and the *fact* that two plus two is four. Existence is not restricted to any particular category or categories. The fact that the number three exists, for example, is more perspicuously expressed by:

(5) Some *e* is such that: $e = 3$.

And the fact that the arithmetical fact just mentioned exists, is represented by:

(6) Some *e* is such that: $e = (2 + 2 = 4)$.

What about 'Tigers exist'? There is no problem:

(7) Some *e* is such that: *e* is a tiger.

Remember that 'some' means 'at least one', and that the 'is a' in 'is a tiger' represents exemplification. Thus to say of an individual thing that it exists is to say that it *is identical with* an existent, while to say of things which have a certain property that they exist is to say that some existents *exemplify* this property.

Perhaps, I have convinced you that my notion of existence does justice to several of our earlier intuitions. It agrees with Kant's conviction that existence is not a property. It agrees with the traditional conception of existence as being the very thing which exists. In this connection, let me make another important historical observation. According to the Aristotelian tradition, an individual thing–Berkeley's apple, for example–is a combination of *matter* and *essence*. From our point of view, it may be said to be a combination of *existence* and *essence*. Existence, if I am correct, plays much of the role which matter plays in that older tradition. But we must first purge this notion of matter of any association with physics or chemistry. Matter, in the meaning of existence, is not to be conceived of as consisting of atoms, or as being some kind of chemical stuff. *It is simply that indescribable ingredient of the world which, when 'informed' by various ordinary and categorial properties, yields the vast and glorious variety of things in the world, from apples to colors, from numbers to facts.*

Existence, I have insisted, belongs to everything. It even belongs to existence itself! How, I asked, could it be otherwise? If existence does not exist, then nothing can exist. My sentiment is forthright, but can we actually *say* that existence exists? Yes, we can. To say that a particular entity A exists, according to my view, is to say that A is identical with some existent. Similarly, to say that existence exists is to say that (all) existents are identical with existents:

(8) 'Existence exists' means 'All e are such that: $e = e$'.

And this comes down to saying that all entities are self-identical. Do you remember Frege's view about the connection between existence and self-identity? According to Frege, to say that A exists is to say that A is identical with itself. I argued that Frege is wrong. To say of A that it exists is to say, rather, that it is identical with an entity. But there is a kernel of truth in what Frege claims. What Frege maintains holds, not for individuals, or properties, or members of other categories, but it holds for existence itself. To say of the entity *entity* that it exists is indeed to say that it is self-identical.

(5) Another look at Heidegger's view

I am rather pleased, you may have noticed, that my explication of existence sheds some light on a number of philosophical convictions, namely, on:

(1) the Kantian claim that existence is not a property;

(2) the traditional suspicion that existence is part of a thing;

(3) the widely accepted definition of existence in terms of the so-called existential quantifier;

and (4) Frege's claim that existence is self-identity.

To this list, I shall now add a fifth item and sixth item:

(5) Heidegger's hints that existence is the substance of man;

and (6) his claim that existence is always individuated.

It goes without saying, that there are vast differences between Heidegger's view and my explication of existence. Most importantly, I have criticized his view that there are modes of existence (or of being). If I am correct, then there is no difference between the existence of an apple and the existence of Heidegger. But this vast difference must not blind us to the fact that my explication has some affinity to the two positions expressed in (5) and (6). I think that this is obvious in the case of (5). Existence, I have said, is the substance of the world. Well, if it is the substance of the world, then it is certainly the substance of every human being in the world. It is that ultimate subject of which we attribute everything, including such properties as those of being a human being, of being wise, of being a philosopher, etc. But existence is, of course, also the ultimate subject of which we attribute all other properties. Nothing could show more emphatically how much our view also differs from Heidegger's.

Caesar exists, and so does Brutus. And, of course, Caesar is not the same person as Brutus. This means, expressed in our philosophical terminology, that some entity is Caesar, that some entity is Brutus, and that the former is not identical with the latter!

(7) Some e_1 is such that: e_1 = Caesar; some e_2 is such that: e_2 = Brutus; and $e_1 \neq e_2$.

In order to express that two entities are not the same, we have to break up the notion of entity (the e) into several separate parts (into several e's). We indicate these different parts by subscripts. Our variable is of only one sort. This is indicated by the letter 'e' which is short for 'entity'. But we need several variables, one for each entity in question. In this sense, existence fragments into many pieces. In this sense, we adopt Heidegger's thesis that existence is always individuated. Existence always appears as *my* existence, or as *your* existence, or as *Caesar's* existence. For I am identical with some entity, e_1, while you are identical with a different entity, e_2, and Caesar is identical with still a different entity, e_3.

We shall now return to the very beginning of our discussion

of Heidegger's view. Heidegger, we saw, starts out with the question of all questions: what is being? But he turns almost immediately to a much narrower question: what is human being? And he never again returns to the first question; the promised answer is never given. But since he raised the question of being in the first place, since he made such a monumental to-do about it, this silence must appear to him and us as an admission that he has failed, not only in the task which he has set for himself, but in his very conception of the task of philosophy. With so much at stake, why does Heidegger never return to the question of being? I think there is a very good reason for his silence, and I shall conclude our discussion of Heidegger with an explanation of this reason.

In a nutshell, the reason is this: Heidegger's conception of Existence as the substance of man is incompatible with his belief that there are many modes of Existence. More generally, the view that existence is the substance of the world is incompatible with the view that there are modes of existence. Let me make out the general case. Assume that we adopt the view that each category of things has its distinct kind of existence. Individuals have one kind of existence, properties have a different kind of existence, relations have a third kind of existence, and so on. Assume also that we locate existence, in the spirit of my explication, in the entity *entity*. This means, more precisely, that we need a number of variables corresponding to the various modes of existence. One kind of variable–the various 'e_1', 'e_2', 'e_3'–will no longer suffice. The existence of individual things, for example, will occur in the form of the variable, 'i_1', 'i_2', 'i_3'. etc.; the existence of properties will occur in the form of the variable 'p_1', 'p_2', 'p_3', etc.; the existence of relations will occur in the form of the variable 'r_1', 'r_2', 'r_3', etc. and so on. To say that Caesar exists is now to say that Caesar is identical with some i; to say that the property of being midnight blue exists is to say that this color is identical with some p; to say the intentional nexus exists is to say that it is identical with some r. And so on.

Let us take as our example the assertion that Caesar exists, which becomes:

(8) Some i is such that: i = Caesar.

Here the 'i' no longer stands just for 'entity' or 'existent'. Rather, it must be read to mean 'entity of the kind of being i'. As soon as we spell out what (8) means, we have to distinguish between existence, on the one hand, and various kinds or modes of existence, on the other. But if we hold that existence forms the substance of the world, then modes of existence become inevitably properties and features of one and the same substance, namely, of existence. There simply cannot be different kinds of existence in a sense of 'kinds' which does not amount to there being different features, characteristics, or properties of existence. To put it differently, the very notion of existence as the ultimate substance precludes the possibility of there being different kinds of existence. *For, existence so conceived allows for no qualitative difference.* All the qualitative similarity and difference there is in the world, traces back to properties and relations. If existence is conceived of as the substance of the world, then there can be many *existents*, but there can be no varieties of *existence*.

If this assessment is correct, then it becomes clear why Heidegger's project is doomed to failure. Heidegger wishes to hold two incompatible views. But if he persists in his view that existence is the substance of the world, then he must give up the view that there is a variety of existence. And if he retains the latter view, then he must reject the former. This lesson goes beyond the confines of Heidegger's version of Existentialism. It holds for all existentialistic ontologies. An Existentialist has no choice. He must either reject the notion that there are modes of being, or else he must give up the view that being is a substance rather than a property. But he cannot do the former, for this would mean giving up his most distinct and cherished thesis, the thesis of the privileged status of human Existence. Existentialism without this thesis is as interesting as macaroni is without cheese. And he is loath to do the latter, for this implies that man is not free. This part of the story is best told in connection with Sartre's philosophy.

Part IV

Jean-Paul Sartre: the quest for freedom

12. The structure of mind

(1) *Being-in-itself and being-for-itself*

In his first philosophical work, *The Transcendence of the Ego* (New York, Farrar, Straus & Giroux, no date), Sartre lays the foundation for one of the main theses of his later philosophy, namely, for the thesis that man is unconditionally free. He argues in this short work that, although there are minds (Sartre uses the term 'consciousnesses'), there are no selves. We shall look at his arguments in a moment, and then I shall also explain what difference there is between a mind and a self. But at first, I would like to explain to you what Sartre's rejection of selves has to do with safeguarding human freedom. In order to understand the connection, we must consider three apparently quite distinct ideas. It is a measure of Sartre's ingenuity that he linked these three ideas together.

The first idea is Husserl's claim that consciousness enjoys a special exalted ontological status. Sartre adopts this view, but wraps it up in a catchy terminology (which he takes from G. W. F. Hegel). Consciousness, he says, has *being-for-itself*, while everything else has merely *being-in-itself*. He claims that there are two modes of being, one enjoyed by consciousness, the other by everything else. But this dichotomy is built not on the commonly used distinction between things which are intentional (mental acts, consciousness) and things which are not, but on Brentano's idea that every mental act is its own awareness.

You may recall the infinite regress argument against the existence of mental acts. If one assumes (a) that every mental act which occurs in a mind is an act of which the mind is conscious, and (b) that such consciousness must occur in the form of a second act, then it follows, as we saw, that whenever there occurs an act in a mind, an infinite number of further acts must also be present in that mind. Some philosophers accepted assumptions (a) and (b) and concluded that, since a mind cannot contain infinitely many mental acts, no mental acts at all can exist. Others concluded from the argument that at least one of the two assumptions must be false. Brentano, I pointed out, rejects assumption (b), while I reject (a). Brentano holds that a mind can be conscious of a mental act without there being a second act which is conscious of the first. But in what does this second consciousness then consist? Brentano answers that every mental act is its own consciousness, that every mental act is self-conscious. A mental act, according to this fascinating doctrine, has two objects: a primary object, for example, whatever happens to be desired, and a secondary object, which is always the act itself. You may also recall that I spoke in this connection of a snake with two heads: a mental act is like such a snake; while the one head strikes at a certain object, the other head bites the snake's tail. And you may further remember that I argued that Brentano's doctrine is almost certainly false.

Now, if Brentano's doctrine were true, then we would have discovered a new feature which distinguishes between mental acts, on the one hand, and everything else, on the other. Mental acts and only mental acts are self-conscious in the way described. Mental acts and only mental acts exist, not only in themselves, but also *for themselves*! Sartre uses Brentano's idea to set mental acts (consciousness) apart from everything else and to endow them with a special kind of being.

So far, we have connected Husserl's idea of the special ontological status of consciousness with Brentano's doctrine about the self-consciousness of mental acts. We can now understand why Sartre argues against the existence of selves. A self would be a mental entity other than a mental act. Hence it would have to be something which is not conscious of itself. Therefore, it would have to have being-in-itself rather than being-for-itself. Consciousness, in the sense of mind, would therefore have to contain a being-in-itself. Consciousness would not be pure and utterly diaphanous. But I better let Sartre himself speak, since he is a master of hyperbole. 'If it [the self] existed', he says, 'it would tear consciousness from itself; it would divide consciousness; it would slide into every consciousness like an opaque blade. The transcendental I [the self] is the death of consciousness' (*The Transcendence of the Ego*, p. 40).

Consciousness, Sartre asserts, must be pure self-consciousness. What remains is to connect this dogma with his defense of freedom. The verbal bridge between the characteristic of self-consciousness and freedom consists of the term 'spontaneity'. Consciousness is unconditionally free, because it is totally spontaneous. And it is totally spontaneous, because it is wholly self-conscious. Here is how Sartre builds the bridge between self-consciousness and spontaneity:

> We call spontaneous an existence which determines its own existence by itself. In other words, to exist spontaneously is to exist for itself and by itself. Then a single reality deserves to be called spontaneous; namely consciousness. For it, in effect, to exist and to be conscious of existing are one and the same. In other words, the great ontological law of consciousness is the following: The only mode of existence for a consciousness is to have the consciousness that it exists. (*L'Imagination*, Paris, Presses Universitaires de France, 1969, 7th edn., pp. 125–6)

It is clear that the crucial step in Sartre's chain of argument is the one from self-consciousness to self-determination. We may agree with Sartre, at least for the sake of the present argument, that consciousness is self-consciousness. We may also agree, for the same reason, that an entity is properly called spontaneous if it creates ('determines') itself. But I think we should balk at Sartre's identification of self-consciousness with self-creation.

At any rate, I hope to have shown why Sartre argues so vehemently against the existence of selves. Selves would not be self-conscious and, hence, not spontaneous. And this means, in turn, that selves would not be free.

(2) *The existence of selves*

A mind is a succession of mental states; and each mental state consists of an experience and the conscious state which is experienced. What is experienced is in every instance, a complicated structure consisting of mental acts, feeling, images, and sensations. The question of whether or not there are selves is the question of whether or not a mind contains an individual thing which is neither a mental act, nor a feeling, nor an image, nor a sensation.

The question of whether or not there are selves was revived in modern times by David Hume. He denies that there are selves in the following famous passage from his book *A Treatise of Human Nature*:

> For my part, if I enter most intimately into what I call *myself*, I always stumble on some particular perception or other, of heat or cold, light or shade, love or hatred, pain or pleasure. I never can catch *myself* at any time without a perception, and never can observe anything but the perception. (book I, part IV, section vi)

Hume appeals to introspection. Whenever he looks into himself, that is, into his mind, so he claims, he finds mental acts and sensations, but he never finds another individual thing, something that may be called a 'self'. Is Hume right? You must decide for yourself. Look into your mind. What do you find? I think that we can all agree that you will find there perceptions, desires, hopes, wishes, fears, questions, etc., and you will also find pains and pleasures, itches and tickles; you will find joy and despair. But do you also find a self? As for myself, I shall surprise you by seeming to be, for once, wishy-washy: In a sense, I do find a self; in another sense, I find no such thing. If by a 'self' you mean a mental entity of a unique kind, different from mental acts, sensations, images, and feelings, then I agree with Hume: I do not find such an entity when I scour the content of my mind. Yet, I do discover something in my mind which is peculiar, something which could easily be mistaken for a self. I shall tell you later on what this thing is.

Sartre sides with Hume: there is no self. We know why he does. A self would cut the mind into two irreconcilable parts. How does Sartre argue for his contention: well, he does not present an argument against the existence of selves, not any more than Hume does. But he tries to refute a traditional argument for the existence of selves. I shall call this argument 'the argument from the unity of the mind'. According to this argument, there must be selves because otherwise nothing would bind the various mental acts, sensations, images, and feelings together so as to form one mind as distinguished from another mind. The argument from the unity of the mind has two parts. Let us look at each one separately.

Imagine that time stands still, so that all the mental things there are in the world are frozen in one moment. At this moment in the world history, there exist then a large number of mental acts, sensations, feelings and images, namely, all of the acts, sensations, feelings and images which human beings experience at that moment. For example, there may exist a certain act of seeing, E_1, a certain desire, D_1, three sensations, S_1, S_2, and S_3, and two feelings, F_1 and F_2. We can now raise the question: does desire D_1 exist in the same mind as the act of seeing E_1? Or we may ask: does sensation S_1 occur in the same mind as feeling F_1? Generally speaking, we may ask which acts, sensations, images, and feelings occur in which minds. We have here another 'bundling problem'. What is there about our frozen world of mental things that tells us how many minds (bundles) there are at that moment and what mental things belong to what minds (bundles)?

The defender of selves claims that this bundling problem is easily solved if we assume that there are selves, while it cannot be solved without them. If there are selves, then our world of mental things will contain, not only mental acts, sensations, feelings, and images, but also a certain number of those selves. Obviously, the number of selves is the same as the number of distinct minds which exist at that moment. Thus we can easily answer the question of how many different minds there are at that moment: We merely have to count how many selves there are. And if we wish to know, for example, whether or not desire D_1 exists in the same mind as the act of seeing E_1, we merely have to establish whether or not D_1 and E_1 belong to the same self. The bundling problem is solved, because we know how many minds there are by counting the selves, and we know what belongs together in one mind by discovering what is associated with one self. This solution to the problem makes two crucial assumptions. Firstly, it assumes that we know how many selves there are at a given moment. Secondly, it takes for granted that we know what mental acts, etc., belong to what selves.

Sartre claims that the problem of the unity of the mind (at a moment) can be solved without selves. But he does not explain how it can be solved. Or, rather, he gives an explanation which makes absolutely no sense to me. So I shall merely cite the relevant passage and let it go at that.

> Now, it is certain that phenomenology does not need to appeal to any such unifying and individualizing *I* [self]. Indeed, consciousness is defined by intentionality. By intentionality consciousness transcends itself. It unifies itself by escaping from itself. The unity of a thousand active consciousnesses by which I have added, do add, and shall add two and two to make four, is the transcendent object 'two and two make four'. Without the permanence of this eternal truth a real unity would be impossible to conceive, and there would be irreducible operations as often as there were operative consciousnesses. (*Ibid.*, p. 38)

Granted that all mental acts of adding two and two, not only Sartre's, but of all the people in the world intend the very same fact, namely, the fact that two and two is four, I simply fail to see how this truth contributes to the solution of the problem of the unity of the mind as I have outlined it. Turning away from Sartre, can we solve this problem in some other way without relying on selves? I think so. Recall our description of a mental state at a moment. Such a state, we said, consists of (a) an act of experience, A_1, and (b) of a conscious state (which contains all the mental things experienced by A_1). Now remember the question before us: does desire D_1 occur in the same mind as the act of seeing E_1? It is obvious how we can answer this question: D_1 and E_1 belong to the same mind if and only if they are parts of the same conscious state. And they belong to the same conscious state, of course, if and only if they are experienced by the same act of experiencing. You can see that mental acts of experience play in our solution to the problem the same role as the selves do in the solution of the proponent of selves. Just as selves are supposed to bundle various mental things so that they form one mind, so acts of experiencing tie together acts, feelings, images and sensation. Our solution to the problem makes the same two assumptions. Firstly, we assume that we know how many acts of experiencing there are, so that we know how many minds there are. Secondly, we assume that we know what mental things are intended by which acts of experiencing. (I cannot resist a remark addressed to the philosophical sophisticates among my readers: the acts of experience of our analysis are what Kant so ponderously describes as 'the transcendental unity of apperception'.)

What I said in the last paragraph is not quite accurate. According to our view, *two* acts of experiencing may belong to the same mind at a given moment. For example, when instead of desiring something at a given moment, you inspect your desire, then you will experience an experience of a desire. In this case, your conscious state contains, not the desire but an experiencing of the desire. Figure 12.1 is a diagram of this situation.

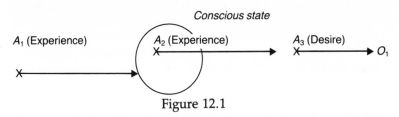

Figure 12.1

In this case, too, there is an act of experiencing, A_1, which determines what belongs to the given conscious state. It is this act which gives unity to the mind at that moment. But it is not true, as I claimed earlier, that you can tell how many minds there are by counting how many acts of experience there are at the moment. Rather, you must count how many acts of experience there are which *are not themselves experienced*. With this slight complication, our solution to the problem of the unity of the mind (at a moment) holds.

The second part of the problem concerns the unity of the mind through time. What ties successive mental states to each other, so that they form a mind that lasts through time? Assume that at a certain moment, t_1, there exists a certain mental state, M_1, and that at a later time, t_2, there exists another mental state, M_2. Under what conditions do M_1 and M_2 belong to the same rather than to different minds? Sartre's answer is short and, this time, to the point. He says: 'It is consciousness which unifies itself, concretely, by a play of "transversal" intentionalities which are concrete and real retentions of past consciousnesses' (*ibid.*, p. 39). In other words, it is memory of past mental things which tells us what belongs to our minds. Assume that M_1 contained a desire, and that M_2 contains a memory of this desire. In this case M_1 is obviously a part of the history of the mind to which M_2 belongs. Of course, the fact that I cannot remember a certain thought, for example, does not mean that I have never had this thought, that it is not a part of my past mind. There are numerous past mental acts of mine which I cannot remember right now, or which I shall not be able to remember at all. On the other hand, the fact that I seem to remember the bed in which I slept as a baby does not mean that I really remember having seen the bed. Our memory of past experiences is notoriously unreliable. But if I do remember a past desire, then I can be sure that it belonged to my mind.

How does the proponent of selves solve the problem? Not surprisingly, his solution is not all that different from ours and Sartre's. It, too, must rely on memory. Whether or not M_1 belongs together with M_2 will depend on whether or not the self connected with M_1 is the same self as the one associated with M_2. The self associated with M_2 must therefore remember what the self of M_1 was. If it remembers what the self of M_1 was, then it compares the two selves and decides whether or not they are the same. But if we assume, as we have all along, that one can only remember one's own mental past, then the comparison becomes superfluous; for if one can remember the past self, then it must be the same as the present self. Moreover, even the memory of the past self becomes superfluous: If I can remember the state M_1, then I already know that it was one of my own mental states. I do not have to consider the self at all.

How do we know that we can only remember our own past mental states? This question is not easily answered. There is much more to the problem of the unity of the mind than we can here discuss. What we are interested in is Sartre's claim that a self is not required to solve the problem. And on this point, I concur with him.

(3) *The transcendence of the ego*

Sartre holds that there is no self, no I, *in* consciousness. But he also maintains that there is an ego, an I, *for* consciousness. To avoid confusion, I shall sharply distinguish between selves and egos. Selves, according to Sartre, do not exist, but egos do. What is an ego, as distinguished from a self? Well, first of all and most importantly, an ego is never part of consciousness, it is never *in* consciousness. Rather, it is always an object *for* consciousness. This means, in our terminology, that an ego is not part of a mental state, but an object for the mind. Secondly, an ego is presented to the mind in a peculiar fashion. It occurs before the mind only, as Sartre puts it, 'in *reflective consciousness*'. I shall not beat around the bush any longer, however, and tell you that an ego is roughly the same thing as a mind. Sartre holds, therefore, that although there are no selves, there are minds. Put this way, his view is scarcely exciting. But he also has a theory about how the mind appears before itself, and this theory deserves our attention.

The ego, Sartre claims, appears only before *reflective consciousness*:

> The fact that can serve for a start is, then, this one: each time we apprehend our thought, whether by an immediate intuition or by an intuition based on memory, we apprehend an *I* which is the *I* of the apprehended thought, and which is given, in addition, as transcending this thought and all other possible thoughts. If for example, I want to remember a certain landscape perceived yesterday from the train, it is

209

possible for me to bring back the memory of that landscape as such. But I can also recollect that *I* was seeing that landscape. (*Ibid.*, p. 43)

Let us translate Sartre's view into our terminology. For 'consciousness' we can in general substitute 'mental act' or 'mental acts'. We can then distinguish between a reflecting mental act and a reflected (upon) mental act. A reflecting mental act is an act which has another mental act for an object. This latter act is the reflected act. When Sartre looked at the landscape from the train window, there occurred, according to him, a certain unreflected act of seeing. Its object was the landscape. Like all mental acts, of course, this act is also its own awareness, as we noted a moment ago. According to Sartre, therefore, we can depict the seeing of the landscape as in Figure 12.2

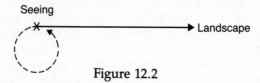

Figure 12.2

According to our analysis, by contrast, the situation would look like Figure 12.3.

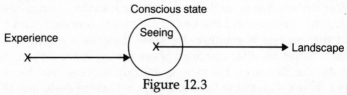

Figure 12.3

Next, we must consider what happens when Sartre remembers that he saw the landscape. There occurs then, according to his view, an act of remembering of an act of seeing. This act of remembering is a reflecting act; it intends the act of seeing. The act of seeing is in this situation the reflected upon act. And the diagram of the situation looks like Figure 12.4.

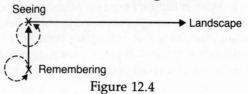

Figure 12.4

210

Again, our analysis yields the quite different diagram in Figure 12.5.

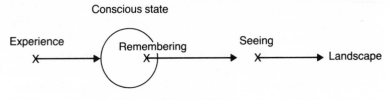

Figure 12.5

Now, according to Sartre, Figure 12.4 is incomplete as it stands; for he holds that the ego appears before the reflecting consciousness. In our specific case, this means that the act of remembering must somehow point, not only at the past act of seeing, but also at something called 'the ego'. Where shall we put the ego? And how shall we diagram it? Sartre does not provide us with too many hints. At one point he says that the *I* is apprehended 'Always inadequately, *behind* the reflected consciousness' (My italics, *ibid.*, p. 53). And at another place he puts it this way: 'Indeed, for this very reason the *I* appears veiled, indistinct, *through* consciousness, like a pebble at the bottom of the water' (my italics, *ibid.*, pp. 51–2). I am not sure that any diagram can do full justice to what Sartre has in mind, but I shall try and propose Figure 12.6 as improvement on Figure 12.4.

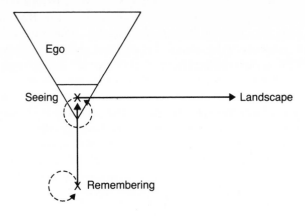

Figure 12.6

211

The triangle which stands on its head is supposed to be the ego (Sartre's 'I'). It is supposed to remind you of an iceberg. Just as only a small portion of an iceberg is visible above the water line, so only a small part of the ego is directly presented to the reflecting consciousness. This small part of the ego is the reflected upon act of seeing the landscape. But just as one is somehow aware of the whole iceberg, even though one can only see its tip, so one may be said to apprehend the whole ego when one reflects upon a tiny part of it, the act of seeing. Whenever one reflects upon a mental act, according to Sartre's view, one is indirectly aware of the whole of which this mental act is a part, namely, of the ego. What Sartre's view should remind you of is Husserl's doctrine of the perspectival aspect of all perception. Just as perceptual object, say an apple, is according to this doctrine given to perception only in part, only from one side, so the ego is presented to reflective consciousness only partially, 'from one side'. Just as there is more to an apple than what you can see, or smell, or taste, etc., from one 'point of view', so there is more to the ego than what you can reflect upon in one act of consciousness. Just as the apple is really a complicated structure consisting of many aspects, so the ego is really a complicated structure consisting of many mental things. If we substitute 'mind' for 'ego', Sartre's view boils down to this: in reflecting consciousness, one is aware of a part of the mind (the reflected upon act); and by being aware of this part, one is indirectly also aware of the whole mind of which this is a part; for to be aware of a part *as a part of a whole*, is to be aware of the whole.

Sartre's insistence that the ego appears only before reflective consciousness poses a problem. How do we know that the ego does not also appear before unreflected consciousness? We cannot possibly 'take a look' at unreflected consciousness in order to find out whether ot not it is presented with an ego; for if we take a look, we turn unreflected consciousness immediately into reflected upon consciousness. But if we cannot take a look, how can we answer the question? The problem does not arise for our analysis. To see this, you only have to compare Figure 12.2 with our analysis as depicted in Figure 12.3. As you can see, there is, according to our analysis, no such thing as unreflected consciousness. The seeing which occurs when Sartre rides the train is, in our view, already reflected upon, namely, by the act of experiencing. Sartre's case of reflected consciousness turns out to be upon our analysis, a case of *doubly* reflected consciousness: An act of experience reflects upon an act of remembering which, in turn, reflects upon an act of seeing. Since there occurs an act of experiencing in Figure 12.3, we could claim that this act informs us that in this case the ego does not appear on the scene. But Sartre has no such act of experiencing. How, then, does he know that the ego does not make an appearance in this situation?

He tries to come to grips with the issue by calling our attention to the broken arrow in Figure 12.2. Since every act is automatically a consciousness of itself, he argues, there exists also a memory which does not consist of a separate act (*ibid.*, p. 46). He claims that the act of seeing is not only a consciousness of itself, but also a memory of itself. This claim makes even less sense than the earlier one about the self-consciousness of all mental acts. I have already argued, in connection with Brentano's view, that a seeing, for example, cannot possibly be its own awareness; for if it were, then a seeing would have to *see* itself, and we cannot see mental acts of any kind. Now Sartre goes even further and claims that a seeing can be its own remembering, that there can be a memory of the seeing without there being a separate act of remembering. How could one possibly diagram this claim? Do we have to add a second broken arrow? But where would it go? If we add it in Figure 12.2, issuing from the act of seeing and pointing at it, we get the absurd result that the seeing is its own memory *while it occurs*. Perhaps, the second broken arrow must be added to the Figure 12.4, issuing from the act of remembering and pointing to the act of seeing. But this would not help to solve Sartre's problem. For Figure 12.4 depicts a case of reflected consciousness, and we know that the ego appears on the scene in such a case. I simply do not see how Sartre can solve the problem before us with the tools of his analysis of consciousness. Nor can I be persuaded when I read how Sartre proposes to reflect upon consciousness without reflecting upon it:

That consciousness [for example, the act of seeing] must not be posited as object of a reflection. On the contrary, I must direct my attention on the revived objects [the landscape], but without losing sight of the unreflected consciousness, by joining in a sort of conspiracy with it and by drawing up an inventory of its content in a non-positional manner. (*Ibid.*, p. 46)

What an intriguing and typically Sartrean thought: The mind conspires with itself against itself!

Reflective consciousness is presented with the ego, that is, with the mind. Now, remember my earlier 'wishy-washy' answer to the question of whether or not there are selves. I sided with Hume and Sartre in claiming that the mind does not contain anything but mental acts, sensations, images and feelings. But I also hinted that it contains something that could easily be mistaken for a self. Sartre's distinction between reflective and unreflective consciousness allows me to make my point clear. I think that one experiences one's self in those situations in which one inspects the content of one's conscious state. If you have a certain desire, you live *in* this desire, and you are directed toward its object. This is a case of unreflected consciousness. But if you now take a look at your desire, if you ask yourself, for example, 'Is it desire or revulsion which I feel for this person?', then you have stepped back, your attention is no longer focused on the object of the desire, but on the desire itself. Now the situation looks like Figure 12.7.

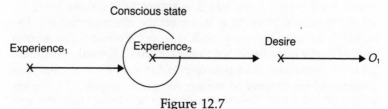

Figure 12.7

What you experience is, not straightforwardly the desire, but an *experience* of the desire. What is now part of your conscious state is, not the desire, but an experience of the desire. It is this experience, I submit, which is the self. What you experience in an introspective situation–Sartre's reflective consciousness–is the kind of mental act which, ordinarily, transcends all of your conscious mental acts. What you experience is precisely the kind of thing which, ordinarily, experiences your desires, wishes, hopes, your images, sensations, and feelings. In short, you experience now what ordinarily experiences your conscious state. And this thing, I suggest, is precisely the self which many philosophers have claimed to have discovered within their minds.

This self is a mental act. But it is a very special mental act. It is the kind of act which lies *behind* all of our mental phenomena. Even in introspection, as our figure shows, the self cannot really look at *itself*. There is another act of experience which is an experience of an experience of the desire. In our introspective situation, this act is the hidden self, the transcendent self. But, and this is the point, this self experiences now a mental act *which is of the same kind* as itself. It experiences *the type of mental act* which in a case of plain desire experiences the desire. It experiences the kind of mental act which is always there, *behind* our conscious states, but which only appears *in* consciousness during introspection.

(4) *The constitution of the ego*

The self which we encounter in introspection is an act of experiencing. The ego of Sartre's analysis, on the other hand, is a complicated structure consisting of various mental things. It is, roughly, what we have called 'a mind'. This ego is the transcendental unity of an infinity of consciousnesses. Just as the apple which you see is, according to Husserl, the transcendental unity of an infinity of perceptions, so the ego is the transcendental unity of an infinity of mental things. But this structure itself consists of substructures, namely, of so-called 'states' and 'actions'. The ego, according to Sartre, is therefore a structure of structures.

Sartre uses hatred as an example of a state. Whenever Sartre sees Peter, the object of his hatred, he feels a profound repugnance. When he reflects upon this feeling, he becomes aware of his hatred for Peter. Thus his hatred for Peter reveals itself through this feeling of repugnance. The feeling is the tip of the iceberg which is his hatred for Peter. Quite obviously, just as the feeling is not all there is to Sartre's ego (mind), so the feeling is not all there is to Sartre's hatred for Peter. This hatred may also reveal itself through its other aspects. And it may be said to exist even at times when Sartre does not think of Peter. In short, Sartre's hatred is a transcendental structure, which is part of a larger structure, the ego, and which appears to consciousness behind particular mental acts, for example, behind acts of repugnance. Figure 12.8 tries to catch these features.

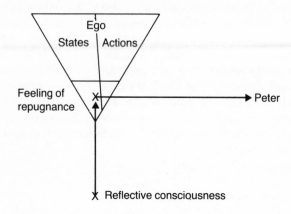

Figure 12.8

Since hatred is a transcendental structure, since it is only presented to us through certain mental acts, we can, according to Sartre, make mistakes about such states. Sartre can be quite sure that at a certain moment he feels repugnance toward Peter. But does this prove that he hates him? Perhaps, it is merely a fleeting emotion. It may not be part of a larger whole, part of a pattern concerning his emotional responses to Peter. Similarly, for love and other states: people may easily make mistakes about them. We know that they may even mistake hate for love, and conversely.

Sartre touches with his description of states on an important topic which we have so far, in our analysis of mind, completely neglected. A mind, I have said time and again, ultimately consists of mental acts, feelings, sensations, images, and of *nothing else*. But this list omits a large number of features and traits which we ordinarily attribute to the minds of human beings. We say that John *loves* Mary. He has *loved* her for many years, and he will *love* her until the day he dies. This *love* cannot be a momentary mental act, or a fleeting feeling. Nor is it a sensation or an image. None of these things lasts as love sometimes does. Nor do they take on the many different aspects which love shows. Yet, love is undeniably a mental phenomenon. Is our analysis then incomplete? Have we left out the most important emotion of them all? It is clear, I think that John's love for Mary somehow *consists* of feelings of pleasure at the sight of her, twinges of desire when he touches her, feelings of affection when he realizes that she needs consolation, and of many more things. But it is not identical with any one of these things. According to Sartre, John's love for Mary is a complicated structure consisting of all of these mental acts, feelings, sensations, and images. I think that this is a splendid solution to the problem of how love can be a mental phenomenon without being identical with any one of the mental contents we have mentioned. But it is not the only solution to the problem. Love, one may hold, is a *disposition*. Let me explain what is meant by a 'disposition'.

A sugar cube is white. It has this particular color, and you can verify that it has this color by looking at it. A sugar cube is also *soluble*. This is another of its properties. But you cannot tell that it has this property by merely looking at it. You must put the cube into your coffee (or some other liquid) and watch it dissolve. To say of the sugar cube that it is soluble is to attribute to it a *dispositional property*, (or disposition, for short), namely, the property to be able to *dissolve, when put into a liquid*. When you attribute this property to the sugar cube, you are in effect saying that it obeys a certain law, namely, the law: if x is put into some liquid, then x dissolves. A dispositional property is really a contracted law of nature. To attribute such a property to something is to say that the thing obeys the law.

Many of the properties which we ascribe to things and persons are dispositional in character. Sugar is soluble, metal is malleable, rubber is elastic, glass is brittle, etc. People are intelligent, brave, considerate, unkind, overbearing, nasty, etc. As you see, all of the so-called character traits are dispositional. To say that John is intelligent is to say that he would behave intelligently under certain circumstances, that is, that he would behave in a certain fashion under these circumstances. For example, if he were given an intelligence test, his score would be high. To say that Mary is brave is to say, similarly, that she would behave in certain ways in certain situations; for example, that she would risk her own life to save her neighbors from a burning house.

There are even dispositions to have dispositions. John, for example, easily falls in love. He has the disposition to have the dispositional property of being in love. To say that he is in love is to say that he has a disposition to act in certain ways under certain circumstances. To say that he easily falls in love is to say that he has the disposition to act repeatedly in these ways under those circumstances. But let us return to John's love for Mary. As I just said, we may think of his love as a dispositional property (concerning Mary). To say that John is in love with Mary is to say that he acts in certain ways in regard to Mary. When Mary enters the room his face lights up; he feels aglow with affection for her. This feeling at this moment is not the whole of his love for Mary. It is merely one manifestation of many. On another occasion, John will be tormented by jealousy, when he sees Mary dancing with someone else. This emotion, too, is merely a small part of his love. If John truly loves Mary, then we expect him to think, feel, and act in certain typical ways toward her. We expect that he thinks, feels, and acts according to a rather vague and unformulated law, the law that governs lovers' behavior everwhere.

Just as we believe that the law about the solubility of sugar has a foundation in the molecular structure of sugar, so we also believe that the law about the behavior of people in love has a foundation in their biological nature and their social environment. Sugar is soluble because it has a certain molecular structure. People act so strangely when they are in love, because they are animals of a very special sort. But there is a difference, of course, between these two examples. We know the law about the molecular structure of sugar and its solubility very well, but we know as yet very little about the biological and social structure of human beings. In either case, though, it is true that the dispositional property encapsulates a rather vague law behind which we search for more precise, more 'scientific', laws.

Sartre mentions dispositions–he calls them 'qualities'–but distinguishes them sharply from states (*ibid.*, pp. 70–1). Hate (and love), he insists, is a state rather than a disposition. But I think that one could reasonably hold that it is the latter. On both views, though, the problem is solved of how love can be a mental phenomenon without being a mental act, a feeling, a sensation, or an image. It is a mental phenomenon, we hold, because it is a disposition (or, in Sartre's view, a state) to react with certain acts, feelings, sensations, and images in certain situations. As always, these mental phenomena in turn, cause certain actions, so that we can tell that John is in love with Mary, not by inspecting his mental acts, feelings, sensations, and images, but by watching him act in certain situations.

Actions, according to Sartre, are the second main kind of transcendent structure that enters into constituting the ego. An action is usually a combination of a series of mental states with a series of bodily movements. In some cases, the bodily movements may be pronounced, for example, when the wide receiver of the American football team runs his pattern and catches a pass from the quarterback. In other cases, the mental activity may be dominant, for example, when someone plays chess. But in almost every case, for an action to occur, certain mental processes as well as certain forms of physical behavior must be present. It is understandable, therefore, why Sartre thinks of actions, too, as transcendent unities. Obviously, the physical behavior of an action transcends the glance of reflecting consciousness. But even purely mental actions, according to Sartre, transcend the grasp of reflecting consciousness; for such actions consist of many consecutive bits of consciousness. The systematic doubt practiced by Descartes is an action and quite different from a single mental act of doubting, say, that Mary will arrive in time for lunch. The latter can be presented to reflecting consciousness, but the process of systematic doubt cannot. This doubt appears to us only through its ingredients, through particular acts of doubting, of remembering, of considering, etc.

Mental states, Sartre here reminds us, are not strung together haphazardly. They form patterns or structures. And it is such a pattern that must accompany certain behaviors for an action to take place.

(5) *The accessibility of the ego*

The ego is the transcendental unity of states and actions. It transcends the grasp of reflecting consciousness. Sartre thinks that this result of his investigation helps to overcome the traditional philosophical distinction between public 'outer' objects and hidden 'inner' mental states (*ibid.*, pp. 94–8.) According to this distinction, a perceptual object can be perceived by several people, while a mental phenomenon can only be presented to the mind in which it occurs. Many people can perceive the same apple, but only one person has access to a given mental act of desire, namely, the person who has this desire. Peter's love, to use Sartre's example, can only be apprehended by Peter himself. All other persons can only speak of his love 'blindly and by analogy' (*ibid.*, p. 94). But if love is a transcendent structure, so Sartre argues, then this theory of privileged access to mental phenomena is false. Peter's love can be presented in intuition, not only to Peter himself, but just as well to other people. Peter can be no more certain about his emotion than anyone else can be.

I think that Sartre is mistaken. It seems to me that his doctrine of transcendent states and actions has no bearing on the traditional distinction. This becomes obvious as soon as we stop using such vague terms as 'being presented to', 'have access to', 'can be apprehended', etc. It is true that the ego, conceived of as a complicated structure of successive mental states, cannot be experienced by a single act of experience. But it is also true that while an apple can be *seen* by many people, a conscious state can only be *experienced* by one person. A desire, to return to one of our examples, can only be *experienced* by one person. Of course, other people may have similar desires, that is, they may experience desires of the same sort for the same things. But they cannot experience Peter's desire. Every person experiences his and only his desires. And, of course, other people can *know about* Peter's desire; it may be written all over Peter's face that he desires Linda. Other people may be affected by Peter's desire; they may be as sure about his desire for Linda as he himself is. But they cannot experience Peter's desire. In this precise sense, mental acts, feelings, sensations, and images are 'private', and

The structure of mind

perceptual objects are 'public'. And Sartre's analysis does nothing to discredit this distinction.

Sartre cannot quite deny the obvious fact that Peter's desire is presented to him differently from other people. He says that Peter's consciousness is 'radically impenetrable', that a 'consciousness cannot conceive of a consciousness other than itself' (*ibid.*, p. 96). Yet, he also insists that there are two kinds of intuition: Peter's intuition of his ego and other people's intuition of Peter's ego. Perhaps Sartre is right on this point, although I have my doubts. But Sartre's analysis of the transcendence of the ego sheds no light on the nature of the kind of intuition which allegedly presents us with other people's egos. My ego is presented to me in reflective consciousness. It appears to reflective consciousness somehow behind the reflected consciousness. But what is this intuition that presumably gets at another person's ego? It cannot be a reflective act of mine; for every such act presents me with my own ego. It must therefore be an instance of unreflective consciousness. Sartre discusses this problem in great detail, several years after the *Transcendence of the Ego* in the chapter called 'The Look' in his book *Being and Nothingness*, and I shall refer you to this book.

(6) *Bad faith*

At the beginning of this chapter, I traced the connection between Sartre's rejection of a self and his quest for human freedom. We saw that Sartre holds that pure consciousness, as pure being-for-itself, is absolute spontaneity. Consciousness, Sartre claims, is a creation *ex nihilo* (*ibid.*, p. 99). Our mental acts do not issue or emanate from a self or even from the ego. They occur spontaneously, of their own accord. But this spontaneity, Sartre goes on to explain, frightens consciousness:

> But it can happen that consciousness suddenly produces itself on the pure reflective level. Perhaps not without the ego, yet as escaping from the ego on all sides, as dominating the ego and maintaining the ego outside the consciousness by a continued creation. On this level, there is no distinction between the possible and the real, since the appearance is the

absolute. There are no more barriers, no more limits, nothing to hide consciousness from itself. Then consciousness, noting what could be called the fatality of its spontaneity, is suddenly anguished: it is this dread, absolute and without remedy, this fear of itself, which seems to us constitutive of pure consciousness. (*Ibid.*, pp. 101–2)

Consciousness therefore tries to hide its own spontaneity from itself. By pretending that all of my consciousnesses, past, present, and future, are parts of this particular structure which is my ego, consciousness feigns limits to its spontaneity. By assigning consciousness to a particular ego, we pretend that it is embedded in that structure, that it is merely a part of a fixed pattern. But in reality there is no such fixed pattern, there is only a spontaneous flow of consciousness. Man is free, not only in the sense that consciousness does not harbor a chunk of being-in-itself in the form of a self, but also in that consciousness is not a part of a rigid structure which is the ego. Consciousness is not a creation of the ego, but creates the ego.

The spontaneity of consciousness is thus responsible for two important features of human existence. Firstly, it is responsible for the dread that pervades our existence. Dread, anxiety, is the fear which consciousness experiences when faced with its own spontaneity. Here we have still another interpretation of the origin and nature of anxiety. Secondly, it is responsible for what Sartre calls 'bad faith'. Consciousness tries to hide its spontaneity from itself. In order to escape from dread, it must lie to itself and deny its own spontaneity. It must pretend to be part of a fixed pattern. It must think of itself as being determined by character or personality. In order to escape from the dread of facing his limitless freedom, man adopts roles and slips into personalities.

Sartre explicitly contrasts his view about anxiety and bad faith with the Freudian view. He mentions the case of a young bride who was in terror, when her husband left her alone at home, of sitting at the window summoning the passers-by like a prostitute. He interprets her fear in this way:

Nothing in her education, in her past, nor in her character could serve as an explanation of such a fear. It seems to us simply that a negligible circumstance (reading, conversation, etc.) had determined in her what one might call 'a vertigo of possibility'. She found herself monstrously free, and this vertiginous freedom appeared to her *at the opportunity* for this action which she was afraid of doing. But this vertigo is comprehensible only if consciousness suddenly appeared to itself as infinitely overflowing in its possibilities the *I* which ordinarily serves as its unity. (*Ibid.*, p. 100)

We have here, presumably, an impressive case of consciousness suddenly confronting its unconditional freedom and reacting with anxiety to this confrontation. A Freudian interpretation would take quite a different turn. Not knowing more about the case than what Sartre relates in a few sentences, I would suspect that the bride's fear has quite a different origin. Perhaps, the young woman learned to be afraid of acting in that promiscuous fashion because her fear keeps her husband at home with her. Or, perhaps her fear was caused by her conviction that in marrying her husband she had already behaved like a prostitute. At any rate, from a Freudian point of view, we can hardly be satisfied with Sartre's explanation.

Sartre's theory about bad faith has some similarity to our view about the nature of neurosis. In bad faith, consciousness lies to itself. In repression, a person lies to himself. Sartre notes this similarity, but denies that a Freudian theory can truly account for the duplicity into which consciousness may enter with itself (compare *Being and Nothingness*, pp. 90–6). His main criticism of the Freudian theory of repression revolves around the contention that this theory splits consciousness into two parts, so that it becomes impossible to account for the fact that in bad faith it is one and the same entity which does the lying and is lied to. It seems to me that Sartre here constructs a dilemma. Either it is one and the same consciousness which lies and is lied to, or else it is not. Freud accepts the second possibility, according to Sartre, he splits consciousness into two parts, the ego and the id. But this will not do, for 'the very essence of the reflexive idea of hiding something from oneself implies the unity of one and the same psychic mechanism and consequently a double activity in the heart of unity . . . ' (*ibid.*, p. 94).

But the first alternative is not acceptable either. Assume that person X deceives person Y into believing P. In this case, X does not believe that *P* is the case. (As a matter of fact, *X knows* that *P* is not the case.) *Y*, on the other hand, believes that *P* is the case. Now, if *Y* is the same as *X*, if *Y* is the same consciousness as *X*, then *X* does not believe that *P* is the case, in so far as it is the deceiver, and *X* also and at the same time believes that *P* is the case, in so far as it is the deceived. But this is a contradiction. It is impossible for one and the same thing, at the same time, to believe *P* and also not to believe *P*. Thus Sartre's view about bad faith implies a contradiction and must be wrong. I have the impression that Sartre simply accepted this contradiction. To our argument, he may have replied: 'So what? Bad faith does indeed involve a contradiction. That is precisely its nature.'

Our way out of the dilemma is clear from our analysis of the process of repression. Anna experiences, at a certain moment, a desire for her father. When she asks herself: 'What is it that makes me feel so strange right now?' when she introspects, she recognizes her desire for what it is. Since she recognizes the desire for what it is, she feels terribly ashamed. But now the thought occurs to her that, perhaps, she is mistaken, that it is really hatred rather than desire which she feels for her father. This thought, though not exactly comforting, is much more acceptable to her than the realization that she desires her father. Since it greatly reduces her shame and guilt, she comes to believe, contrary to the fact, that it is hate she experiences rather than desire. In a sense, she learns to deceive herself. In a manner of speaking, Anna is lying to herself. But our story shows, I think that it is a lie merely in a manner of speaking, and that we must not take this kind of talk about lying too seriously. What happens is much more accurately and succinctly described by saying that Anna learns to believe that she hates her father, even though she desires him, because the truth is too shameful to her. She does not believe that she desires her father and, at the same time, also believe that she does not desire her father. Rather, even though she realized at one time that she desires her father, she later on comes to believe that she does not desire her father. Later on, there exists only this belief and not also the belief that she desires her father. There is no contradiction.

It may be replied that Anna must believe later on that she desires her father, for she still has the desire, and one cannot have a desire without knowing and, therefore, believing that one has it. What is wrong with this argument is the assumption that to have a desire, to experience it, is to know that one has it. On the contrary, to have a desire–to experience any kind of mental act–is precisely not to know that one has it. Experience, in our technical sense of the word, is not knowledge. In order to know that one has a desire, there must occur first an introspection of the desire. One must turn inward, so to speak, and ask oneself: 'What precisely is it that I experience at this moment?' And the answer which one gives to this question may or may not be true. Anna, we have seen, learns to give the wrong answer. Introspection, plain experience shows everyday, is not infallible. What makes Anna's case different from a case of being just plainly mistaken about one's feelings is the fact that she, at one point, clearly recognized her state of mind, but chose to believe otherwise, since it makes her feel better.

I conclude, therefore, that our analysis of the process of repression and of the nature of the unconscious clearly shows in what sense consciousness may be said to deceive itself. And our analysis, in contrast to Sartre's theory of bad faith, does not involve a contradiction.

13. The origin of nothingness

---

(1) *The nature of negation*

Sartre's quest for freedom has three themes. We discussed one in the last chapter: man is free because consciousness is pure spontaneity. We turn now to a second thesis: man is free because consciousness is the origin of nothingness. I shall again begin with an outline of Sartre's train of thought. Being-in-itself, the world around us other than consciousness, contains bits and pieces of nothingness. But these bits and pieces, so Sartre reasons, cannot be the product of being-in-itself. Being-in-itself, he says, is sheer positivity. Whence, then, comes nothingness? It can only be projected into the world by being-for-itself, that is, by consciousness. Man, therefore, is the origin of nothingness. But how could consciousness project nothingness into the world if it were merely a causal effect of being-in-itself? How could consciousness bring nothingness into the world, if it could not disengage itself from the world of being-in-itself? Thus the appearance of nothingness presupposes that consciousness can sever its causal connection with being-in-itself. But to stand apart from the great causal chain of being-in-itself is to be free. Hence consciousness is free.

I think that you can understand from this outline the drift of Sartre's discussion of freedom. But in order to understand fully the complexity of his thought, we must go rather deeply into his analysis of nothingness. And first we must take a look at negation and its place in the world.

Among the furniture of the world, there are quite obviously facts. It is a fact that the earth is round, a fact that whales are mammals, a fact that every mental act has an object, and a fact that two plus two equals four. These are four 'positive' facts. Are there also negative facts? It seems obvious to me that there are. It is a fact that the earth is *not* flat, a fact that whales are *not* fish, a fact that *not* all mental acts are desires, and a fact that two plus two is *not* five. As evident as it seems to be that there are these and many more negative facts, many philosophers have stubbornly denied their existence. 'There is implanted in the human breast', Bertrand Russell once said, 'an almost un-quenchable desire to find some way of avoiding the admission that negative facts are as ultimate as those that are positive' (B. Russell, *Logic and Knowledge*, ed. R. C. Marsh, London, George Allen & Unwin, 1956, p. 287). And he also tells us that when he lectured at Harvard and maintained that there are negative facts, this nearly produced a riot (*ibid.*, p. 211). I shall brave the prospect of a riot among my readers and just as boldly as Russell assert that negative facts are part of the world.

But in order to give you a taste of how philosophers have tried to eliminate negative facts and also to prepare you for later discussion, we shall briefly look at one attempt to do away with negative facts. This particular ploy rests on the assumption that there are two opposite mental acts of affirming and denying. And it holds that to affirm a particular negative fact *not-P* is in reality nothing else but to deny the corresponding positive fact *P*. For example, when it looks as if someone affirms that the earth is not flat, he denies, in reality, that the earth is flat. If someone seems to affirm that it is not the case that all swans are white, then, in reality, he denies that all swans are white. And so on.

There are at least three weighty objections to this reduction of negative facts to the denial of positive facts. Firstly, the question arises whether there really are these two distinct opposite mental acts, or whether one of them is merely the negation of the other. For example, to disbelieve is nothing else but *not* to believe. If so, then to say that someone disbelieves *P* is to say that he does *not* believe P and, hence, to state a negative fact about him. Now, if to deny P is, similarly, to affirm that P is *not* the case, then the reduction has failed. But let us grant that affirmation and denial are equally fundamental, genuine, mental acts. Then the further question arises, secondly, of whether or not denying P is really the same as affirming not-P. It seems to me to be quite clear that it is not the same. It seems to me that one can affirm P and also in different circumstances, affirm not-P; and that one can deny P and also, in a different situation, deny not-P. The case is even more obvious if we turn to belief and doubt. To believe not-P seems quite clearly different from doubting P. To believe that the earth is not flat is not the same as to doubt that it is flat. Finally, and thirdly, there is the all-important question of what fact accounts for the truth of the denial of P or the doubting of P. To believe that the earth is not flat is, according to the view under discussion, the same as to doubt that it is flat. Now, this doubt is true rather than false. What fact of the world accounts for its truth? Of course, it is not the fact that the earth is flat; for, firstly, this is not a fact, and, secondly, it would make the doubt false rather than true. Is it then the fact that the earth is round? It cannot be this fact either; for even if the earth was not round but, say, pear-shaped, the doubt would be true. If you think this matter through along the line suggested, you will eventually conclude that the only fact that fits the doubt is the negative fact that the earth is not flat.

I am quite sure, as I said, that there are negative facts. I am less sure of how to analyze them, however, There are several plausible theories about the nature of negation. All of these theories must accommodate the fact that negation co-ordinates to every positive state of affairs precisely one negative state of affairs, and conversely. For example, it co-ordinates to the state of affairs that the earth is round the negative state of affairs that the earth is not round; to the positive state of affairs (not fact!); that two plus two is five, there belongs the negation: two plus two is not five; and the state of affairs that all whales are mammals has as its negation the state of affairs: it is not the case that all whales are mammals. As this last example shows, one must be careful to insert the 'not' of negation at the right place. It would be a mistake to think of the negation of the state of affairs that all whales are mammals as the state of affairs: All whales are not mammals. Since negation assigns to every positive state of affairs precisely one negative state of affairs (and conversely), one may think that there exists a certain relation, call it 'the relation of incompatibility', which has the following feature. Whenever you assert a negative state of affairs, you are really asserting that there exists a fact which is incompatible with the positive twin of the negative state of affairs which you assert. For example, if you assert that the earth is not flat, you are asserting that there exists a fact, not further specified, which is incompatible with the state of affairs that the earth is flat. When you believe that it is not the case that all swans are white, you believe that there exists a fact which is incompatible with the circumstance that all swans are white. Negation according to this theory, resides in the incompatibility relation. It is a relation between states of affairs.

This relation holds in every case between a fact, on the one hand, and a 'mere state of affairs' which is not a fact, on the other. In our first example, the relation is said to hold between a fact, not further specified, and the mere state of affairs that the earth is flat. It is supposed to hold between a fact and something that is not the case. One may argue that the theory under discussion fails for this reason alone, namely, because there can be no such relation. But we cannot use this argument; for we have already admitted that the intentional nexus is precisely of this abnormal sort: If someone believes that the earth is flat, then his belief is connected by means of the intentional nexus with the mere state of affairs that the earth is flat. If we hold that there are relations which can connect with nonexistent states of affairs, then we cannot very well reject the incompatibility relation on the ground that it is such a relation.

But another consideration speaks against the existence of this relation. What precisely is this relation? Notice how I explained it to you. In effect, I said that there is supposed to be a relation which holds between some state of affairs P and a given state of affairs Q if and only if it is the case that if P is a fact, then Q is *not* a fact; and it is the case that P is a fact. Clearly, I suppose here that you already know what a negative state of affairs is. If we cannot find any other way of understanding the alleged incompatibility relation except in terms of negative states of affairs, we may be justifiably suspicious of its existence.

Another analysis of negation assumes that there exists a negative exemplification relation in addition to the familiar positive one. To assert that the earth is not flat is to assert, according to this theory, that this negative exemplification holds between the earth and the property of being flat. Of course, to say that the earth is round is to say that the earth (positively) exemplifies the property of being round or, in ordinary English, that it *is* round. We could agree to use 'not' as a word for this negative exemplification relation, so that sentences of the form '*A* is not *P*' would be re-written as '*A* not *P*', in analogy to the positive sentence '*A is P*'. There are then two equally important and fundamental relations, the familiar copula represented by 'is' (or some tensed form of 'to be'), and the presumed copula represented by 'not'.

This view is plausible as long as we consider relatively simple states of affairs of the form *A is not F*. But how are we to treat the fact that it is not the case that all swans are white? According to the rules of logic, this fact is equivalent to: something is a swan and is not white. Here negation occurs in connection with the property of being white, so that we can again treat it as negative exemplification. What the original negative fact turns out to be is the fact that something positively exemplifies being a swan and negatively exemplifies being white. I cannot bring myself to believe that the former negative fact concerning all swans is the *same* fact as the latter.

Furthermore, there is the objection that this theory explains negation only for states of affairs involving exemplification. But there are other kinds of state of affairs as well. For example, there is the fact that my left shoe does not belong to the set of things which are on my desk before me. Expressed in more technical terms, there is the fact that my left shoe is *not a member of the set* of things on my desk. Here, we are dealing with the membership relation between things and sets and not with exemplification. Or consider the fact that a certain belief does not intend the state of affairs *P*. This fact, too, does not involve exemplification. What is negated, speaking loosely, is the nexus of intentionality. One could, of course, add to negative exemplification negative membership and negative intentionality.

But this extension of the theory would fly in the face of what I consider to be a basic feature of negation, namely, that negation is the same, no matter in what kind of fact it occurs. Negation is of one piece. It does not fragment into numerous different relations.

According to a third popular view, negation exists in the world in the form of negative properties. The fact that the earth is not flat is analyzed into the earth, the nexus of exemplification, and a certain property, namely, the property of not-being-flat. The earth is said to exemplify this property. This particular example is not very flattering to the view under discussion; for there clearly is no separate property of not-being-flat. Rather, what we have here is simply the *negation* of being flat. But there are also facts more amiable to a treatment in terms of negative properties. Consider the fact that Peter is *not* here in the restaurant. We may have said instead that Peter is *absent* (from this restaurant). Being absent seems to be just as genuine a property as being present, albeit a negative one. English contains a number of *simple* predicates for negative properties; and so do other languages. But this does not prove that the present view must be correct. In most cases, there is no simple predicate and we must build the negative predicate with the help of negation. Moreover, this view faces all the problems mentioned in connection with the attempt to explicate negation in terms of negative exemplification. There is the problem of how to treat the fact that it is not the case that all swans are white. And there is the, to my mind, insurmountable problem of how to treat negative facts which do not involve properties at all. (The fact that my left shoe is not a member of the set of things on my desk poses no problem, since it is generally assumed that to every set there corresponds its complement set. But no treatment is available for the fact that two plus two is not five.)

For the reasons I have mentioned, I believe that negation exists neither in the form of a relation nor in the guise of properties. I think that it is an entity of an entirely different sort, one of a kind, in a class all by itself. This entity occurs in every negative fact, irrespective of whether the fact concerns the exemplification of properties, or set-membership, or relations among numbers, or the intentional nexus, etc., and irrespective of whether the fact is simple or very complicated. A negative fact, in my opinion, can be most perspicuously represented by a sentence of the form 'It is not the case that *P*' or, for short, 'Not *P*'. Every negative fact, in other words, consists of two distinct parts, negation and a certain state of affairs. The state of affairs, obviously, is not a fact; it does not obtain; it is not the case; it does not exist. How negation can attach itself to a nonexistent state of affairs is a mystery which I cannot explain.

(2) *The givenness of negation*

We return now to Sartre. It is an axiom of Sartre's philosophy that being-in-itself contains no negation. Thus Sartre denies what I have affirmed, namely that there are negative facts independent of minds. According to him, negation is somehow transported into the world by consciousness. In particular, it is the *question* which reveals to us the 'permanent possibility' of non-being. 'In every question', he says, 'we stand before a being which we are questioning'. (*Being and Nothingness*, p. 35). And we question being either about its ways of being or about its being. The reply to our question will in either case be a yes or no. For example, I may ask: 'Is this pencil before me on my desk black?' Here I question the pencil, to use Sartre's quaint way of talking, about its way of being; we may say that I question it about its so-being. The answer may be either 'Yes, it is black' or 'No, it is not black.' In the latter case, we are confronted with a negative state of affairs. Or you may question a being about its being by asking: 'Does the Loch Ness monster exist?' Again, the answer will be either 'Yes, it exists' or 'No, it does not exist.' In the latter case, we have again a negative state of affairs. In short, whenever you raise a question, you must be prepared to get a *negative* answer. According to Sartre, it is the questioning attitude of consciousness which reveals non-being to us.

But now, as Sartre says, 'someone will object that being-in-itself cannot furnish negative replies' (*ibid.*, p. 36). This someone will go on to claim that ordinary experience cannot disclose non-being to us. Negation, he will say, 'could appear only on the level of an act of judgment by which I should establish a comparison between the result anticipated and the result obtained' (*ibid.*, p. 37). Sartre is determined to refute this view. His discussion is not very clear, partly because his opponent's view is not explained in detail, partly because Sartre's own position is somewhat obscure. Let us try to bring some lucidity to the issue.

It is likely that the view which Sartre attacks is a view expressed by the French philosopher Henri Bergson (1859–1941). I shall assume that it indeed is and quote a passage from Bergson in order to introduce you to his thought about negation:

> Thus, whenever I add a 'not' to an affirmation, whenever I deny, I perform two very definite acts: (1) I interest myself in what one of my fellow-men affirms, or in what he was going to say, or what might have been said by another *Me*, whom I anticipate; (2) I announce that some other affirmation, whose content I do not specify, will have to be substituted for the one I find before me. Now, in neither of these two acts is there anything but affirmation. The *sui generis* character of negation is due to superimposing the first of these acts upon the second. (*Creative Evolution*, trans. Arthur Mitchell, New York, 1911, ch. 4)

Bergson's example is the negative state of affairs that the ground is not damp:

> Keep strictly to the terms of the proposition, 'The ground is not damp', and you will find that it means two things: (1) that one might believe that the ground is damp, (2) that the dampness is replaced in fact by a certain quality x. This quality is left indeterminate, either we have no positive knowledge of it, or because it has no actual interest for the person to whom the negation is addressed. (*Ibid.*)

Bergson's view has two parts. Bergson explains, firstly, how an affirmation of a negative state of affairs comes about; why we are moved to make such a judgment. And he explains, secondly, what the true state of affairs is which is affirmed. Filling in a few details, let us first consider how the assertion of a negative state of affairs is supposed to come about. I am walking toward a picnic area near the lake. It has recently rained and I expect that the ground near the lake–where the best view is–will be damp. Firstly, there is in this case an expectation of the positive state of affairs that the ground will be damp. When I get to the preferred spot by the lake, I see that the ground is actually dry. My expectation is not fulfilled. Secondly, there occurs therefore a perception of the positive state of affairs that the ground is dry. I, thirdly, form the judgment, in response to my earlier expectation, that the ground is not damp. If it were not for my expectation, no such judgment would be made. I would simply be satisfied with the observation that the ground is dry. This shows what role the expectation plays in the eventual formation of the negative judgment. Furthermore, if it were not for the observation that the ground is dry, I could not asssert that it is not damp. I *conclude* that my expectation is not fulfilled by reasoning that since the ground is dry it cannot be damp. This shows what role the observation plays in the eventual appearance of the negative judgment. And it also shows that this judgment is the result of a process of reasoning rather than an immediate perception. This last point is the important one, so let me repeat it in other words. That the ground is not damp is a state of affairs, according to Bergson, which we can *judge* to be the case, on the basis of some observation, but which we cannot *perceive* to be the case. We can only perceive positive states of affairs. For example, we can perceive that the ground is dry or we can perceive that the ground is damp. But we can never perceive that it is not dry or that it is not damp. This we can only judge to be the case on the evidence of having observed some positive state of affairs first. I said that this contention is the important one because it is the bone over which Sartre fights with Bergson. According to Sartre, negation is given to us, not only through judgment, but in immediate perception. According to him, we can literally see with our eyes, not only conclude from what we see, that the ground is not damp.

According to the second part of Bergson's view, the judgment which occurs as the result of my reasoning is a judgment that the ground has some quality *x* other than the expected quality of being damp. The state of affairs judged, is precisely speaking, not of the form *the ground is not damp*, but has the different structure: *the ground has a quality x which is incompatible with the quality of being damp.* You see that Bergson's view is a version of the view, according to which negation appears in the form of the incompatibility relation. If so, then Bergson does not deny the existence of negative states of affairs. He merely denies that such states of affairs contain, as I believe they do, a unique entity represented by the word 'not'. Rather they are characterized by containing the incompatibility relation. Sartre seems to me to misunderstand Bergson's position when he says that, according to this position, 'negation would be simply a quality of judgment' (*ibid.*, p. 37). There is, of course, the further possibility that Bergson himself did not realize that his view implies the existence of a negative state of affairs.

As I see it, the real issue between Sartre and Bergson is whether a negative state of affairs—however it may be analyzed— can be presented in perception (and other 'immediate' intuitions) or can only be the intention of a judgment. Sartre claims that one can *see*, for example, that Peter is *not* here (not in this café), and I wholeheartedly agree with him on this point. When Sartre describes how Peter's absence haunts the café, he is at his best in describing the phenomenon (*ibid.*, p. 40–2). I can see that Peter is not here. I can hear that the radio is not playing. I can taste that the wine is not sweet. I can feel that the pain is not getting worse. And so on. Our mental acts present us with negative states of affairs just as directly as they present us with positive ones.

Why would anyone wish to deny that I can see, with my eyes, and without any inference, that the pencil in front of me is not black? I shall venture a guess. Perhaps it is true, as a matter of brute psychological fact, that I always see first that the pencil before me has a certain color, yellow, before I see that it is not black. Perhaps, Sartre must see first some of the things and persons that are present in the café before he can see that Peter is absent. Perhaps, in short, a perception of a negative state of affairs is always preceded by the perception of one or more relevant positive states of affairs. If so, then one may be misled into arguing that the negative fact must be *inferred* from the observed positive facts and cannot itself be observed. Since I first see that the pencil before me is yellow, one may reason, and since I *can* infer from this fact that it is not black, *I must have arrived* at the fact that it is not black by inference rather than by perception. But this argument is fallacious. If someone tells you that my pencil is yellow, you can infer that it is not black, without having seen the pencil at all. From the fact that this inference is possible, however, it does not follow that it must always occur. In my own case, with the pencil before me in plain view, I can just take a look and see that the pencil is not black.

(3) *The nature of nothingness*

Negation, Sartre tells us, has its origin and foundation in *nothingness*: 'In order for negation to exist in the world and in order that we may consequently raise questions concerning Being, it is necessary that in some way Nothingness be given' (*ibid.*, p. 56). We must therefore take a look at this infamous existentialistic notion of nothingness. Unfortunately, there is not just one such notion. Sartre uses the word 'nothingness' to mean several quite different things. I shall once again try to clarify the terminology and the philosophical issues involved, before we consider Sartre's view.

We must sharply distinguish between three very different things which Sartre constantly confuses with each other. Firstly, there is *negation*. We have discussed this notion in the last section, and I shall merely remind you that it is expressed by the word 'not' as it occurs in the sentence 'The earth is not flat.' Secondly, there is *non-being*. To have non-being is simply *not* to have *being*. Since we have rejected modes of being in favor of existence, we can also say that to have non-being is the same as *not* to *exist*. Ghosts have non-being, that is, they do not exist. Hamlet has non-being, that is, he does not exist. A round-square has non-being, that is, there is no such thing. And so on. It is obvious that the notion of non-being consists of the two notions of negation and of being. It is a complex notion. We could form, analogously, the notion of non-squareness. To be non-square, to have non-squareness, is the same as not to be square. Oscar, for example, has non-squareness. Thirdly, there is the notion of *nothing* (ness). This notion, I cannot too strongly emphasize, is entirely and utterly different from the notions of negation and non-being. It is the notion of what logicians and philosophers call 'a quantifier'.

Consider the statement: nothing is both green and red all over at the same time. This statement tells you, in effect, *how many* things have a certain complex characteristic, namely, the feature of being red and green all over at the same time. It tells you that *no thing*, as contrasted with *all things* or *three things*, has this feature. The statement is therefore similar to such assertions as:

Everything is identical with itself.

Something is a whale.

Three things (persons) ran for the office of Mayor.

The first assertion states that *every* thing (or *all* things) has the characteristic of being self-identical; the second asserts that *some* things are whales; the third that *three* things were candidates. Here, too, we have complex notions: in each case we can distinguish between what I shall call 'a quantifier word', on the one hand, and the word 'thing(s)', on the other. 'Nothing' consists therefore of the quantifier word 'no' and the word 'thing'. Nothingness is in the same pot as such notions as somethingness, allthingness, threethingness, etc. What distinguishes among these notions is the quantifier proper, the idea that gives you the quantity involved: *no, some, all, every, three,* etc.

Nothingness, let me say it again, is not the same as negation or non-being. The quantifier *no*, no matter what the word for it may sound like, is not intimately related to the negation *not*. Rather is it the brother of *all* and the sister of *some*. Nor does it have anything to do with non-being. To fix this firmly in our minds, let us look at some further statements. Consider the following three assertions:

(1) Nothing does not exist.

(2) Something does not exist.

(3) Everything does not exist.

The thing to note is that their truth or falsehood depends on what we mean by a 'thing'. If we use this expression in its widest sense, so that it means what we have previously called an 'object', then we get the following results. (3) is clearly false; for there is at least one object, the apple called 'Oscar', that does exist. (2) is clearly true; for there is at least one object, say the flying elephant Dumbo, which does not exist. And (1) is obviously false for the same reason for which (2) is true. On the other hand, if we mean by a 'thing' an existent, then the following is the case. (3) is clearly false since it states that every existent does not exist. (2) is also false, since it says that some existent does not exist. And (1) is true; for it says that no existent has the feature of non-existing. So far, I think, everything is clear. But now we turn to the statement:

(4) Nothingness does not exist.

What we mean to say by means of (4) is that the object *nothing* does not exist. In a similar vein, we may assert that something-ness does not exist. Is (4) true or false? Sartre maintains that nothingness is not, that it has no being (*ibid.*, p. 57). Hence he would say that (4) is true (assuming that we mean by 'existence' the same as by 'being'). I think that (4) is false. Nothingness does exist. It is part of the furniture of the world. Just as somethingness and everythingness is. If the entity *something* did not exist, it seems to me, then there could be no such fact as that something is a whale; for this entity is an essential ingredient of the fact. Similarly, if the entity *nothing* did not exist, then there could be no such fact as that nothing is both red and green all over at the same time, and for the same reason. I admit, though, that this is a very hotly disputed issue. Whether or not the quantifiers exist is a question on which there is no agreement among philosophers. But what I shall insist on is the fact that whether or not nothingness exists is a question made from the same cloth as the question of whether or not somethingness exists. And it must, moreover, be sharply distinguished from the question of whether or not non-being has being (non-existence exists).

Let us venture another step into this maze of nothingness, non-being, and negation. Assume that someone confuses nothingness with non-being. Thus (4) means to him:

(5) Non-being has no being.

In order to show that (5) is true, he may argue as follows. If non-being had being, then it would have to have both non-being, *for that is what it is*, and also being. But this is impossible. Therefore, non-being cannot have being, and (5) must be true. Perhaps this is how Sartre arrived at his belief that nothingness has no being. If so, then he reasoned fallaciously. To see this clearly, you must realize that the question *is not* whether *something* can both have being and non-being. The answer to this question is obvious: it cannot. No, we are not asking whether *something* can both be and not be, but rather whether *non-being* has being. Next, you must also realize that non-being 'in order to be what it is' need not *have* the feature of non-being. Perhaps this will become clearer if we consider the analogous assertion: (the color) green is not green. Someone may argue that this assertion must be false, green must be green, because if it were not green, then it would have to be both green (*for this is what it is*) and also not green, and this is impossible. Green, of course, is what it is: this particular *property* of individual things. But in order to be this property rather than something else, it obviously need not have the color green. As a matter of fact, it does not have this color. An apple may be green, a sweater may be green, but the color green is not green. It does not *have* this property even though it is (identical with) this property. The crucial point is that there is an ambiguity in the phrase 'for that is what it is'. From the fact that the color green is what it *is*, namely, the color green, it does not follow that it must *have* itself as a property.

Similarly, for non-being. Non-being is what it is and not something else. In particular, it is not the same thing as being. It is not *identical with* being. But from this fact does not follow that it cannot *have* being. From the fact that non-being is not the same as being, it does not follow that it cannot have the feature of being. As a matter of fact, I think that non-being–just like negation and nothingness–has being. (5), in my opinion, is false. If non-being had no being, so I would argue, how could anything not be? If there were no such thing as non-existence, to put it my way, how could it possibly be the case that the round-square does not exist? How could some objects (not: entities!) possibly have the feature (not property!) of non-existing, if there were no such feature?

It is at any rate true that in order to answer some of the difficult questions which we have raised in the last few paragraphs, we must carefully distinguish between negation, non-being, and nothingness. Sartre, as I said, does not do so consistently. 'Nothingness', it appears to me, is for him a kind of umbrella term, covering negation, non-being, and a few other things. Seldom if ever does he mean by it the quantifier. Otherwise, why would he make such a fuss over nothing and not also over something?

(4) *Being and non-being*

In his criticism of Hegel's view, Sartre clearly has non-being in mind when he speaks of nothingness. The question is: what is the nature of non-being? Sartre takes Hegel to hold a view that can be summed up in the following three propositions. (1) Being and non-being are two abstractions. (2) They are on equal footing, neither one more fundamental than the other. (3) They are dialectical opposites which ultimately shade into each other and amount to being the same thing. Sartre's main objection against Hegel's view is that being is primary and not on the same level with nothingness. He says:

> This is what we mean when we say that *nothingness haunts being*. That means that being has no need of nothingness in order to be conceived and that we can examine the idea of it exhaustively without finding there the least trace of nothing-ness. But on the other hand, nothingness *which is not*, can have only a borrowed existence, and it gets its being from being. Its nothingness of being is encountered only within the limits of being, and the total disappearance of being would not be the advent of the reign of non-being, but on the contrary the concomitant disappearance of nothingness. *Non-being exists only on the surface of being*. (*Ibid.*, p. 49)

Notice how Sartre here switches without a moment's hesitation from nothingness to non-being, as if they were one and the same thing.

Before we try to evaluate Sartre's objection, let us look at Hegel's reason for holding that being and non-being are equal opposites. As Sartre interprets him, Hegel starts out with a notion of being as 'the indetermination which precedes all determinations, the undetermined as the absolute point of departure' (*ibid.*, p. 45). Perhaps it is not too far fetched to see in Hegel's characteristic of being an anticipation of our view that being (existence) is the ultimate substance of the world. Existence, in our view, has no properties as such; it is not even a category. It is not an individual, nor a property, nor a relation, etc. The entity *entity*, as such, is not green, nor is it a shape, nor is it a property etc. An entity, as an entity, is *not* this, that, or the other. But this means, so Hegel argues, that pure being is *absolute negation*, and absolute negation is nothingness. Therefore, being and nothingness are ultimately one and the same undifferentiated thing.

Pure being, the entity *entity*, we agree, is *not* this, that, or the other, but does it follow, as Hegel maintains, that being therefore is absolute negation and, hence, non-being? I do not think so. From the fact that all *properties* must be negated of being, it does not follow that *being* must be negated of being. From the fact that being has no *properties*, it does not follow that it has no *being*. That it does not follow becomes obvious as soon as we recall that being is not a property. Hegel's view, at least in our interpretation, implies both that being is the substance of the world as well as that it is merely a property among properties. But even though being does not have properties, it has being. The entity *entity* is an entity, even though it does not have properties.

Sartre argues that being and non-being are not equal opposites because non-being is subsequent to being. Non-being is being first posited and then denied (*ibid.*, pp. 47–9). Non-being, as we would put it, is negated being. It is a composite of being and negation. It is not a primitive, unanalyzable thing like being. The contrast between being and non-being is comparable to the contrast between the property of being square and the 'property' of being non-square. There really is no such property as being non-square. Being non-square is not simple as the property of being square and the property of being round are. The notion of the 'property' of being non-square is the notion of something's *not* being *square*. It consists of the two notions of negation and of the notion of squareness. Given any property P, we can always assert that something does *not* have this property. And this leads us to speak of the 'property' of not being P. But it is clear that our understanding of this alleged property rests entirely on our prior understanding of negation and the property P.

Being is indetermination, to use Hegel's terminology. But non-being, Sartre objects, is not identical with this indetermination. Rather, it is this indetermination negated. Sartre says: 'Whatever may be the original undifferentiation of being, non-being is that same undifferentiation *denied*' (*ibid.*, p. 47). It may be true, he argues, that being has no properties, but it could not

241

be true that it has no being; for the very assertion that *it* has no being implies its being. I let Sartre once more speak for himself: 'Thus, let anyone deny being whatever he wishes, he can not cause it *not to be*, thanks to the very fact that he denies that it is this or that. Negation cannot touch the nucleus of being of Being, which is absolute plenitude and entire positivity' (*ibid.*, p. 48).

I agree with Sartre that being is primary and non-being derivative. But notice that this is not to say that nothingness is derivative. Being and nothingness are not opposites. The opposite of nothing is something. Hence the opposite of nothingness is somethingness. Now, what holds for non-being relative to being does not hold for nothingness relative to somethingness. Nothingness is not secondary to somethingness. Rather, nothingness and somethingness are both primary, they are equals, neither one is reducible to the other. It is true that logicians can get along without the quantifier *nothing* by construing logically equivalent expressions in terms of 'everything' or 'something'. But this does not imply that the quantifier *something* (or *everything*) is primitive and *nothing* merely derived from it. For by the same method we can also replace contexts with the quantifier expression '*something*' by logically equivalent expressions with the quantifier expression 'nothing'. The case of being and non-being is quite different from the present case. There we do not have two primitive, unanalyzable notions, but only one such notion, the notion of being. Non-being can only be understood, can only be conceived, as the negation of being.

(5) *Everything and nothing*

Being done with Hegel, Sartre turns next to Heidegger's view on nothingness. In Sartre's interpretation, Heidegger's view looks like this. Human being, according to Heidegger, is being-in-the-world. The world in which a human being finds itself is, in Sartre's words, 'A synthetic complex of instrumental realities' (*ibid.*, pp. 50–1). The world appears as the *world* to human beings only if they transcend it; if they look at it, as it were, from the point of view of nothingness. One has to position oneself in nothingness in order to grasp the world as a whole. Nothingness is the other to the world. As Sartre sees Heidegger, nothingness is the opposite of the world, and it appears to human beings only when they transcend the world: 'Here then is nothingness, surrounding being on every side and at the same time expelled from being. Here nothingness is given as that by which the world receives its outlines as the world' (*ibid.*, p. 51).

Nothingness, according to Heidegger, is the opposite of the world. Can we make sense of this notion? The world, of course, is *everything* there is. It is the totality of existents. It consists of all existents. Outside of the world there is nothing. Outside of the world no thing exists. Every existent is thus contrasted with no existent. This is obviously not the same contrast as the one between being and non-being. We must carefully distinguish, as I said before, between non-being and nothingness. But we must also be clear whether we are talking about things in the sense of existents or in the sense of objects of the mind. Since we are contrasting nothing with the world, and the world consists of existents rather than objects, nothing is here the notion of no existent. (We have discovered, therefore, an even deeper contrast, a contrast the existentialists do not even see, namely, the contrast between every object and no object.)

Sartre raises two main objections against Heidegger's conception of nothingness. The first one is reminiscent of his objection to Hegel. Negation, he declares, is indeed founded upon nothingness, but only because nothingness envelops the not (*ibid.*, p. 52). But the nothingness of Heidegger is the nothingness of being-other-than-the-world. It is the negation of being as part of the world. Thus it is a composite of negation and world, of negation and being. It is not primary and primitive:

> Nothingness can be nothingness only by nihilating itself
> expressly as nothingness of the world, that is, in its nihilation
> it must direct itself expressly toward this world in order to
> constitute itself as a refusal of the world. Nothingness carries
> being in its heart. (*Ibid.*, p. 52)

This time, I think, Sartre is half right and half wrong. He is right in regard to being, but he is wrong in regard to negation. Nothingness, in the sense of no-existent, is indeed not a simple notion. It is not irreducible. It is not unanalyzable. It consists of the two notions of *no* and of *existent*. It consists of the notion of the quantifier and of the notion of being. But we must also stress that the notion of every-existent is equally complex. It, too, is not simple, irreducible, unanalyzable. It, too, consists of the notion of a quantifier, *every*, and of the notion of an existent (being). The world, as the totality of existents, is thus also a complex notion. And both notions, the notion of the world as everything and the notion of nothing, equally contain the notion of existence. Sartre is therefore right when he maintains that nothingness is relative to the world, relative to everything. But he is wrong when he claims that this nothingness is the *negation* of the existents of the world. The notion of no-existent does not involve negation. It must not be confused with the notion of not-an-existent (non-being). The verbal difference between the two phrases may be small and subtle, but the difference in things is tremendous. What lies beyond the world, the world conceived of as the totality of existents, is not non-being, but no existent. Heidegger's nothingness is not the same as Hegel's.

Sartre's second main complaint is that Heidegger's extra-mundane nothingness cannot account for the appearance of non-being in the midst of the world:

> If I emerge in nothingness *beyond* the world, how can this extra-mundane nothingness furnish a foundation for those little pools of non-being which we encounter each instant in the depth of being. I say 'Pierre is not there', 'I have no more money', etc. Is it really necessary to surpass the world toward nothingness and to return subsequently to being in order to provide a ground for these everyday judgments? (*Ibid.*, p. 53)

Here you have another illustration of Sartre's sliding back and forth between the three crucial notions of our discussion. Pierre's *not* being there is cited as an example of those little pools of non-being. But it is not a case of non-being at all; it is a case of *not* being at a certain place. And nothingness as we are now considering it has little to do with negation of this sort.

It is clear that Sartre's criticism hits the mark only if Heidegger holds that nothingness is all there is to negation. We agree with Sartre that negation is part of the world. The world is full of negative facts. Furthermore, what lies beyond every existent, nothingness, does not touch upon, does not found, does not concern these negative facts. On the other hand, it is true, as Heidegger emphasizes, that nothingness is opposed to the totality of existents, including, in our view, all negative facts.

Let me sum up these rather difficult inquiries into the nature of nothingness. Following Sartre's example, we considered Hegel's and Heidegger's notions of nothingness.The first of these, I assumed, is the notion of non-being; the second, the notion of no-existent. I agreed with Sartre that non-being is parasitic on being. Non-being is the negation of being; it consists of the notion of negation and of the notion of being. The opposite of no-existent, on the other hand, is not being, but everything, all existents, in short, the world. Both notions, the notion of everything and the notion of nothing, involve the notion of being. Both are parasitic on the notion of being. In addition to the notion of being, each one of these two notions contains the notion of a quantifier. The first, contains the notion of the quantifier *every* (all); the second, the notion of the quantifier *no*. These two quantifiers are of equal status. Nor does the latter have anything more to do with negation than the former. From my point of view, there are three fundamental, irreducible, and important notions: Negation, being, and the quantifier *no*. Nothingness is not the metaphysical king of the hill. Rather, it is being. When combined with negation it yields non-being. When wedded to the quantifier, it brings forth nothing.

(6) *Questioning being*

I believe that negation, being, and the quantifier are part of the furniture of the world. In other words, negation is an existent, and so is existence and the quantifier. Furthermore, I do not see why these existents should depend for their existence on consciousness, that is, on there being minds. To speak ponderously like Heidegger: the being of these three beings is independent of the being of human beings! Would it not be a fact that the earth is *not* flat if there were no human beings who wonder about the shape of the earth? Of course, it would. Would it not be a fact that elephants *exist* and a fact that mermaids do not *exist*, if there were no human beings to feed elephants and to fear mermaids? Of course, these would be facts. And would it not be a fact that *nothing* can be red and green all over at the same time, if there were no human beings who tried to imagine such an impossible situation? Of course, it would. All of these facts would exist if there were no minds. And how could these facts possibly exist, unless their main ingredients exist?

Sartre, as we saw, insists that negation is not a creation of judgment. It is presented to us in ordinary perception. But he also holds that negation is in some sense a creation of consciousness. A certain metaphysical axiom forces Sartre into this position. According to this axiom, being-in-itself is sheer plenitude and full positivity (See, for example, *ibid.*, p. 43 and p. 56). And there is also his conviction, a conviction so firm that no philosophical argument can touch it, that the world without consciousness has no structure at all. Perhaps these two dogmas are just two sides of the same coin. But be that as it may, I think that there is a noticeable tension between Sartre's metaphysical beliefs and his phenomenological insights. There is a tension, for example, between his belief that it is the mind that structures the world, on the one hand, and his convincing appeal to the phenomenological fact that negation is given in straightforward perception, on the other. There is a tension between his belief that being-in-itself is full positivity and his pronouncement that 'nothingness lies coiled in the heart of being–like a worm' (*ibid.*, p. 56).

Here is how Sartre sees the dialectic of the situation:

> Nothingness must be given at the heart of being, in order for us to apprehend that particular type of realities which we have called *negatités*. But this intra-mundane Nothingness cannot be produced by Being-in-itself; the notion of Being as full positivity does not contain Nothingness as one of its structures. We cannot even say that Being excludes it. Being lacks all relation with it. Hence the question which is put to us now with a particular urgency: If Nothingness can be conceived neither outside of Being, nor in terms of Being, and if on the other hand, since it is non-being, it cannot derive from itself the necessary force to 'nihilate itself', where does Nothingness come from? (*Ibid.*, p. 56)

The alternatives are clear. Nothingness does not lie beyond being, but dwells in its midst. But it cannot be part of being, for being is full positivity. Nor can it have created itself, for since nothingness is not, it could not have done anything. Where, then, does it come from? But does not this question presuppose what Sartre denies, namely, that there is nothingness? If nothingness is not, if it does not have being, what sense does it make to ask where it comes from? This is one of Sartre's predicaments: If nothingness is, then it makes sense to ask for its origin; but then it is also part of being. On the other hand, if it is not, then there is no question. Sartre tries to get around this difficulty:

> But Nothingness is *not*. If we can speak of it, it is only because it possesses an appearance of being, a borrowed being, as we have noted above. Nothingness is not, Nothingness 'is made to be', Nothingness does not nihilate itself; Nothingness is 'nihilated'. It follows therefore that there must exist a Being (this cannot be the In-itself) of which the property is to nihilate Nothingness, to support it in its being, to sustain it perpetually in its very existence, *a being by which Nothingness comes to things*. (*Ibid.*, p. 57)

I do not think that Sartre shows us a way out of his predicament. If nothingness is not, then it cannot be nihilated, it cannot be supported in its being (*sic*), it cannot be sustained in its existence (*sic*), and it cannot come to things, neither by being-in-itself nor by consciousness, that is, being-for-itself. But let us waive this objection. How does being-for-itself bring nothingness to things? Sartre answers: human beings can project nothingness into the world because they contain nothingness. In distinction to being-in-itself, being-for-itself is not sheer positivity. It contains nothingness at its very core.

But how is Sartre to make plausible this claim that nothingness lies at the core of human being? He seems to be casting around for a reasonable explanation. He remembers that he started out with the assertion that nothingness is revealed to us through the question. How does the fact that human beings can question being show that they contain nothingness? When we question being, Sartre claims, 'we realize a nihilating withdrawal in relation to the given, which becomes a simple *presentation*, fluctuating between being and Nothingness' (*ibid.*, p. 58). Assume that I have forgotten whether I left a black or a red pen on my desk. While I am away from my office, I ask myself: is the pen on my desk black? It is clear that this mental act of questioning is not an act of perceiving something in my environment. Nor is it an act of desiring something present, or an act of fearing something before me. It concerns something, the pen on my desk, of which I am merely *thinking*, which is a mere 'presentation'. As soon as I raise the question, I disengage myself from the things around me.

This kind of 'nihilating withdrawal' from the things around me becomes in Sartre's next step of argumentation a disassociating from the causal series. The questioner, Sartre maintains, must be capable of withdrawing from the causal series of events. Only then is questioning intelligible: 'Thus in so far as the questioner must be able to effect in relation to the questioned a kind of nihilating withdrawal, he is not subject to the causal order of the world; he detaches himself from Being' (*ibid.*, p. 58). I am at home, away from my office. I wonder whether the pen left on my desk is black. My mental act of questioning is caused neither by the things around me nor by the pen. The table before me, when I have dinner at home, is the cause for seeing it. My mental act of seeing it is caused by it. But nothing in my environment at home can cause, in the same sense, my mental act of questioning the color of the pen in my office. Nor can the pen cause this question. If a tiger should suddenly walk through the patio door, while I am eating dinner, the tiger would cause me to be afraid. It would be the cause of my mental act of fear. But neither the tiger nor anything else present could cause, in the same sense, my question about the color of the pen. In short, questions are not caused by the things around us as perceptions and perhaps certain other mental acts are. In this sense, the questioner 'is not subject to the causal order of the world'. (But how does this agree with Sartre's assertion that we can question the carburator before us? Does not the carburator in front of us cause us to question it? And is it really the tiger that causes me to be afraid or is it my seeing the tiger?)

Man contains nothingness in the sense that he is not subject to the causal chain of being-in-itself. An act of questioning is a kernel of nothingness because it stands outside the causal process that connects being-in-itself with being-in-itself. But to stand outside of this process is to be free. In this way, Sartre connects the nothingness in human beings, which brings nothingness to the world, with their freedom:

> For man to put a particular existent out of circuit is to put himself out of circuit in relation to that existent. In this case he is not subject to it; he is out of reach; it can not act on him, for he has retired *beyond a nothingness*. Descartes following the stoics has give a name to this possibility which human reality has to secrete a nothingness which isolates it–it is *freedom*. (*Ibid.*, p. 60)

While I have dinner at home and before the question about the pen occurs to me, I am *thinking* that tomorrow I have to grade a lot of papers. I think that I always grade papers with red rather than black pen. This leads me to *wonder* whether the pen I left on my desk is red or black. If it is black, I realize, I had better take a red pen with me when I go to my office in the morning. The question about the color of the pen in my office occurred to me *because* I *remembered* having to grade tests. It occurred to me *because I want to* grade the tests, as I usually do, with red rather than black pen. Thus a certain mental process, a train of thought, a series of connected mental acts, *caused* me to wonder about the color of the pen in my office. It is true, as we have conceded for the sake of advancing the discussion, that the *direct* cause of my question was nothing in my environment, nor was it the pen itself. But as our story reveals, this does not imply that my question had no cause. It was caused by other things that went on in my mind. The mental act of questioning is a part of a whole series of causally connected mental acts, some of which are directly caused by my environment. For example, I was reminded that I will have to grade tests by the fact that I saw one of my daughter's school books on the couch, beyond the dinner table, in the dining room. And this act of seeing was caused by the book on the couch. So the book caused a perception, the perception caused a remembering, and the remembering eventually caused a questioning.

But if my mental acts are part of a causal order which

intermingles acts caused by perceptual objects with acts caused by other acts, how could they be said to be free? Even if Sartre is correct when he maintains that the act of questioning is not caused by being-in-itself, he has not shown that it is not caused at all and, hence, free. In order to prove that man is truly free, Sartre must argue that consciousness is not a causal process. He must prove that mental acts themselves do not form a causal chain. He must argue that mental acts are, not only causally disengaged from the things in the world, but also from prior mental acts. And this is precisely his next task.

14.   The pliancy of the past

An explication of determinism

The third main theme of Sartre's attempt to prove that man is free is that man is free because he creates his own past. We saw in the last chapter that in order to prove that consciousness is not part of a causal process, it is not enough to prove that it can disengage itself from the causal influence of the world of being-in-itself. Sartre must also show that past mental states do not determine present ones. He tries to show this by arguing that a past state of consciousness is what it is only for a present state. Only through the interpretation of the past which takes place in the present does the past get its meaning. How then, so he asks rhetorically, can a past which is only fixed by the present influence the present? Obviously it cannot. But is there really no past mental state, independently of what we think of it, independently of what we make of it in the present? No, there is not. To think of past states of consciousness as somehow 'being there, once and for all', Sartre claims, is to turn them into little chunks of being-in-itself. But consciousness is not of this kind. In and by itself it is nothing. Only through consciousness does consciousness get its peculiar sort of being. Such is Sartre's main argument. Now, again, to the details.

Is man free? The answer depends, of course, on what you

mean by 'free'. In one sense, there can be no doubt that man is free. If you mean: can a person deliberate, make up his mind, decide to follow a certain course of action, etc., then man is undoubtedly free. It is obvious that we think about future possible actions, that we weigh their consequences as best we can, that we try to make up our minds about what to do in the light of these deliberations, that we change our minds in the end and consider still different possibilities, and so on. These mental processes do occur, and if their existence means that we are free to act as we choose, then nobody can doubt that we are free. In this sense of the term, a tree is not free, for it experiences no mental acts at all. In this sense of the term, even a dog may not be said to be free. For even though it undoubtedly experiences certain mental acts—it feels pain, for example—we do not believe that it is capable of higher mental processes, that is, of making decisions about future actions in the light of practical consequences and moral values. This is the plain and plausible reason why we do not hold trees and dogs morally responsible for their behavior. And it is also the reason why we do not even hold certain persons morally responsible for what they do, namely, those persons who resemble trees and dogs in that they are incapable of deliberation in the relevant sense of the word.

But this notion of freedom is not the one that has always excited philosophers and theologians. Granted that normal human beings experience certain sophisticated mental processes, processes of deliberation and choosing, the great debate centers on the question of whether or not these mental processes are *determined*. I may consider what to do tonight. Should I go out to meet with friends, have a beer or two, talk about the latest follies of the university administration, or should I stay home and start the spaghetti sauce for tomorrow's dinner? I weigh the advantages and disadvantages of both actions. There is the fact to be considered that my friends may not show up at the tavern. And there is the further fact that I will not have much time tomorrow afternoon to make the sauce. But, of course, I could start the sauce in the morning before I go to my office. After a while, I make up my mind: I shall go out and make the sauce tomorrow. (You probably knew from the beginning that this is what I was going to do!) But was not this decision of mine to go out determined? Was it not determined by my thoughts, by my wishes, by my desires, my hopes and fears? Was it not determined by my general inclination to prefer a good time with friends to slaving over a hot stove? In short, are not all of my deliberations, all of my choices, just part of a vast network which connects the past with the present and which determines for any given moment what goes on in my mind?

We must be clear that the view that all of our mental states are determined is not a view capriciously invented by philosophers and scientists. It is part and parcel of common sense. You relied on this piece of common sense, for example, when you expected me to go out for a beer. You knew or thought you knew that my eventual decision was already determined and that I was just going through the motions of weighing the two alternatives. We are quite sure, in many cases, that we can predict the actions of other people because we know their inclinations, preferences, shortcomings, fears, etc. Furthermore, all of our beliefs in the possibility of educating, civilizing, or rehabilitating people rest on an implicit belief in determinism. If we really believed that our actions are not determined by what happens to us at earlier times (in conjunction with what happens at the present), then it would make absolutely no sense to try to bring up children correctly or to rehabilitate criminals. A belief in determinism, I claim, is part of common sense. But it is a very inarticulated part. Although we all act as if we believed in determinism, we also tend to profess to free will, when specifically asked about our theory. In order to rid ourselves of this contradictory attitude, we must clarify what determinism is and what it is not.

Let us start with a very abstract example. Consider a system S, of ten bodies, $A, B, C, \ldots$ and assume that each one of these ten bodies has precisely three properties, $m, p,$ and v. Assume that we can measure these properties, so that we can assign numerical values to them. At any given moment in time, t_n, the system S will be in a certain state, S_{t_n}, determined by the numerical values of the three properties for each body. The state of the system at moment t_1, for example, is completely given by the following list of thirty values:

$A: m_7, p_{13}, v_4$

$B: m_9, p_2, v_{78}$

$C: m_{24}, p_8, v_{32}$

....

....

$J: m_4, p_{16}, v_2.$

The numerals have no special significance. They merely indicate, for example, that the property m of A at t_1 has a specific value, namely, the value 7. For every moment in time, there exists such a list of thirty values, that is, a state of the system for that moment. At t_{935}, for example, the value of p for body C may be 94. Since we have assumed that the ten bodies of our example have precisely these three properties and no others, the description of the state of the system for a given time t_m constitutes what we may call 'perfect knowledge' of the system (for that time). There is nothing more that we could wish to know about the system.

Assume, finally, that there is a law of nature, L, which is of the following sort: from a description of the system at a given moment t_n and L there follows logically a description of the system for any other moment in time, earlier than t_n as well as later than t_n. *In this case, we say that S is deterministic.* Let me say the same thing in different words: a system S is deterministic if and only if there exists a certain kind of law, L, such that any state of the system, S_n, together with L determines every other state of system S.

It will shed some light on this notion of determinism if we explain what it means for our ability to *predict*. We shall make the following three assumptions:

(1) We shall assume that we can accurately *measure* the state of the system for a given moment in time,

(2) that we have *discovered* the law L which connects the various states,

(3) and that we can *compute* the states of the system from the given one and the law L.

If these three conditions are fulfilled, then we can *predict* (or postdict) the state of the system for any given moment in time from the state of the system for any other moment in time. For example, you will be able to predict what value p had for body C for any given moment in time.

The pliancy of the past

It is of the utmost importance to realize that a system may very well be deterministic, even though we are not able to predict its states. It may be the case, for example, that the system is much too complicated for the measurement of one of its states. Imagine that the system consists of billions of bodies and that each body has hundreds of properties. It may then be impossible to measure all of these properties for all of these bodies for a given moment. But even if we are able to measure the state of a complicated system, the second of the three conditions may not be fulfilled: We may not have discovered the relevant law L, or we may never be able to discover it. Finally, it may be the case, for a given system, that the computation is much too complicated for us, so that even the fastest and best computer may not be able to predict the states of a system from a given state and the law L. Whether or not a given system is deterministic, to stress it again, does not depend on us human beings. A system is deterministic, whether we know it or not, if it obeys a certain kind of law. Whether or not we can predict the behavior of a system, on the other hand, depends quite obviously on us. It depends on our ability to measure, to discover, and to compute. But there is an obvious connection between determinism and predictability. This connection can best be illustrated if we assume that there is an all-powerful and all-knowing God. Such a God would not be hampered by the restrictions contained in the three conditions mentioned above. Hence, if a system is deterministic, this God could predict and postdict all of its future and past states.

The system of ten bodies which I described in abstract terms does actually exist. It is deterministic and, wonder of all wonders, we are actually in the position of God in regard to it. It consists of the nine planets and the sun. The letters 'm', 'p', and 'v' stand for the three 'properties' of mass, position, and velocity, respectively. (Position divides into three co-ordinates, but I wanted to keep the example simple. Notice also that the value for the mass does not change from one state to another.) We can actually measure the values for these three 'properties'. We have also discovered the relevant law; it consists of certain differential equations in time. Finally, we are able to compute future and past states of the solar system. This means, for example, that we can predict the future mass, position, and velocity of the earth for any moment in time. And this means, for example, that we can predict the position and velocity of the earth for 10 January 1988.

Is the physical universe, the sum total of all elementary particles, a deterministic system? This is the important question. Does the universe as a whole, with all the stars and nebulae, black holes and what-have-you, behave like the solar system, that is, deterministically? We know, precisely, what this question means: is there a law (or conjunction of laws) such that the state of the universe at any given moment is determined by the state of the universe at any other moment and the law? You realize now, I trust, how big the gulf is between determinism and full predictability. Even if the universe is deterministic, it is rather doubtful that we should ever be able to predict its future states. For it is rather doubtful that we could ever measure all of the properties of all of the elementary particles in the universe for a given moment in time. It is doubtful, in other words, that we can ever know the state of the universe for a given moment. And think also of how unlikely it is that the other two conditions will ever be fulfilled. I am pretty confident, therefore, that we shall never be able to predict the future of the universe as a whole. But this does not mean, to say it once again, that the universe may not be deterministic. Nor does it mean that we shall never be able to have perfect knowledge of parts of the universe, of isolated simple systems like the solar system.

Well, then, is the universe as a whole deterministic? After all this to-do you should be able to see that the answer is obvious: I do not know. Nor does anyone else. Nobody knows whether or not there exists a law of the required kind (or a conjunction of such laws). We know many deterministic laws for smaller systems, and we may *believe* that there must be one for the universe as a whole, but we do not *know* that there is one. The thesis of determinism, namely, that the universe as a whole obeys deterministic laws, is just that, a thesis. Scientists accept this thesis. They act as if it were true. They hope that it is true. But nobody knows for sure whether or not it is true.

At this point of our exposition, we must complicate matters even further and distinguish between deterministic laws, on the one hand, and probabilistic laws, on the other. Consider again the system *S*. But assume that after an exhaustive search we can only come up with the following sort of law: given the state of the system at t_1, five of the ten bodies will at t_2 have a value of v larger than a given number and five will have a value smaller. Similarly, for other moments in time. This law tells us *something* about the behavior of the system, but it does not tell us *everything*. In particular, it does not tell us which ones of the ten bodies have the value of v smaller than the given number and which ones have the larger value. It does not tell us, for example, whether the earth will at t_2 have a smaller or larger value. But it does tell us that 50 per cent of the bodies will have a value smaller and that 50 per cent will have a value larger than the given number.

Our example is a little silly, but the principle is quite clear. Given certain information about the age, sex, religion, educational level, economic level, dietary habits, etc. of certain bodies (persons), we know a law that will tell us how many of these bodies will die within a year, but we cannot predict individual deaths. Here we know probabilistic laws about the life expectancy of persons. Given certain information about a die and how it is to be thrown, we know a probabilistic law that tells us that on the average one in six throws will yield a three. The laws of gambling are probabilistic in our sense of the term. If the die is unbiased and if it is thrown in an unbiased way, then the probability of getting a three is one/sixth. This law, I want you to realize, is as iron-clad, as unbendable, as objective as the law that regulates the motion of the planets. We discovered this law about unbiased dice just as we discovered the law that governs the planets.

These two examples of probabilistic law show in what sense we tend to believe in determinism, even if we cannot prove its thesis. That we can predict the death of a given person only with probability, we attribute to our ignorance and not to the way the universe ultimately behaves. If we just knew more about the causes of death and other factors, and if we could just find certain complicated laws, so we believe, we could predict individual deaths. We make do with probabilistic laws because we cannot, at the present time, do any better. But we believe that the world really is deterministic. If we knew more about the precise force and angle with which the die is cast, and if we know certain other facts and had the relevant laws, then we could predict the outcome of the next throw of the die. But the belief that the universe as a whole is ultimately deterministic rather than probabilistic, we know, is nothing more than a belief. The world may be deterministic. Or it may be probabilistic. All we know for sure is that certain systems are deterministic and that other systems, usually the more complicated ones, are probabilistic.

(2) *Freedom versus determinism*

So far, we have talked about the physical universe only. It is time to bring back the mind and fit it into our picture. We know that certain, very complicated, chemical structures give rise to mental processes. Whenever we find a highly developed nervous system, we also find certain mental phenomena. Let me simplify this scientific story, without loss of philosophical relevance, by saying that human brains are co-ordinated to mental processes. I spoke of brains 'giving rise to' and of 'being co-ordinated' to mental processes. Here is a vagueness which we shall now try to remove. Common sense believes, and science concurs, that brain states are lawfully connected with mental states. We know, for example, that a prefrontal lobotomy will lead to apathy, lack of emotions, docility, etc. And we know that if certain parts of the brain are destroyed, certain mental functions will be impaired. What precise brain changes cause what precise mental changes is a matter to be investigated by the scientist. As philosophers, we are only interested in the following two aspects of the situation. Firstly, in the fact that in addition to brain states there are mental states. And, secondly, that there is a lawful connection between the two. Next, I shall simplify once more and assume that the relationship between brain states and mental states is a one-one relationship. This means that to every brain state there corresponds precisely one mental state, and conversely. This assumption may well be false, and I am inclined to believe that it is false. It seems to me plausible that minute differences in brain states will not be accompanied by differences in mental states, so that to several brain states there corresponds only one mental state. But for the sake of simplicity, I shall pretend that the relationship is one to one. Finally,let us pretend that a certain person P is a closed system, unaffected by any outside stimuli. We can then diagram the physiological and mental processes in Figure 14.1.

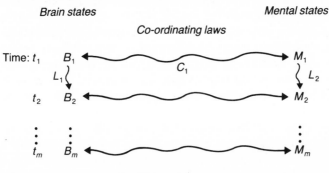

Figure 14.1

The wavy arrows stand for lawful connections, L_1 between brain states and brain states, L_2 between mental states and mental states, and C_1 between brain states and mental states.

Assume that the brain states of person P form a deterministic system. In this case, there is a law such that the state of the brain at any moment, B_m, is determined by this law and any other state of the brain B_n. For example, brain state B_1 determines, together with the law, in what state the brain will be in at the later time t_2. If we know B_1, if we know the law, and if we can compute, then we can predict B_2. Next, add our assumption about the one-one co-ordination between brain states and mental states. You can see that then all of the mental states are determined as well. Given that the brain is in state B_1, the mind will be in state M_1. But B_1, by means of the law, determines all other brain states. Hence it determines also all other mental states. Thus if determinism holds for the brain states, it holds *ipso facto* for the mental states. The whole person P, consisting of body and mind, forms a deterministic system. Notice the following interesting point. Assume that at t_m there occurs the mental state M_m. What *caused* M_m? You may with equal justification say that it was the prior brain state B_1 or that it was the prior mental state M_1. B_1 may be said to have caused M_m because it caused B_m, by means of the deterministic law L_1, and B_m is co-ordinated, by means of the co-ordinating law C_1, to M_m.

Or you may say that M_1 caused M_m, either directly by means of the deterministic law L_2, or indirectly by means of being co-ordinated to B_1. In this fashion, you can trace a causal path from any brain state or any mental state to any other brain state and any other mental state.

But assume now that the physical universe is not deterministic. In this case, there exists no deterministic law L_1 which, together with some one brain state, determines all other brain states. Therefore, no mental state is determined either. Even if we had all the relevant information and computational ability, we could not predict later brain states or mental states on the basis of earlier ones. But this means that we could not, in principle, predict person P's later *actions*. (Please remember that we are making the rather staggering assumption that P forms a closed system which is not influenced by outside stimuli.) We may ask: will P tomorrow mail a letter to his mother? If determinism is true, then this action–which is a complicated pattern of bodily movements and mental processes–is determined by the present state of P. We may not be able to predict what P will do, that he will not mail the letter, for example. But what P will do, whether or not we are able to predict it, is determined by his present state (or any other state, for that matter). But if determinism is not true, as we now assume, then P's action is not determined, and there is no possibility that we could ever predict it. In this case we may say that P is *free* to do anything tomorrow, either mail the letter or not mail the letter. (We must not say that he is free to do what he *wants to do*; for that is the case, even if determinism is true. What he wants to do however, is determined.) In this manner, freedom is opposed to determinism. To get the complete explanation of this notion of freedom, we simply drop the assumption that we are dealing with just one person conceived of as a closed system. We now consider the whole universe, consisting of all physical bodies and of certain mental things which occur in connection with brains. The actions of a person in such a universe may be said to be free if they are not determined, that is, if determinism is not true for this universe. Is man free in this precise sense? You can anticipate my answer: I do not know. Since I do not know whether or not determinism is true, I do not know whether or not man is free in this sense. Nor does anyone else.

The universe either is deterministic or it is not deterministic. It cannot be just a little deterministic. There either exists the deterministic law or else there does not. There is no third possibility. But the universe may be *lawful* without being deterministic. It may be probabilistic. It may be the case, for all we know, that the states of the universe (including mental processes) are connected with each other, not be a deterministic law, but by a probabilistic one (or a conjunction of such laws). It may not be determined, for example that P will not mail the letter to his mother. But the probability that he will not mail the letter may be precisely one-tenth. And if we have the relevant information, if we know the probabilistic law, and if we can compute, then we can predict that the probability of P's action is one-tenth. If the universe is probabilistic rather than deterministic, then the laws which connect its states are just as objective, as I already pointed out, as deterministic laws would be.

The possibility of a probabilistic universe calls our attention to another notion of freedom. Man may be said to be free if the universe is neither deterministic nor probabilistic. Man may be said to be free if his actions follow neither deterministically nor probabilistically from earlier states of the universe. In this sense, man is free only if his actions are not *lawfully connected* with earlier states of the universe. Is man free in this sense? I am convinced that he is not. Although I do not know whether or not there are comprehensive probabilistic laws governing the universe as a whole, I know that there are a number of probabilistic laws which govern human behavior. In regard to human behavior and probabilistic laws, we are in a position similar to the one in which we are in regard to the solar system and deterministic laws. We do not know whether or not the universe as a whole is deterministic, but we do know that this particular system is deterministic. Similarly, I do not know whether or not the universe as a whole is probabilistic, but I am relatively confident that human behavior is governed by probabilistic laws.

We have distinguished between three different notions of freedom. Human beings may be said to be free (to have free will) if they can contemplate alternative courses of actions, choose among these possibilities, decide what to do, and sometimes even change their minds at the last minute and reconsider their decisions. Since these mental processes do indeed occur, there can be no doubt whatsoever that human beings are free in this sense. By contrast, stones, dogs, and certain 'insane' persons are not free to act as they choose in the light of the moral consequences of their actions. But the fact that human beings are free in this sense raises a further question: are these mental processes, which constitute choosing, determined or not? That they occur, nobody can deny. But is their occurrence determined? In another sense of the word, human beings can only be said to be free if their deliberations and choices are not determined. In order to explain what is involved in this notion of being determined, we had to delve into the possibility of a deterministic universe. I confessed that I do not know whether or not human beings are free in this second sense. Finally, we saw that even if the universe is not deterministic it may still be lawfully governed by probabilistic laws. And this possibility led us to consider a third notion of freedom. Human beings may be said to be free only if their deliberations and decisions are not lawful at all, if they do not even obey probabilistic laws. I am convinced that man is not free in this sense. The field of human behavior seems to me to be one of the most outstanding examples of probabilistic lawfulness. We know of numerous probabilistic laws that connect a person's behavior with his past experiences.

So, where do we stand in regard to human freedom? Man is free in so far as he can choose. He may or may not be free in so far as his choices are determined. And he is not free in so far as his choices are lawful.

(3) *Freedom and reasons for actions*

Sartre claims that man is totally, unconditionally free. Nothing whatsoever restricts his freedom. This claim clashes with everything we know about human behavior. And it clashes with everything we do. It clashes with our practice of education. It clashes with our attempts at rehabilitation. It clashes with our hope for the progress of civilization. Sartre's task is therefore quite Quixotic. He must try to convince us, in spite of all we know and do, that nothing whatsoever can influence our actions. His argument, not surprisingly, is heroic. In outline, it comes to this:

(1) You can only look at your past mental states from the standpoint of the present. (2) This means that a past mental state can only exist for you as the object of a present mental act. (3) But this means that a past mental state can only exist as the object of present consciousness. (4) To put it differently, mental states can only exist *for* consciousness; they cannot exist *by and in themselves*. (5) But if they can only exist as objects of present consciousness, then they cannot have determined or otherwise influenced present consciousness. (6) Hence no mental state can be determined or influenced by an earlier mental state. (7) Therefore, every mental state is totally free.

I think that (1) is a truism and immediately to be granted. (2) is merely another formulation of (1), except that it contains two fatal words, namely 'for you'. The crucial step of the argument occurs from (2) to (3). In effect, you get from (2) to (3) by simply dropping what looks like a harmless phrase, the 'for you' just mentioned. But dropping these two words makes all the difference in the world. For what (3) asserts is the most amazing contention. It asserts that your past mental states do not exist independently of your present mental states. It asserts that there are really no past mental states of yours, only present ones which are about past ones. But this last sentence of mine cannot be correct. If there are no past mental states, then present ones cannot be about them. You see, I trust, how absurd Sartre's contention is. It is so absurd that it is hard even to formulate it. Let me try again. What (3) claims is, in effect, that there are no past mental states, but only present mental states which may be about other mental states which, for some reason, appear to be past mental states. Since (3) is the crucial assertion, we shall have to scrutinize it carefully. I take (4) to be another, more sophisticated way of stating (3). Hence I have to grant it if I accede to (3). I also agree with (5). Thus, if I accepted (3), I would have to agree to (6). And (7) would then follow by what we mean in this context by 'free'.

What (3) says is that there exists no fixed past mental process, that our mental past is what we make it be in the present. Our past is totally pliant. Sartre's example of an action done freely is the Frankish king Clovis's conversion to Catholicism. What was the cause, if there was any, of Clovis's conversion? Sartre's first point is that the cause, if there was any, is the same as the reason for his action. And the reason for an action, Sartre says, is 'the state of contemporary things as it is revealed to a consciousness' (*ibid.*, p. 577). It is the situation as viewed by the person who acts. In this sense of reason, the reason for Clovis's conversion was, according to Sartre, 'the political and religious state of Gaul; it is the relative strength of the episcopate, the great landowners, and the common people' (*ibid.*, p. 575). This is what Sartre actually says, but we must correct him. What he must mean to say is that the reason for Clovis's conversion is Clovis's *perception* of the political and religious state of Gaul; etc. The reason for Clovis's conversion cannot be, for example, the state of Gaul as assessed by a modern historian with the advantage of hindsight. Why did Clovis convert? What was his reason? Clovis thought that the episcopate was the strongest force in Gaul and would be able to help him the most in achieving his goal, namely, the conquest of Gaul.

Notice that when I just stated Clovis's reason for converting, I mentioned not only his estimate of the powers in Gaul, but also his goal and the belief that one of the powers would better help him achieve this goal. Why did Clovis convert? He wanted to conquer Gaul, and in order to achieve this goal he looked around for help. He thought that the episcopate was the strongest force in Gaul and hence would be the most powerful ally. He believed that he could secure the help of this ally by converting to Catholicism. This, in outline, was his reason. As you can see, his reason is a very complex mental process, involving his intentions, his beliefs, his estimates, his desires, his hopes, etc. *Because* this particular mental process occurred, Clovis converted. Sartre, however, sees it differently. He wants to isolate Clovis's conception of the political situation in Gaul from his intentions, hopes, other beliefs, etc.

> The cause of Clovis's conversion is the political and religious
> state of Gaul; . . . Nevertheless, this objective appreciation
> can be made only in the light of a presupposed end and
> within the limits of a project of the for-itself towards this end.
> In order for the power of the episcopate to be revealed to

Clovis as the cause of his conversion (that is, in order for him to be able to envisage the objective consequences which this conversion could have) it is necessary first for him to posit as an end the conquest of Gaul. If we suppose that Clovis has other ends, he can find in the situation of the church causes for his becoming Arian or remaining pagan. . . . We shall therefore use the term *cause* for the objective apprehension of a determined situation as this situation is revealed in the light of a certain end as being able to serve as the means for attaining this end. (*Ibid.*, pp. 575–6)

At the beginning of this quotation, Sartre says that the cause is (Clovis's estimate of) the political and religious state of Gaul. At the end of it, he says something quite different, namely, that the cause is Clovis's estimate of the situation in Gaul *as revealed in the light of a certain end* etc. There is a reason for this ambiguity. Sartre wants to argue that the reason for Clovis's conversion is *not* a cause for it, in the sense of determining or influencing it. Clovis acted freely when he converted. What we call 'the reason' for his conversion did not in any sense cause his conversion. To make this contention plausible, Sartre does two things. Firstly, he isolates Clovis's estimate of the situation in Gaul as his reason for converting. He does not allow, as we do, other things to enter into what constitutes Clovis's reason. In particular, he does not admit Clovis's goal (intention) of conquering Gaul as part of his reason for converting. Secondly, Sartre claims that Clovis's estimate of the situation in Gaul is shaped, formed, colored, or what-have-you by his consequent action of converting. His line of reasoning clearly is that if the reason for the action is only created through the action, then it cannot have been a cause of the action:

Therefore the cause, far from determining the action, appears only in and through the project of an action. It is in and through the project of imposing his rule on all of Gaul that the state of the Western Church appears objectively to Clovis as a cause for his conversion. (*Ibid.*, p. 578)

There are lots of things wrong with Sartre's line of reasoning.

Firstly, as I said before, it seems to me quite clear that the reason for Clovis's conversion involves, not only his estimates of the situation in Gaul, but also his ambitions, his beliefs about other matters, his hopes, etc. Secondly, but granted for the sake of the argument that Clovis's reason was his estimate of the situation in Gaul, it seems to me to be obvious that this estimate is not created by the subsequent action of converting. As Sartre himself admits, Clovis may have made the same estimate with other goals in mind and, hence, may have acted differently. But perhaps, thirdly, I am misinterpreting Sartre at this point. Perhaps, Sartre means not that the action carves out of all possibilities the estimate of the situation in Gaul, but rather that Clovis's having a certain goal, the conquest of Gaul, gives meaning to his estimate of the situation in Gaul. If so, then there in some truth in what he says. We agree that *because* Clovis had this particular goal he tries to figure out what the distribution of power is in Gaul. His having this goal causes him to evaluate the situation in Gaul. But this means that his evaluation of the situation came about as a consequence of his intentions. It does not mean that the action of converting was not caused, at least in part, by this evaluation. The one thing has nothing to do with the other.

There is one final twist to Sartre's attempt to make the reason for Clovis's action depend on the action rather than the other way around. In the last quotation, Sartre no longer speaks of *the* reason for Clovis's conversion, but of what *appears to Clovis* as reason for his conversion. The two, of course, need not be the same. What someone takes to be the reason for his action need not be the real reason. Have we, then, been talking all along not about the reasons for actions, but rather about what people take in hindsight to be the reasons for their actions? I do not know. This is just one more of the many ambiguities of Sartre's discussion. But if we do turn to Clovis's retrospective analysis of the reason for his action, then we arrive at long last at what I alleged to be Sartre's main argument at the beginning of this section. The reason for Clovis's action, *after the action has taken place*, can only appear to Clovis as an object of a later mental state. And this means, as I described Sartre's argument, that it can only exist through Clovis's later mental states. Hence it could not possibly have determined his action. In a word: since the past is what we make of it in the present, it could not have determined the present.

If we try to protest that this is surely absurd, that the past is what it is and cannot be changed by our thinking about it in the present, Sartre threatens us with his metaphysical club: to think of past mental processes as being what they are in and by themselves, is to treat them as things among things, as having being-in-itself (*ibid.*, pp. 567–8). Absurd as Sartre's defense of total freedom may appear to be, it is of one cloth with his basic metaphysical axiom: things are what they are, consciousness is what we make of it. And this axiom is with him a matter of faith or, rather, of wishful thinking. If being-for-itself is what we make of it, then we can make it be whatever we wish it to be. Man is free because he can make himself be whatever he wants to be, merely by looking at himself in a different way. I think of this as the ostrich view of the human condition.

(4) *Freedom and original choice*

We believe that Clovis converted because he wanted to secure the help of the church for his attempt to conquer Gaul. If Sartre were correct, then there is no reason at all for his conversion. Of course, Sartre speaks of causes and reasons, but he insists that they make absolutely no difference to what happens. But if actions are not lawfully connected with mental processes, other actions, and environmental factors, are they not purely gratuitous? Does it not follow from Sartre's view that all actions occur at random? If Sartre were correct, then it would make no sense at all to try to explain why people do the things they do. Nor would it make any sense whatsoever to try to influence their actions. By insisting that actions are totally free, Sartre has jumped from the frying pan into the fire. As abhorrent as it may be to contemplate the possibility that our actions are determined, as repugnant is it to face the prospect that they are utterly capricious. Sartre is aware of this dilemma. 'Someone, nevertheless, may object and ask how if my act can be understood *neither* in terms of the state of the world *nor* in terms of the ensemble of my past taken as an irreducible thing, it could possibly be anything but gratuitous' (*ibid.*, p. 584). Sartre looks

for a way out. Actions, he wishes to hold, are totally free, not
lawfully connected with the world and mental states. Yet, he
cannot admit that they are, therefore, capricious and incomprehensible. His way out consists in invoking the notion of an
'initial project' or 'original choice'.

Clovis's action was not caused by anything. Is there then no
explanation at all for it? Did it just happen out of nowhere? Did
it just pop into existence? No, there must be some way of
understanding this action, of relating it to other things, without
placing it into a web of causes. It must be viewed as part of a
structure, so that it can get its meaning from this structure, but
this structure must not be the causal network which, according
to our view, holds the world together. Sartre calls this structure
the 'initial project' or 'the original choice'. Clovis's action,
though not caused by anything, can nevertheless be understood
as part of Clovis's original choice of himself, as a constituent of
Clovis's initial project of himself. Clovis could have acted
otherwise; he did not have to convert. But in a sense he could
not have acted otherwise; for he could only have acted
otherwise at a price, namely, at the price of having to modify
fundamentally his original choice of himself. Clovis's action is
not gratuitous because it fits into a pattern. This pattern is laid
down by his original choice.

What, precisely, is this original choice? Here is Sartre's
explanation:

> My ultimate and initial project–for these are but one–is, as
> we shall see, always the outline of a solution of the problem
> of being. But this solution is not first conceived and then
> realized; we *are* this solution. We make it exist by means of
> our very engagement, and therefore we shall be able to
> apprehend it only by living it. (*Ibid.*, p. 596)

Clovis's action is an integral part of the project which is his life.
It does not stand alone by itself, unrelated to other parts of his
life, and therefore incomprehensible. It can be understood as
part of a project, and we know that Clovis could not really have
acted otherwise, unless he had changed this project. There is
some truth to all of this, we feel, but does it really afford a way
out of the dilemma? Clovis's action fits into a pattern. He

wanted to be ruler of Gaul. He wanted to be a powerful ruler. But what does this mean if not that his ambitions, his personality traits, hopes and fears, explain in a lawful manner his actions? If Clovis had decided, for some reason or other, to give up his project to conquer Gaul, if he had changed his life's ambition, he might have acted differently, he might have abdicated, he might have become a beggar, he might have committed suicide. He could have acted otherwise, but only at the price, as Sartre puts it, of changing his choice of himself. Does this mean anything more than that to understand an action as an essential part of a human being's life is to understand it as being embedded in a network of *causal factors*?

We are still not clear about the notion of original choice. What, for example, was Clovis's original choice? Was it to be ruler of all of Gaul? Was it to be the most powerful person in the Western world? Was it to be a decent and just servant of the people? And when did Clovis make his choice? As a baby? As a young adult? Sartre, I believe, would accuse us of misunderstanding his view, if we seriously pursued these questions. The choice is not first made and then realized. We live this choice at all times. And we can only apprehend it by living it. But what kind of choice is this, a choice that is not made at some time or other, a choice that cannot be apprehended when it is made? At any rate, the original choice supposedly explains how man can be free, but not too free. It supposedly explains how man's actions can be free without being capricious. Man is utterly and totally free to choose his ultimate project, but he is only conditionally free to make other choices; for these have to conform to his original choice. Let us make the ridiculous assumption that Clovis's very first thought was to conquer Gaul one day in the future. Much of what he does later on can be explained in terms of this ambition. We can explain, for example, why he converted. It is therefore true that his life's project, his basic ambition, his over-riding purpose, limits his actions. But is it also true that his original choice was totally free? And if it was utterly free, was it not then capricious? We see that Sartre's dilemma has not been avoided but merely shifted. Clovis's conversion, though presumably free, was not capricious, because it fits into the pattern of Clovis's original choice. But what about this choice itself? It appears to be completely capricious and totally incomprehensible.

Nor is this all. Sartre's way out of the dilemma is threatened from another direction as well. If Clovis's conversion is really a part of a pattern, how can it be free? Is it not then *determined* by this pattern? We encounter here still another notion of freedom, a notion which we can best discuss in connection with Leibniz's story of the creation of Adam. According to this story, Adam consists of a nature which God endows with existence. This nature contains all of Adam's properties, including the property of taking a bite from the apple. When God created Adam, he considered various possible persons. He reviewed all kinds of possible natures. Then he picked one of these, Adam's nature, and added existence to it. This story implies, as we noted, that Adam was not free to choose whether or not to eat the apple. As surely as Adam is Adam, that is, as surely as he has this nature and no other, as surely had he to eat the apple. If 'he' had not eaten the apple, 'he' would have had to be someone other than Adam.

As you can imagine, Leibniz's view is anathema to Sartre. He abhors the idea that God chooses Adam's nature and, hence, is ultimately responsible for all of Adam's actions (*ibid.*, pp. 602–4). But there is a superficial similarity between Adam's nature as conceived of by Leibniz and the ultimate project of Clovis's life as envisaged by Sartre. Just as all of Adam's actions are determined by his nature, since they are but parts of that nature, so all of Clovis's actions threaten to be determined by his ultimate project, since they are but parts of that project. If we seriously think of Clovis's ultimate project as a pattern of which his conversion is a part, then the conclusion seems to be inescapable that his conversion was no more freely chosen than Adam's action of eating the apple was.

But there is an important difference and Sartre is quick to point it out. Clovis's original choice, in distinction to Adam's nature, is merely a *pattern*, a pattern which does not completely determine its parts. What Sartre has in mind harks back to our discussion of the origins of Gestalt theory and the nature of structures. To use one of the favorite examples of Gestalt psychologists, one and the same melody can exist in different keys and, therefore, does not determine what tones must occur in it. To use our own earlier example, remember the two series of even and of odd positive integers. These two series, we saw, are isomorphic to each other. Now, we may call a series of things which is isomorphic to either one of these two series of numbers 'a progression'. The term 'progression' is then a word for a pattern in the sense in which we are now talking about it. Every structure which is a progression is isomorphic to every other such structure. All these structures have something in common, so to speak, that makes them progressions. Now, the important point to notice is that being a progression does not determine the nature of the parts of the progression. One of our progressions, the series of even integers, consists of the numbers 2, 4, 6, etc., and the relation of being the next larger even number; the other progression consists of completely different numbers, namely of the numbers 1, 3, 5, etc., and of a quite different relation, namely, the relation of being the next larger odd number. To know that something is a progression, is to know that it has a certain structure–that it is isomorphic to the series of the positive even integers, for example–but it is not to know as yet what its parts are.

What Clovis chose when he made his original choice was a pattern in this meaning of the term. His choice does not determine the parts of this pattern, but merely its structure. In this precise sense, Sartre explains how Clovis's act of conversion is not capricious and yet free. It is not capricious because it fits into the pattern; one can understand it as part of this rather than some other patterns. It is free because some other action would fit the same pattern equally well; another action would equally well be meaningful as part of the same pattern. But this explanation leaves many questions unanswered. What, precisely, is this pattern chosen by Clovis? It cannot be Clovis's life; for his life is not a pattern, but an instance of the pattern. Is it the goal of becoming the ruler of Gaul? If so, then Sartre's view amounts to nothing more than the truism that people have grand ambitions, life-long plans, etc. which they try to fulfill and carry out by using diverse means. For example, some other action, other than his conversion to Catholicism, may equally well have served Clovis's over-all plan to become ruler of Gaul. In this case, though, it would still make sense to ask why Clovis chose this other action rather than conversion, and we would expect that his choice was lawfully connected with other mental and non-mental factors. For example, we could explain this alternative action by pointing at Clovis's ultimate goal to conquer Gaul and some further thoughts of his about the strength (or weakness) of the church. In short, Sartre's appeal to the ultimate choice merely invokes the truism that our goals in life, though they are partial causes for our actions, do not in and by themselves determine what we do on each particular occasion.

(5) *Metaphysical freedom*

I closed our discussion of Heidegger with the remark that Existentialists are caught between the devil and the deep blue sea. On the one hand, they insist that existence is the substance of the world. On the other hand, they assert that there are modes of existence. These two views, however, are incompatible with each other. One of them has to go. This is where the dilemma lies. If the Existentialist gives up the idea that there are modes of existence, he abandons what is essential to existentialistic thought. If he rejects the view that existence is the substance of the world, he loses his most powerful defense of freedom. Let us look at this last consequence in these concluding pages.

Leibniz's story of the creation of Adam (and of everything else in the universe) implies that the essence of a thing precedes its existence. First, there exists in God's mind a notion of Adam's nature, his essence, then God adds to this nature existence, and in this fashion creates the person Adam. Adam's essence exists thus in God's mind, before Adam exists in reality. And this implies, as we have seen, that Adam is not free. Existentialists, therefore, reject this and any other conception which implies the precedence of essence over existence. They maintain that the order is reversed: existence precedes essence. Sartre says: 'For us, on the contrary, Adam is not defined by an essence since for human reality essence comes after existence. Adam is defined by the choice of his ends; . . . ' (*ibid.*, p. 603). A human being first of all exists, and he creates his nature as he goes along, so to speak, within the framework of his original choice. In this way, human freedom is assured.

But this existentialistic view implies that existence is the ultimate substance of the world, that is, that it is the basic subject of all predication. If existence were a property or feature instead, even a transcendent property or feature, then it would have to be such a property or feature of *something else*. This something else would be the ultimate substance of the world. It could not be the case then that man exists first and only afterwards acquires his properties. There would have to exist something which has the feature of existence, and what could this something possibly be? Not some formless matter; for consciousness does not consist of matter. The original choice, perhaps? But would this not imply that man is not free or, at least, that he is only a little bit free? For we know that the original choice determines, within certain limits, what a person will do. So, if what originally has existence, is the original choice, then man is only free to the extent that he has to live through the consequences of his original choice. The only difference between Leibniz's story and Sartre's, then, is that Leibniz's concept of nature contains every single one of Adam's properties, while Sartre's notion of the original choice contains only the most important of Clovis's properties. Freedom then would merely be a matter of degree and not the unconditional, total condition which Sartre wants it to be. Nor would it be possible, as Sartre envisages, that the original choice could be aborted, taken back, changed. If it exists, if it has this feature of existence, then there is nothing that can change it. Just as Adam must eat from the apple as long as he is Adam, so Clovis must convert to Catholicism or perform an equivalent action, as long as he is Clovis, that is, as long as he is this particular original choice and no other.

Sartre avoids this consequence by holding that the original choice is nothing complete, nothing fixed, nothing given once and for all. It unfolds, so to speak, during a lifetime. It is the pattern of a life as it emerges during the life. But this conception is no longer possible if we think of the original choice as the something which has existence in so far as Clovis has existence. This something, in order for *it* to have existence, must be whole and complete when it gets its existence. It cannot be one thing at one time, and something else again later on. No, to assume that Clovis's original choice is the substance of Clovis which has the feature of existence is to restrict Clovis's freedom only slightly less than to assume that it is Clovis's essence which receives existence.

If we conclude that existence is indeed Clovis's substance as well as Adam's, so that the existence of these substances does not by itself determine what properties they shall have, then we are forced, as I said, to repudiate the Existentialist's distinction between modes of being. Though human beings are vastly different from stones, they do not partake in a different sort of existence. Both human beings as well as stones are therefore 'metaphysically free'. In so far as they are small bits of existence, they have no natures, no essences. In so far as they are mere pieces of existence, their properties are not determined.

Index

accident: essence and, 17, 80, 86, 89; substance and, 4–5, 17, 23, 89
act-properties, 45–6
Adam's nature (Leibniz's example), 26–8, 180, 270, 272–4
Anaximander, 171
Anna (example of anxiety), 56–8, 73–6, 224–5
anxiety, 56, 71–6, 159–61, 222
apple (examples), 14–15, 22, 34–5, 41, 59, 194, *see also* Oscar
Aquinas, St Thomas, 3
Aristotelian tradition: Brentano and, 46; Descartes and, 3, 172; essences and accidents, 80, 86; existence and, 183, 194; Heidegger and, 172, 178; nominalism, 81; Platonic mind and, 87; relations and, 40; substances, 80, 86
Aristotle: distinction between substance, essence and accident, 79–80; essence, 180; logic, 185; metaphysics, 137; Plato and (example of relation), 41–3, 46; Scholastic philosophy and, 3
aspects, Husserl's theory of, 115, 117, 122, 127, 129
awareness, acts of, 51–3

bad faith, 222–5
Barcelona (example), 55
Being, 173–7
being: and becoming, 79, 81, 86–7, 113, 168; and existence, 173, 177, 179; Heidegger's question, 150–3, 163, 178, 197; modes of, 154, 163–77, 236; non-being and, 240–3, 245; Russell's notion of, 47–8, 173
being-for-itself: 201, 203, 221, 267; nothing-

ness and, 226, 247
being-in-itself: 201, 203, 232, 251, 267; nothingness and, 226, 246, 248–9
being-in-the-world, 157–62, 164, 242–3
being-there (Dasein), 168
Bergson, Henri, 233–5
Berkeley, George, 12, 20–6, 40, 150, 155
billiard-balls (example), 9, 19, *see also* Max and Moritz
birch-tree, hallucinated, 140–1
Boethius, 83–4
brain, 8–10, 258–60
Brentano, Franz: 29–67; distinction between mental and physical phenomena, 31–6, 117; Husserl and, 11, 89; mental act, its own awareness, 202, 213; theory of intentionality, 32–48, 92–3, 134, 160, 170
bride (example), 222–3
British Empiricists, 16, 19
bundle view: 17, 24–7, 59, 150; Berkeley and, 21–2, 26; Brentano and, 29–30, 59; relations and, 40–1; Twardowski's, 115–17

Caesar, 7, 173, 177, 189–90, 194, 196–7
caring, 158
categories, 150–1, 169, 170
choice, 28, 252–3, 262, 268–72
Clovis's conversion (Sartre's example), 264–74
color: 12–17, 21–5, 94; Berkeley on, 21–2, 24; Brentano on, 31, 35–6; Descartes on, 12, 14–17, 35; Gestalt view of, 67; Husserl on, 117–22
configurations, 59–60
consciousness: Brentano on, 202; Husserl

275

Index

Index